Comments from elementary teachers who have participated in professional development workshops based on *Teaching Physical Science through Children's Literature:*

"Good information, great ideas, wonderful science ties."

"This approach of using reading, science, and math for a completely integrated program will be a key in developing our new science program."

"Good concepts, very valuable, non-threatening science activities. I can't wait to use these lessons with my second graders."

"Provides opportunities for integration without being forced or contrived."

"The literature is terrific and there's a tremendous amount of science."

"I especially appreciate the explanations of the science principles. I feel that is extremely important."

"Great choice of literature."

"I am impressed. These are by far the most complete, well-thought-out, comprehensive, cross-curricular materials I have seen."

"The lessons are clearly framed and articulated."

"Excellent materials with quality literature and quality activity-based ideas to use with young children. I am delighted."

Teaching Physical Science through Children's Literature

20 Complete Lessons for Elementary Grades

Susan E. Gertz
Dwight J. Portman
Mickey Sarquis

Terrific Science Press,
with funding from the
National Science Foundation

**LEARNING
TRIANGLE
PRESS**

▲

*Connecting kids, parents, and teachers
through learning*

An imprint of McGraw-Hill

McGraw-Hill

A Division of The McGraw·Hill Companies

Terrific Science Press
Miami University Middletown
4200 East University Blvd.
Middletown, Ohio 45042
513/727-3269
cce@muohio.edu

pbk   1 2 3 4 5 6 7 8 9   MAL/MAL   9 9 8 7 6

Photos provided by Miami University Applied Technologies.

Support for *Teaching Physical Science through Children's Literature* was provided by a grant under the federally funded Dwight D. Eisenhower Mathematics and Science Education Act, administered by the Ohio Board of Regents.

This material is based upon work supported by the National Science Foundation under Grant Number TPE-9055448. This project was supported, in part, by the National Science Foundation. Any opinions, findings, and conclusions or recommendations expressed in this material are those of the authors and do not necessarily reflect the views of the National Science Foundation.

Library of Congress Cataloging-in-Publication Data

Teaching physical science through children's literature : 20 complete
  lessons for elementary grades / by Terrific Science Press, Susan E. Gertz,
Dwight J. Portman, and Mickey Sarquis.
     p. cm.
  Includes index.
  ISBN 0-07-064723-2 (pbk.)
  1. Science—Study and teaching (Elementary) 2. Children's
literature—Study and teaching (Elementary) I. Terrific Science
Press.
LB1585.T435 1996
372.3'5—dc20
                                        95-48084
                                          CIP

Acquisitions editor: Kimberly Tabor

Contents

Section 1: Properties of Objects and Materials

Section 2: Light, Heat, Electricity, and Magnetism

Section 3: Position and Motion of Objects

Appendices **233**

Acknowledgments

The authors wish to thank the following individuals who have contributed to the development of this book.

Contributors

Baheejah Hasan, Taft Elementary School, Middletown, Ohio
Served as co-instructor of the Science-Literature Integration Development course.

Paula Ellis, Trailwoods School of Environmental Studies, Kansas City, Missouri
Contributed to the development of the Building Bridges section of each activity.

Phoebe Ingraham, Arlington Primary School, Lockland, Ohio
Contributed information on classroom centers.

Terrific Science Press Design and Production Team

Document Production Manager: Susan Gertz
Technical Coordinator: Amy Stander
Technical Writing: Lisa Taylor, Amy Hudepohl
Technical Editing: Amy Stander, Lisa Taylor
Illustration: Thomas Nackid
Design/Layout: Susan Gertz, Stephen Gentle, Thomas Nackid
Production: Stephen Gentle, Amy Hudepohl, Anne Munson, Thomas Nackid, Lisa Taylor
Laboratory Testing: Andrea Nolan, Annette Souder

Reviewers

Sarah Dowhower, Miami University, Oxford, Ohio
Phoebe Ingraham, Arlington Primary School, Lockland, Ohio
Beverley Taylor, Miami University, Hamilton, Ohio
Linda Woodward, University of Southwestern Louisiana, Lafayette, Louisiana

Science-Literature Materials Development Teachers

These teachers, through their participation in the development project at Miami University, helped to develop lesson ideas, performed classroom testing, and provided valuable reviews.

Susan Baker, West Carrollton, OH
Sharon Beckett, Wilmington, OH
Terrie Beckman-Hurley, Miamisburg, OH
Paul Briese, Lebanon, OR
Vicki Brunner, Hamilton, OH
Jerry Bruns, Toledo, OH
Mary-Frances Cahill, Hamilton, OH
Bonnie Calvin, Middletown, OH
Cordelia Carter, Wilmington, OH
Opal Chambers, Middletown, OH
Jill Clayton, Toledo, OH
Audrey Cleveland, Dayton, OH
Carole Colegate, Hamilton, OH
Katherine Collins, Hamilton, OH
Brenda Conley, Hamilton, OH
Barbara Dehm, Salem, OR
Cherie Dixon, Wilmington, OH
Laura Dowers, Hamilton, OH
Elaine Dunkle, Kettering, OH
Sandra Edgington, Dayton, OH
Marilou Enslein, Dayton, OH
Teresa Fedor, Toledo, OH
Peggy French, Loveland, OH
Richard French, Loveland, OH
Mary Jo Gardener, Kalispell, MT

Peggy Gass, Washington C.H., OH
Mary Gayhardt, Wilmington, OH
Elizabeth Haas, West Carrollton, OH
Sue Hanna, Wilmington, OH
Baheejah Hasan, Middletown, OH
Patrick Hayes, Cincinnati, OH
Deborah Howard, Cincinnati, OH
William Huth, Hamilton, OH
Maria Jeffers, Middletown, OH
Virginia Kasper, Miamisburg, OH
Patricia Kenney, Cincinnati, OH
Margaret Kulczewski, Monmouth, IL
Brenda LaBoffe, Hamilton, OH
Betsy Lavelle, Dayton, OH
Michele Leatherbury, Kettering, OH
Daniel Lundgard, Huber Heights, OH
Jane Maasen, Mason, OH
Elizabeth McCardle, OH
Joan Mollman, Miamisburg, OH
Christine Moore-Goad, Kettering, OH
Anne Moran, West Carrollton, OH
Melinda Myers, Wilmington, OH
Mary Neises, Dayton, OH
Jody Nelson, Hamilton, OH
Jane Newcomer, Darlington, MO

Linda Olinger, Wilmington, OH
Stephen Peterson, Toledo, OH
Philip Preston, Cincinnati, OH
Janet Priest, West Carrollton, OH
Delores Pugh, Dayton, OH
Sarah Roberts, Dayton, OH
Charliemae Rose, Toledo, OH
Suzanne Rumbalski, Cincinnati, OH
Susan Saettell, West Carrollton, OH
Linda Schaffer, Ramey, PR
Patricia Seta-Giddings, OH
Lori Seubert, Toledo, OH
Ann Spahr, Jeffersonville, OH
Elizabeth Staggenborg, St. Bernard, OH
Cynthia Stanford, Cincinnati, OH
Jill Stelzer, Englewood, OH
Jan Stickles, Toledo, OH
Susan Sturgill, Hamilton, OH
Sue Swigert, Jeffersonville, OH
Lorry Swindler, Wilmington, OH
Marilyn Temple, Middletown, OH
Julie Thompson, Miamisburg, OH
Marjorie Tudor, Kettering, OH
Susan Voyles, Middletown, OH
Kimberly Weibler, Toledo, OH

Introduction

Teaching Physical Science through Children's Literature offers 20 complete lessons for teaching hands-on, discovery-oriented physical science in the elementary classroom using children's fiction and nonfiction books as an integral part of that instruction. Each lesson in this book is a tightly integrated learning episode with a clearly defined science content objective supported and enriched by all facets of the lesson, including reading of both fiction and nonfiction, writing, and, where appropriate, mathematics. Along with the science content objectives, many process objectives are woven into every lesson.

These lessons are not a stand-alone curriculum; rather, the lessons are intended to complement and enrich your own curriculum. We encourage you to consider how these lessons can meet the needs of your students and fit your own teaching style. See Getting the Most Out of This Book, pages 3–19, for suggestions for doing so.

Why Teach Science through Literature?

Like most elementary teachers, you probably spend much more time in your classroom on reading and language arts than on science. You may experience one or more of the common barriers to including physical science instruction in elementary classrooms:

- Time—Elementary teachers already have extensive curricular requirements. Making time for another subject is challenging: If you add more science, what should you omit?
- Experience—Many elementary school teachers have little experience teaching activity-based, discovery-oriented science.
- Familiarity—When science is taught, teachers usually focus on the more familiar and comfortable life and earth science topics.

Our goal is to support you in your effort to improve the quantity and quality of physical science instruction in your classroom by providing a very familiar starting point that already has a place in your curriculum: children's fiction and nonfiction literature.

When science is taught through literature, the time for science need not come at the expense of other subjects. Integrating science with literature not only makes more elementary science education possible; it also results in more effective science teaching. Typically, cross-curricular teaching emphasizes the process skills common to many subjects rather than rote memorization of content facts. When students are building and testing a musical instrument in "Rubber Band Banza," investigating optical color mixing with a spinning top in "Whirling Colors," or watching a model of the water cycle in "Making Clouds and Rain," they are also developing effective reading skills by using process skills such as observing, communicating, classifying, predicting outcomes, and drawing conclusions.

Support for the Development of This Book

The lessons in this book were developed through the support of two professional development programs for teachers offered at Miami University in Ohio: the Ohio Board of Regents-funded Science-Literature Integration project and the National Science Foundation-funded Teaching Science with TOYS program. These projects promote children's literature and toys as ideal mechanisms for activity-based, discovery-oriented science instruction because stories and toys are a part of the students' everyday world and carry a user-friendly message.

The goals of the Science-Literature Integration project are to enhance teachers' knowledge of physical science and to encourage activity-based, discovery-oriented science instruction. The Science-Literature Integration project includes two major components: materials development and implementation. Teachers who have participated in the materials development component of the program developed, reviewed, and classroom-tested the literature-based physical science lessons in this book. Teachers participating in the implementation component of the course learn basic physical science content and gain experience conducting science investigations.

The goals of Teaching Science with TOYS are to enhance teachers' knowledge of chemistry and physics and to encourage activity-based, discovery-oriented science instruction through the use of toys. Many of the science investigations in this book are adapted from activities used in the TOYS program. Additionally, TOYS program participants participated in the development and testing of the lessons in *Teaching Physical Science through Children's Literature*.

Through Science-Literature Integration, Teaching Science with TOYS, and their affiliated programs, many teachers have brought literature- and toy-based science into their classrooms. Through written materials such as this book, many more teachers and students can share in the fun and learning of the Science-Literature Integration and Teaching Science with TOYS projects.

For more information about professional development opportunities for teachers at Miami University, see Appendix A.

● Getting the Most Out of This Book

We hope that you find this book helpful in preparing fun, exciting, and informative scientific investigations for your classroom. However, each of the lessons in this book contains much more than just the instructions for a science investigation. To help you get the most out of using this book in your classroom, this section presents some of the pedagogical concepts behind the lessons as well as many tips and suggestions. The six topics covered in this section are as follows:

- Meeting the Needs of Your Students presents suggestions for adapting the lessons in this book for students of different grade levels and abilities.
- Standards for Science Education discusses published standards for science education and how this book relates to them.
- Integrating Practices of Reading Instruction presents suggestions for using practices of good reading instruction to effectively enhance the development of the total science concept.
- Teaching with Classroom Centers explains the concept of centers as used in this book and presents suggestions for setting up and using centers in your classroom.
- Using Science Journals presents suggestions for integrating journal writing into your students' science investigations.
- Other Pedagogical Approaches discusses additional instructional approaches that you may use with the lessons in this book.

Meeting the Needs of Your Students

This book was written and classroom-tested with a focus on the needs and abilities of students in grades 1–4. However, the science content is rich enough to enable you to easily adapt the lessons for upper elementary grades as well. Additionally, whether you teach in a traditional or multi-age classroom, the individual needs of your students will span a great range, requiring adaptation. As you read the various lessons in this book, you will see that the science, reading, and writing represent a wide span of challenges and learning experiences; not all of them are appropriate for every grade. In our testing, teachers of various grades adapted each part of the lessons to fit the needs of their classrooms. We encourage you to do the same.

The first table on page 4 (Adapting Lessons to Meet the Needs of Your Students) provides a general example of how to adapt the science content objectives, students' use of the literature, and the writing extensions in these lessons to meet the needs of your students. The second table on page 4 (Adapting "Are Mittens Warm" to Meet the Needs of Your Students) provides an example of how to apply the ideas presented in the first table to a specific lesson. A discussion of adapting the science content objectives, use of the literature, and writing extensions is provided on page 5.

Adapting Lessons to Meet the Needs of Your Students

	Grades K–2	Grades 2–4	Grades 4–6
Science Content Objectives	The objective should be an introduction to this concept.	The objective should be fully explained. Some students will understand the concept while many will still be developing their understanding.	The objective should be mastered by most students.
Listening and Reading	Encourage students to listen to the story for a purpose and reread, assisted or unassisted.	Encourage students to listen to the story for a purpose, reread the book unassisted, and do some independent reading of provided related material.	Encourage students to listen to the story for a purpose, reread the book unassisted, conduct independent research, and read new material.
Writing to Learn	Encourage drawing or writing about the topic as a whole class or independently.	Encourage students to write factual descriptions of their work and to begin to use what they have learned in original fiction or nonfiction writing.	Encourage students to write descriptive analyses in which they apply their new knowledge.

Adapting "Are Mittens Warm?" to Meet the Needs of Your Students

	Grades K–2	Grades 2–4	Grades 4–6
Science Content Objectives	Students learn that they must adapt their clothing to the weather.	Students learn that mittens and other clothing are not in themselves warm but can trap our body heat to help us stay warm.	Students learn objectives as stated for grades 2–4, are introduced to the concept of insulation, and design and conduct new experiments on clothing and insulation.
Listening and Reading	Students listen to *Mama, Do You Love Me?* and look for different types of warm clothes worn by the characters. They have opportunities for rereading the story.	Students read as described for grades K–2, hear the nonfiction story *Eskimo Boy*, and have opportunities for rereading both.	Students read as described for grades 2–4 and also research and read nonfiction sources on clothing, climate, and insulation.
Writing to Learn	Students draw and/or write about what they wear as the weather changes.	Students write about a character who lives in a cold climate and describe the character's clothing.	Students design new coats for people traveling through a variety of climates and create a catalog of garments to purchase.

Science Content Objectives

The purpose of the science content objectives is to let you know exactly what the important science idea in each lesson is. We understand that a science objective as we have stated it may not be appropriate for your grade level and expect you to adapt the objective to meet the needs of your students and curriculum. Some of the science content objectives addressed by the lessons in this book are very basic, such as in "Glitter Wands": *Students observe the three states of matter and identify matter in each of these states.* Other science objectives are more challenging, such as in "Whirling Colors": *Colors of objects depend on the colors of light that are reflected, and colors and patterns can mix visually on spinning objects.* A complete science explanation is included in each lesson, giving you all the information you need to decide exactly what to teach your students about the science concept.

Use of the Literature

The lessons in this book were written with the assumption that students would initially listen to the featured fiction book being read out loud and later reread the book themselves. Some of the books, such as *The Rainbow Fish* and *Carousel,* are fairly simple to listen to, understand, and reread. Other books, such as *The Black Snowman,* are much more challenging, both in content and in reading difficulty. In some cases, the difficulty of the book and the difficulty of the science objective may not seem to match. However, all the books, whether familiar or new, easy or difficult, will be experienced by your students in the context of these lessons. Therefore, even if *Planting a Rainbow* is very basic reading to your fourth graders, they probably never considered it from the point of view presented in the lesson "Chromatography Garden."

Besides the featured fiction book, some of the lessons include a featured nonfiction book to be read aloud. Almost all lessons include suggestions for further reading. Appendix B contains an alphabetical listing of all featured fiction and nonfiction books used in the lessons as well as all books listed as suggestions for further reading. Older students may also conduct independent research to find related reading materials.

Writing Extensions

The writing extensions in these lessons span a range of levels, from emergent to fluent. The suggested writing extensions are intended to give students different types of opportunities to communicate what they have learned about the science objective. As such, these extensions can serve as assessment tools. For example, in "Making Clouds and Rain," students write a "before and after" book to compare and contrast what plants, animals, people, and the earth are like before and after rain. "Glitter Wands" suggests students work at home with family members to make lists of solids, liquids, and gases in or around the house.

Standards for Science Education

Many scientists, educators, policy-makers, and parents share a vision of education in America in which *all* students will become literate in science, mathematics, and technology. This vision has been translated into sets of standards for science education, most notably the *Benchmarks for Science Literacy* compiled under the direction of the American Association for the Advancement of Science and the *National Science Education Standards* compiled under the direction of the National Research Council. This book is organized around the Physical Science Content Standard for Grades K–4 from the *National Science Education Standards*. The lessons in this book are consistent with the recommendations of both *Benchmarks for Science Literacy* and the *National Science Education Standards*.

In your day-to-day teaching you probably do not work directly with these standards. Instead, you probably work with the required science curriculum that has been developed for your district. So why do you need to know about *Benchmarks for Science Literacy* and the *National Science Education Standards* and how this book relates to them? You need to know for several reasons:

- Your local curriculum may be based on one or both of these standards.
- You may be part of your district's efforts to develop new science curricula based on one or both of these standards.
- Your current science curriculum may be inadequate, and you may need information to prepare you to encourage your school system to reform the curriculum.
- You may serve on a committee to select science textbooks for your district and need a frame of reference for selecting the best materials.
- You may need to justify the added expense of hands-on, minds-on science education to supervisors, colleagues, and parents.
- You may need to justify the instructional value of the lessons in this book to supervisors, colleagues, and parents who are not familiar with activity-oriented science.

In the following sections, we discuss two major categories of standards found in both *Benchmarks for Science Literacy* and the *National Science Education Standards:* standards for understanding the nature of science and content standards for physical science.

Understanding the Nature of Science

When we think about teaching physical science, we often begin by thinking about content objectives, such as the following: Students will learn that magnets attract iron, students will learn that air takes up space, or students will learn the properties of each of three states of matter. But each experience students have with science investigations in the classroom does more than teach science content; it also helps to shape student perceptions of what science is and what scientists do. Thus, every lesson in this book has been developed with the goal of shaping students' ideas about science and about how they can work as scientists.

The *National Science Education Standards* states that as a result of activities in grades K–4, students should develop the abilities necessary to do scientific inquiry and to understand the process of scientific inquiry. *Benchmarks for Science Literacy* has student goals relating to understanding the scientific world view and the process of scientific inquiry. The table below provides examples of how lessons in this book support specific student objectives from these sources in understanding the nature of science.

Process Skills

Science investigations and reading are information-processing procedures that have many skills in common. Through classroom experiences that enable them to understand what science is and what scientists do, students integrate the process skills common to science and reading as well as many other subjects. As students do science investigations, follow scientific procedures, and think as scientists, they also develop effective reading skills by observing, communicating, classifying, predicting and verifying outcomes, and drawing conclusions. Thus, students can improve science and reading skills simultaneously. The table on page 10 titled Examples of Process Skills Related to Science and Language Skills presents specific examples of process skills that are shared by science and reading.

Using This Book with the *National Standards for Science Education** and *Benchmarks for Science Literacy***		
	"Ramps and Cars"	"Shrinky Plastic"
Understanding the Nature of Science	(NS) Students employ simple equipment to gather data. *(Students use stopwatches to measure elapsed time and adding machine tape to measure distance.)* (NS) Students will understand that scientists use different types of investigations, including experiments. *(Students use a controlled experiment to gather data.)* (B) When a scientific investigation is done the way it was done before, we expect to get a very similar result. *(Students do repeated trials to confirm results.)*	(NS) Students will understand that scientists use different types of investigations, including systematic observations. *(Students make careful observations of plastic samples.)* (B) People can learn more about things around them by doing something and watching what happens. *(Students heat polystyrene and observe what happens.)* (B) Describing things as accurately as possible is important in science because it enables people to compare their observations. *(Students trace their plastic shapes on graph paper and post results to share with the class.)*
Physical Science Content	(NS) Position and motion of objects can be changed by pushing or pulling. *(Students observe that pushing the car makes it go up the ramp.)* (NS) An object's motion can be described as its change in position over time. *(Students measure elapsed time and change in position.)* (B) Earth's gravity pulls things towards it. *(Students observe the effect of gravity as it pulls the car down the ramp.)*	(NS) Objects have many observable properties, including size, weight, shape, and color. (NS) Objects are made of one or more materials and can be described and sorted by the properties of these materials. *(Students observe and describe the properties of an assortment of plastic objects.)* (B) Heating and cooling cause changes in the properties of materials. *(Students observe that heating causes polystyrene film to shrink.)*
*NS = National Standards for Science Education **B = Benchmarks for Science Literacy*		

Physical Science Content Standards

An understanding of the physical world is an essential component of scientific literacy. To help you teach physical science concepts, the lessons in this book are grouped into three sections based on the Physical Science Content Standard for Grades K–4 from the *National Science Education Standards:* Properties of Objects and Materials; Position and Motion of Objects; and Light, Heat, Electricity, and Magnetism. An important idea to remember is that students are expected to develop an understanding of these concepts as a result of observation and manipulation of objects and materials in their environment. Every lesson in this book gives students the opportunity to develop their understanding through such experiences. In *Benchmarks for Science Literacy,* the physical science content is divided into four categories: structure of matter, energy transformations, motion, and forces of nature. The table on page 7 provides examples of how lessons in this book support specific student objectives from these sources for knowledge of physical science.

The Particle Nature of Matter

An important issue that arises when teaching physical science content in the elementary grades is how to approach teaching about the particle nature of matter. To be able to explain the nature and interactions of matter, it is necessary to know about the nature of the particles that make it up. As adults, you have probably heard and used the terms atoms, molecules, and ions. Remember, however, that young children do not have the conceptual background to correctly distinguish between these three terms. In the elementary grades, we strongly recommend that you use the general term "particles" with students to prevent creating misconceptions that will later be difficult—if not impossible—to correct. Additionally, with elementary students, limit your discussion to the general idea that all matter is made up of particles that are too small to be seen by the human eye and that, in spite of our inability to see these particles, their existence accounts for matter as we know it. The discussion of the various types of particles (atoms, molecules, ions) should be held to later years in the curriculum when the students are conceptually ready for this level of detail. Our recommendations are consistent with those of the American Association for the Advancement of Science *Benchmarks for Science Literacy* and the National Science Foundation-funded S_2C_2 (School Science Curriculum Conference) report, a joint report of the American Chemical Society and the American Association of Physics Teachers.

Assessment

Assessment and learning are two sides of the same coin. Assessments enable students to let teachers know what they are learning, and when students engage in an assessment exercise, they should learn from it. Paper-and-pencil tests are a familiar and ubiquitous form of assessment. But in light of what we are hoping to teach students about both the process and content of science, traditional tests requiring students to choose one of a few given answers or fill in the blank measure only a fraction of what we need to know about their science learning. The *National Science Education Standards* advocates using diverse assessment methods, including performances and portfolios as well as paper-and-pencil tests.

Emerging from among a host of terms describing current assessment options (for example, authentic, alternative, portfolio, and performance), the term active assessment has been proposed by George Hein and Sabra Price in their book *Active Assessment for Active Science*. They define "active assessment" as a whole family of assessment methods that actively engage the learner and can also be interpreted meaningfully by the teacher. Almost any of the experiences that make up the lessons in this book can also serve as active assessments. For example, brainstorming sessions, science journal entries, data and observations from science investigations, and writing extensions can all be part of developing a picture of what students are learning. For this reason, we have not identified any particular portion of the lessons in this book as assessments. We hope that as you use the lessons in this book, you will engage in many different forms of active assessment, thus maximizing the opportunity for all students to demonstrate their accomplishments and understanding.

References

American Association for the Advancement of Science. *Benchmarks for Science Literacy;* Oxford University: New York, 1993.

Hein, G.E.; Price, S. *Active Assessment for Active Science;* Heinemann: Portsmouth, NH, 1994.

National Research Council. *National Science Education Standards;* National Academy: Washington DC, 1996.

Padilla, M.; Muth, D.; Padilla, R.L. "Science and Reading: Many Process Skills in Common," *Science Learning: Processes and Applications.* 1991; 14–19.

Examples of Process Skills Related to Science and Language Skills		
Process Skills	Science Skills	Language Skills
Observing	Using one or more of the five senses to gather information. May include use of equipment.	Discriminating shapes, sounds, syllables, and word accents.
Predicting and Validating	Forming an idea of an expected result. Depends on observation and judgment that is based on past experiences. Validation is based on current observations.	Forming an idea of an expected event or outcome through observation and judgment based on past experiences. Validation is based on current observations.
Collecting Data	Measuring and recording information in an organized way. Being precise and accurate.	Taking notes. Using reference materials. Using different parts of a book. Recording information in an organized way. Being precise and accurate.
Investigating	Using observations to collect and analyze data to draw conclusions and solve a problem.	Asking questions. Investigating possible relationships. Following organized procedures.
Interpreting Data	Reading tables, graphs, and diagrams. Explaining the information presented and using it to answer a question.	Recognizing cause-and-effect relationships. Organizing facts. Summarizing new information. Thinking inductively and deductively.
Classifying	Grouping or ordering objects or events according to an established scheme based on observations.	Comparing and contrasting characteristics. Arranging ideas and ordering and sequencing information. Considering multiple attributes.
Forming Conclusions	Generalizing. Critical analysis. Establishing relationships. Using information in other situations.	Generalizing. Critical analysis. Identifying main ideas. Establishing relationships. Using information in other situations.
Communicating Results	Giving or exchanging information orally and/or in writing.	Arranging information logically. Sequencing ideas. Describing clearly.

Integrating Practices of Reading Instruction

Although this book is not specifically about teaching reading, it is about enhancing the teaching of science through the reading of fiction and nonfiction. Thus, throughout these lessons we have suggested using many of the practices of good reading instruction to effectively support the development of the total science concept being taught.

Background Knowledge and Schemata

Researchers from many disciplines agree that learning is a constructive process. That is, learners construct their own meanings through an interaction of past experiences and current information. This constructive process occurs in both science and reading. Thus, the background knowledge that a student brings to listening to a story or conducting a scientific investigation has strong implications for comprehension. A major view of how background knowledge affects the construction of meaning is the theory of schemata, frameworks of knowledge that organize related concepts. You might think of schemata as frameworks for interpreting incoming information. For example, the phrase "lack of facilities" is ambiguous until you have a framework of "washing clothes." With this framework in mind, you would probably interpret "lack of facilities" as meaning not having a washing machine. It is very easy to assume that students have the same schemata that we do, and we tend to assume that our schemata are the right ones. These assumptions may or may not be correct.

With these ideas in mind, we have included the Building Student Knowledge and Motivation portion of the lessons as an opportunity for students to share some experiences that relate to the topic of the lesson. For example, in "Catch the Wind," students begin the lesson by spending time in a classroom science center looking at magazines and books on sailing and the force of air. They also observe a wind sock hanging outside the classroom window. This gives all students a frame of reference before beginning the class discussion on things that catch the wind in the Getting Ready to Read portion of the lesson. For at-risk students who may have limited home enrichment, the experiences provided by the Building Student Knowledge and Motivation activities can be crucial. Ideally, the experiences in Building Student Knowledge and Motivation span several days prior to the beginning of formal instruction, giving students a chance to absorb and reflect upon what they have read and done.

Listening for a Purpose
Hand in hand with the concept of students constructing knowledge while listening to a story is the idea of listening for a purpose. In this book, the stories being read aloud to students are intended to be part of a lesson about a specific science concept. As students hear the story, they should be thinking about the story in the context of the lesson as a whole. Students' experiences in Building Student Knowledge and Motivation set the stage. Through class discussion in Getting Ready to Read, students organize their thoughts and focus on a purpose for listening to the story. For example, in "Catch the Wind," students brainstorm and make a class list of things that catch the wind. The teacher then explains that in the story they are about to hear, Mirandy wants to catch the wind, and then asks,

"Do you think she can? Why do you think she would want to catch the wind?" With these predictions, students set their own individual purposes for reading that support the overall purpose of the lesson: to learn that wind can be used to do work.

In other cases the teacher sets the purpose. For example, in "Are Mittens Warm?" the teacher asks students to look for examples of warm clothes worn by the characters in *Mama, Do You Love Me?* This book could be listened to with many other purposes in mind, but the stated purpose supports the overall objective of the lesson.

Graphical Organizers

Constructing graphical representations to organize ideas is a powerful tool. The lessons in this book require students to organize observations and information from Building Student Knowledge and Motivation, Getting Ready to Read, the story itself, and the science investigation. Throughout the lessons, the Science Chart icon shown at left indicates the use of graphical organizers.

Graphical organizers can help the learner classify, comprehend, summarize, and synthesize ideas. Several types of graphical organizers are used in these lessons. For example, a Venn diagram is used in "Keep Your Balance" to compare different types of balance toys. In "Making Clouds and Rain," students develop a web diagram to organize their weather observations. In "Whirling Colors," students compile a class observation chart to summarize their observations of spinning objects. Students use a Know-Wonder-Learn chart throughout "Colors of the Rainbow."

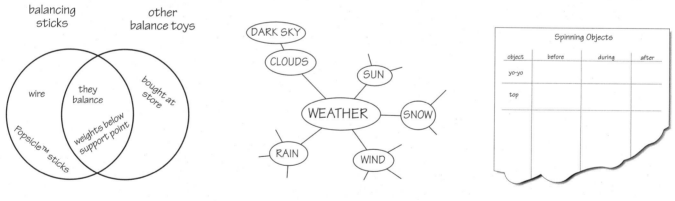

Venn Diagram

Web Diagram

Observation Chart

In most lessons, the class begins developing a chart during the "Getting Ready to Read" portion of the lesson. This chart is usually referred to and expanded upon throughout the rest of the lesson. We suggest that as you complete various lessons in this book you leave all the science charts in an accessible place so that students can add to them throughout the year. Many of these lessons cover interrelated topics, and students may have insights that they want to add to older charts. In this way, the charts become graphical organizers within individual lessons and between lessons as well.

Repeated Listening and Reading

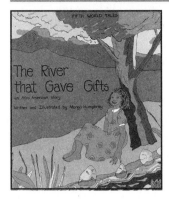

Repeated listening and reading are proven instructional tools for both remedial and developmental readers. Repeated listening to the same story helps students' story comprehension and encourages deeper questioning. Several of the lessons in this book suggest repeated listening to excerpts from the featured fiction book. Because the lessons in this book lead students to integrate many ideas and experiences, rereading provides an important opportunity for students to reflect upon what they have read and done. For example, in "Colors of the Rainbow," students investigate different ways to make a rainbow in the classroom. The story they listen to prior to the science investigation, *The River that Gave Gifts*, presents a make-believe view of how rainbows can form. The teacher rereads relevant excerpts from the book during a class discussion about the differences between the make-believe rainbows in the book and the real rainbows in the classroom. Even where not specifically suggested, repeated reading of the featured fiction or nonfiction books may be incorporated into any of the lessons in this book.

Repeated reading may be assisted or unassisted. Unassisted repeated reading involves independent practice in which no model is used. Alternatively, assisted repeated reading involves a model such as an audiotape of the story being read. Many of the lessons in this book suggest returning the relevant fiction and nonfiction books to a center after the whole group instruction portion of the lesson is completed. Revisiting the center after the whole group instruction gives students an opportunity for either assisted or unassisted rereading of those books.

References

Bernhardt, E.B. "The Text as a Participant in Instruction," *Theory into Practice.* 26(1), 32–37.

Dowhower, S.L. "Repeated Reading: Research into Practice," *The Reading Teacher.* March 1989, 502–507.

Dowhower, S.L. "Repeated Reading Revisited: Research into Practice," *Reading & Writing Quarterly: Overcoming Learning Difficulties.* 1994, 343–358.

Jones, B.; Pierce, J.; Hunter, B. "Teaching Students to Construct Graphic Representations," *Educational Leadership.* December 1988–January 1989, 20–25.

Tierney, R. *Reading Strategies and Practices,* Simon & Schuster: Needham Heights, MA, 1990.

Teaching with Classroom Science Centers

Nearly all of the lessons in this book refer to the use of classroom science centers. Centers are small areas of a classroom set aside for independent learning. You also might call them stations or learning areas. Science centers can be an integral part of everyday classroom instruction, or they can be used as temporary learning stations for a specific activity. A center is not just a physical space to work on tasks such as ditto sheets or workbooks. Rather, centers should provide opportunities for creativity, problem solving, critical thinking, and learning by doing. Science centers can provide motivation to take on difficult challenges while helping younger children develop the concentration skills necessary to complete multiple-step activities.

The center environment has many advantages. Centers allow for cooperation among students. Centers also allow for activities that vary in ability level, so that every child is able to complete some tasks with success, but each child is also challenged. Centers encourage independence and self-sufficiency; within the established structure, students take responsibility for their own learning.

Nearly all of the lessons in this book suggest beginning the lesson by setting up a science center that small groups of students will visit over a period of days. Typically, the center includes a variety of materials for students to manipulate, read, and look at. For example, in "Folded Paper Kites," the center contains sample kites of several styles as well as books that show traditional kites from many cultures. The assigned task in the center is to look at the different types of kites and write a brief description of each. Students use these descriptions later in a class discussion about categorizing the kites by different attributes. In "Is It Really Magic?" students work in a science center to practice and try to explain commercial magic tricks they have seen the teacher demonstrate.

Some of the lessons in this book specifically suggest having the students do the science investigation independently in a science center, rather than simultaneously in small groups or as a whole class. For example, in "Searching for Empty Space" students take turns visiting a center that has three different investigations for students to complete. Depending on how you wish to use centers in your classroom, most of the science investigations in this book could be done independently by groups of students in centers.

Many of the lessons in this book also suggest returning the science materials and relevant fiction and nonfiction books to the center after the whole group instruction portion of the lesson is completed. Revisiting the center after the whole group instruction gives students an opportunity to summarize and synthesize ideas as well as pose new questions.

Making and Using Flip Card Booklets

Masters for flip card instructions are provided for many lessons. These flip cards can be used by students working independently in classroom science centers, as instructions for students working in small groups, as a reference during whole group instruction, or as a set of instructions for a take-home activity. Throughout the lessons, the flip card icon shown at left indicates the use of flip card instructions.

To make flip card booklets for your classroom, follow these steps:

1. Photocopy and cut out the numbered flip cards.

2. Glue each card to a 4-inch by 6-inch index card. Make sure to leave room at the top of the index card for binding the booklet. Laminate if desired.

3. If using rings to bind the booklets, punch two holes at the top of each card. If using plastic comb binding, punch holes with an appropriate binding machine.

4. Bind the flip card booklets as desired.

Reference

Ingraham, P. *Creating and Managing Learning Centers: A Theme-Based Approach;* Crystal Springs: Peterborough, NY, 1996.

Using Science Journals

Writing is an integral part of the process of scientific inquiry. When working as scientists, students must record observations and data, organize and summarize results, and draw conclusions. Often they must communicate both the process of the investigation and its results to others through words and/or pictures.

Writing can be viewed as hands-on thinking: It gives students opportunities for reflection and active processing of learning experiences. As a result of regular writing experiences, students gain a better understanding of what they know.

Regular use of science journals throughout the lessons in this book will give students many opportunities to practice writing skills in the context of doing science. We have provided masters for three styles of science journal pages for you to make available to your students. The first style (page 17) has a large area for drawing and a few primary-ruled lines. The second style (page 18) has a smaller area for drawing and a larger area of notebook-type ruled lines. The third style (page 19) has four specific questions that can apply to any science investigation in this book.

References

Saul, W. *Science Workshop: A Whole Language Approach;* Heinemann: Portsmouth, NH, 1993.
Zikes, D. *Reading & Writing Across the Curriculum;* Dinah-Might Activities: San Antonio, TX, 1994.

Other Pedagogical Approaches

The activities in this book were developed with the following idea in mind: No single instructional strategy best meets the needs of all students at all times. Howard Gardner, author of *The Unschooled Mind*, views each learner as possessing a distinctive profile of "intelligences" or ways of learning, remembering, performing, and understanding. These differences are thought to dramatically affect what instructional approach is most likely to be effective for a given student. In keeping with this idea, a variety of instructional approaches can be effectively used to present the literature-based science lessons in this book. Some of these have been specifically discussed in the previous pages, but many other options are open to you. We encourage you to use these lessons as a starting point and integrate other instructional approaches to meet the needs of your students.

Reference

Gardner, H. *The Unschooled Mind: How Children Think and How Schools Should Teach;* Basic Books: New York, 1991.

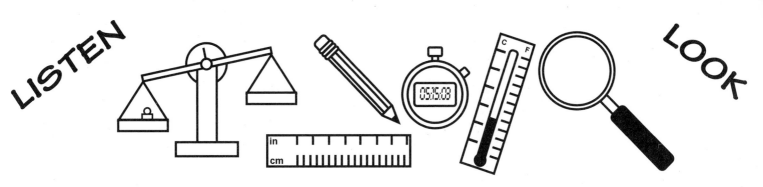

LISTEN

LOOK

_____
_____
_____
_____
_____
_____
_____
_____
_____
_____
_____
_____
_____
_____
_____
_____

What question did you try to answer with this science investigation?

_____

_____

_____

Explain what you did to answer the question.

_____

_____

_____

_____

_____

Draw your science investigation.

```
┌──────────────────────────────────────────────┐
│                                                │
│                                                │
│                                                │
│                                                │
│                                                │
│                                                │
│                                                │
│                                                │
│                                                │
└──────────────────────────────────────────────┘
```

What did you find out?

_____

_____

_____

● Organization of the Lessons

Each lesson in this book provides complete instructions for using the lesson in your classroom. These lessons have been classroom-tested by teachers like yourself and have been demonstrated to be effective, safe, and practical in elementary classrooms. The first page of each lesson includes photographs of the featured fiction book and activity materials or setup as well as overview information to help you decide how the lesson can fit into your curriculum. The rest of the lesson is organized into four parts: Building Bridges, Science Activity, Lesson Extensions, and For Further Study. Following For Further Study are masters for any reproducible pages referred to in the lesson. Each part of the lesson has several sections. These are described below and on the following pages.

Key to the First Page of Each Lesson

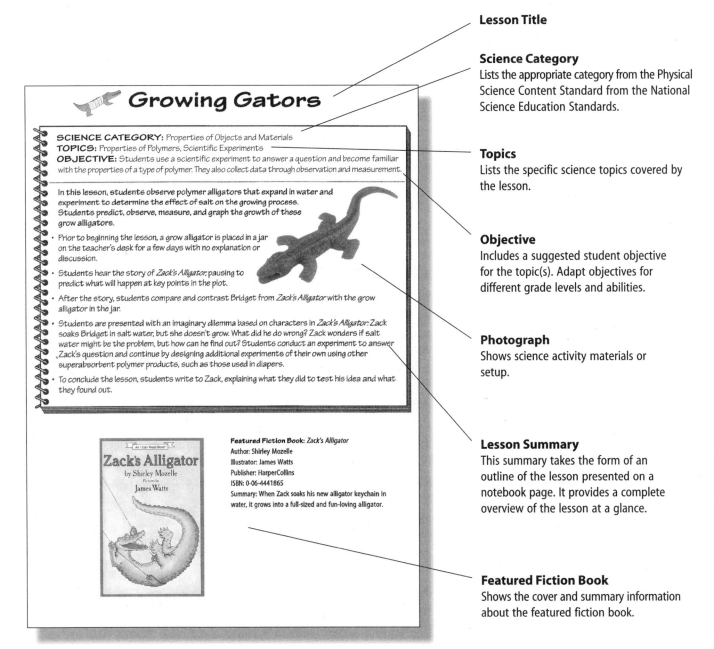

Lesson Title

Science Category
Lists the appropriate category from the Physical Science Content Standard from the National Science Education Standards.

Topics
Lists the specific science topics covered by the lesson.

Objective
Includes a suggested student objective for the topic(s). Adapt objectives for different grade levels and abilities.

Photograph
Shows science activity materials or setup.

Lesson Summary
This summary takes the form of an outline of the lesson presented on a notebook page. It provides a complete overview of the lesson at a glance.

Featured Fiction Book
Shows the cover and summary information about the featured fiction book.

Within the illustrated lesson page:

Growing Gators

SCIENCE CATEGORY: Properties of Objects and Materials
TOPICS: Properties of Polymers, Scientific Experiments
OBJECTIVE: Students use a scientific experiment to answer a question and become familiar with the properties of a type of polymer. They also collect data through observation and measurement.

In this lesson, students observe polymer alligators that expand in water and experiment to determine the effect of salt on the growing process. Students predict, observe, measure, and graph the growth of these grow alligators.

- Prior to beginning the lesson, a grow alligator is placed in a jar on the teacher's desk for a few days with no explanation or discussion.

- Students hear the story of *Zack's Alligator*, pausing to predict what will happen at key points in the plot.

- After the story, students compare and contrast Bridget from *Zack's Alligator* with the grow alligator in the jar.

- Students are presented with an imaginary dilemma based on characters in *Zack's Alligator*: Zack soaks Bridget in salt water, but she doesn't grow. What did he do wrong? Zack wonders if salt water might be the problem, but how can he find out? Students conduct an experiment to answer Zack's question and continue by designing additional experiments of their own using other superabsorbent polymer products, such as those used in diapers.

- To conclude the lesson, students write to Zack, explaining what they did to test his idea and what they found out.

Featured Fiction Book: *Zack's Alligator*
Author: Shirley Mozelle
Illustrator: James Watts
Publisher: HarperCollins
ISBN: 0-06-4441865
Summary: When Zack soaks his new alligator keychain in water, it grows into a full-sized and fun-loving alligator.

Notes and Icons

Icons appear throughout the book in the left-hand margins and are described below.

Science Chart—indicates the use of graphical organizers.

Flip Cards—indicates the use of flip card instructions.

Student Data Sheet—indicates the use of student data sheets.

Just for Fun—indicates student activities that are included just for fun.

➤ *Notes are preceded by an arrow and appear in italics.*

⚠ *Cautions are preceded by an exclamation point and appear in italics.*

Part 1: Building Bridges

- Building Student Knowledge and Motivation—This section includes an idea for a science center activity that serves as an opening strategy for the lesson. These activities help students develop common background knowledge prior to reading the story and doing the featured science activity.
- Getting Ready to Read—This section includes ideas for activities and/or discussions. These activities and discussions draw upon the student experiences from Building Student Knowledge and Motivation and set the stage for reading the story.
- Bridging to the Science Activity—This section includes ideas for activities and discussions that follow the reading of the story and help students link the story to the featured science activity.

Part 2: Science Activity

- Materials—Materials are listed for the Procedure and for any Science Extensions. Materials are divided into amounts per class, per group, and per student. Most materials can be purchased from grocery, discount department, or hardware stores. Quantities or sizes may be listed in English measure, metric measure, or both, depending on what is clear and appropriate in each case. Sources are listed for unusual items. In addition, a shopping list for unusual items is provided in Appendix C.

- Safety and Disposal—Special safety and/or disposal procedures are listed if required.
- Getting Ready—Information is provided in Getting Ready when preparation is needed before beginning the activity with students.
- Procedure—The steps in the Procedure are directed toward you, the teacher, and include cautions and suggestions where appropriate.
- Science Extensions—Extensions are methods for furthering student understanding of topics.
- Science Explanation—The Explanation is written to you, the teacher, and is intended to be modified for students.

Part 3: Lesson Extensions

- Writing Extension—This section provides suggestions for extending the activity into writing.
- Math Extension—This section provides suggestions for extending the activity into math instruction.
- Cross-Cultural Integration—This section describes how the fiction book or science activity relates to various cultures from around the world and throughout history. It is intended for teacher background. You may wish to use the information in this section to develop age-appropriate activities for your classroom.

Part 4: For Further Study

- Additional Books—Provides suggestions for additional fiction and nonfiction books for students.
- References—Cites reference materials used to develop the lesson.

Reproducible Materials

Many of the lessons in this book include masters for reproducible materials, including student data sheets and flip card instructions for centers. Permission is granted to copy these for classroom use. Flip cards can be used independently in classroom science centers, as a reference during whole group instruction, or as a set of instructions for a take-home activity. See Using Classroom Science Centers for instructions on assembling and using flip cards.

Safety

The hands-on science investigations in this book will add fun and excitement to science education in your classroom. However, even the simplest activity can become dangerous when the proper safety precautions are ignored, when the activity is done incorrectly, or when the activity is performed by students without proper supervision. The science investigations in this book have been extensively reviewed by classroom teachers of elementary grades and by university scientists. We have done all we can to assure the safety of the activities. It is up to you to assure their safe execution!

Be Careful—and Have Fun!

- Always practice activities yourself before performing them with your class. This is the only way to become thoroughly familiar with the procedures and materials required for an activity, and familiarity will help prevent potentially hazardous (or merely embarrassing) mishaps. In addition, you may find variations that will make the activity more meaningful to your students.

- Activities should be undertaken only at the recommended grade levels and only with adult supervision.

- Read each activity carefully and observe all safety precautions and disposal procedures.

- You, your assistants, and any students observing at close range must wear safety goggles if indicated in the activity and at any other time you deem necessary.

- Special safety instructions are not given for everyday classroom materials being used in a typical manner. Use common sense when working with hot, sharp, or breakable objects, such as flames, scissors, or glassware. Keep tables or desks covered to avoid stains. Keep spills cleaned up to avoid falls.

- Recycling/reuse instructions are not given for everyday materials. We encourage you to reuse and recycle the materials according to local recycling procedures.

- In some activities, potentially hazardous items such as hot-melt glue guns or ovens are to be used by the teacher only.

Section 1:
Properties of Objects and Materials

Chromatography Garden

SCIENCE CATEGORY: Properties of Objects and Materials
TOPICS: Mixtures, Chromatography
OBJECTIVE: Students discover that many colored inks are actually mixtures of colors.

In this lesson, students use chromatography to explore the properties of water-soluble ink and make beautiful flower-like designs in the process. Students also practice using expressive language to communicate scientific observations.

- Prior to beginning the lesson, students record the colors they see in a real flower bouquet and in seed catalogs.

- Through a class discussion, students draw on their observations to compile a class list of the colors they have seen in the catalogs and bouquet.

- Students hear the story *Planting a Rainbow* and watch for colors of flowers shown in the story.

- Students are presented with an imaginary dilemma: They are working for a book company and have been assigned the job of illustrating a book about flowers. Unfortunately, they have only three pens. How can they finish the illustrations? Students use chromatography to solve the problem.

- To conclude the lesson, students use booklets made with flower seed packets to record their observations.

Featured Fiction Book: *Planting a Rainbow*
Author and Illustrator: Lois Ehlert
Publisher: Harcourt Brace Jovanovich
ISBN: 0-15-262610-7
Summary: A mother and child plant a rainbow of flowers in the family garden.

Part 1: Building Bridges

Building Student Knowledge and Motivation

Set up a classroom center with a number of flower seed catalogs and an assortment of real or artificial flowers. Prior to the lesson, have groups of students visit the center and look for different colors in the catalogs and in the bouquet. Have them record the colors they see. (Masters for several types of science journal pages are provided in the Using Science Journals section at the beginning of the book.)

Getting Ready to Read

Turn to a clean sheet on your science chart and divide it into four columns: "Colors in Bouquet," "Colors in Catalogs," "Colors in *Planting a Rainbow*," and "Colors in Chromatography Garden." Through a class discussion, have students draw on their observations in the center to compile a class list of flower colors for the "Colors in Bouquet" and "Colors in Catalogs" columns on the chart.

Lead students to discuss how one color, red for example, is actually a range of different shades. Show students two different red flowers, and have them describe how the colors are different. Are there different color names they can use instead of red? Display a large box of crayons (64 or 96 colors). Have students pick out all the crayons they call red (or blue or green or yellow) and discuss why the crayons are named the way they are. Discuss why having special words to describe things like color is important, bringing out the idea that we need to communicate clearly.

Show students the cover of *Planting a Rainbow*. Ask, "How do you think the author came up with the title?" Tell students to watch for colors of flowers as you read aloud.

Bridging to the Science Activity

Ask students what colors they saw in the book. Use student responses to fill in the column titled "Colors in *Planting a Rainbow*." Have students count the number of colors they recorded in each column of the science chart. Ask "How many colors would you want to use if you were drawing pictures of a garden?"

Present students with an imaginary dilemma: "You work for a book company and have been assigned the job of illustrating a book about flower gardens. Unfortunately, you have only three pens to work with. How can you make beautiful and colorful illustrations with only three pens?" Tell students they will use a process called chromatography to solve the problem.

Part 2: Science Activity

Materials

For the Procedure

Per group
- 3 water-soluble, fine- or medium-point felt-tipped pens (Make sure each group gets only three colors.)

➤ *Use several brands of each color so that groups will get different results. Vis-a-Vis® and Crayola® brands work well. Test other brands in advance. Do not use water-soluble markers sold as "washable." These markers produce poor results. If you plan to do "Kente Chromatography," do not use black markers in this lesson so the students will not have seen the color separation of black markers before the "Kente Chromatography" activity.*

Per student
- clear plastic cup
- water
- paper circles, 9–15 cm in diameter (round filter paper or coffee filters)

➤ *Chromatography on filter paper produces a much clearer color separation than chromatography on coffee filters, but coffee filters are much less expensive. You may wish to let each student do several flowers on coffee filters and then do one design on the more expensive filter paper. Filter paper with a 9-cm diameter (#80-060-4009) and a 15-cm diameter (#80-060-4086) can be ordered from Delta Education, P.O. Box 3000, Nashua, NH 03061-9913; 800/442-5444.*

- piece of a fluffy pipe cleaner (about 4 inches in length, or a little less than the height of the plastic cup)

➤ *Large, fluffy pipe cleaners are available at craft and discount stores. The cost is minimal. Be sure to use the very fluffy ones. The more common (less fluffy) pipe cleaners do not work well.*

Per class
- sharpened pencil, nail, or similar tool to poke a 2-mm to 3-mm hole in paper
- scissors

For the Science Extension

Materials listed for the Procedure plus the following:

Per class
- 9-inch pie pan with a clear plastic lid
- paper towel
- large piece of filter paper

➤ *Large filter paper with a 24-cm diameter (#09–795J) can be ordered from Fisher Scientific, 1600 W. Glenlake Ave., Itasca, IL 60143; 800/766-7000.*

Safety and Disposal

No special safety or disposal procedures are required.

Getting Ready

Test each type of pen to make sure that the ink will migrate and/or separate on the paper. All water-soluble pens do not work equally well. (Specifically, washable markers do not work well.) Poke a small hole in the center of enough paper circles for Steps 1 and 2 of the Procedure. You need not poke holes in the paper circles for Steps 3 and 4 because the students can easily poke wet pipe cleaners into the paper without making a hole in advance.

Procedure

1. Tell students that before they make the flowers, you want them to observe just the paper and water. Have each group do the following steps:

   a. Roll a wedge-shaped piece of filter paper into a cone and stick the pointed end through the hole in the paper circle. (See Figure 1.)

   Younger students may need help rolling the paper wedges.

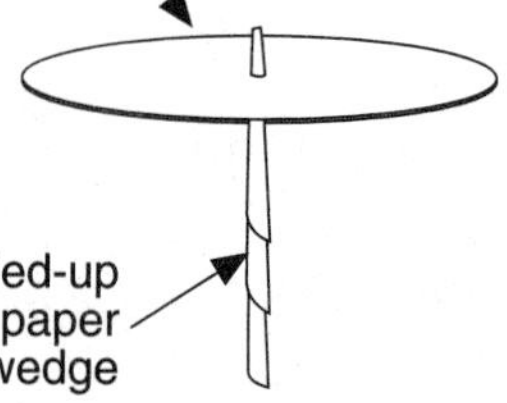

   b. Put enough water into a cup so that the bottom of the cone will dip into the water.

   c. Put the paper circle on top of the cup with the bottom of the cone touching the water.

filter paper

rolled-up filter paper wedge

Figure 1

2. Have students watch the paper for a few minutes. Ask, "What happened?" *The water moved up the paper cone and wet the paper.* "Do things usually go up by themselves? Why or why not?" *No. Because of gravity.* Explain that water moves up the paper cone and across the circle because the water is attracted to the paper. Tell students that the movement of water is an important part of making chromatography flowers.

3. Model the following steps for the students:

   a. Write your name lightly in pencil on one side of the paper circle.

   b. Use the markers to make a quarter-sized ring of small dots approximately around the center of the paper circle, alternating all three colors.

   c. Put enough water into a cup so that the bottom of the pipe cleaner will dip into the water.

   d. Completely wet a piece of pipe cleaner and stick it in the center of the paper.

   Although using rolled-up paper wedges is an alternative in this Procedure, pipe cleaners are easier to use and reusable.

   e. Put the paper on top of the cup with the bottom of the pipe cleaner touching the water.

   f. When the water gets near the edge of the paper, remove the paper from the pipe cleaner and set the paper aside to dry.

4. Have students make their chromatography flowers using the flip cards (provided) as a reference. Give students a chance to complete one or more flowers.

Flip Cards

SCIENCE CHART

5. Bring out the science chart from Getting Ready to Read. Talk again about how the class used different words to describe different red flowers and crayons. Tell students that scientists need to be able to describe their observations just as the class described the different crayon and flower colors. Ask students to name the colors they see in their chromatography flowers. Use student responses to fill in the column titled "Colors in Chromatography Garden." Have students count the number of colors listed in this column. Ask, "How many colors did we start with?" *Three.* "How many did we end with?"

Teaching Physical Science through Children's Literature

6. Ask students where they think the additional colors came from. Through a facilitated discussion, lead students to understand that the colors were in the ink all along and that many inks are mixtures of several colors.

7. Put some chromatography flowers in the center along with materials to make more flowers. Add a selection of nonfiction books about colors. Give students opportunities to visit the center over the next week or so, and encourage them to add any new observations to the science chart.

Science Extension

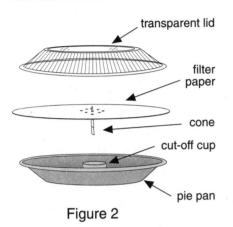

transparent lid

filter paper

cone

cut-off cup

pie pan

Figure 2

Make a giant chromatography flower: Cut the top off a plastic cup so that when it sits in the pie pan it is not taller than the sides of a 9-inch pie pan. (See Figure 2.) Fill the cup about ¾ full of water. Dry the rim of the cup with a paper towel. Place the cup in the center of the pan. Poke a hole in the center of a large, round piece of filter paper. With three markers, make five or six dots around the center hole. (Make proportionally larger dots than in the Procedure.) Insert a cone of filter paper through the large, round piece of filter paper. Place the paper on the pie pan so the cone extends into the cup of water in the center of the tray. (The rim of the cup supports the center of the paper, and the rim of the pan supports the edges.) Place a clear plastic lid over the setup to give a clear view of the spreading colors. Allow about one hour for this giant chromatography flower to develop.

Science Explanation

The following explanation is intended for the teacher's information. Modify the explanation for students as required.

Although the ink in a marking pen appears to be just one color, it often consists of more than one color. That is, the ink is a mixture, made up of two or more substances, each of which retains its own properties within the mixture. One characteristic of a mixture is that the component substances can be separated from one another by physical processes. In this activity, a process called chromatography is used to separate the components of the ink mixtures. Chromatography requires a stationary phase (such as paper) and a mobile phase (such as water).

When the paper circle and pipe cleaner are put into contact with water, the water travels up the pipe cleaner and outward through the paper circle by capillary action. The capillary action is strong enough to overcome gravity and move the water up the pipe cleaner. The leading edge of the water moves across the paper because of the attraction of water particles to particles in paper; the trailing water follows along because of strong attraction between water particles themselves. When the water contacts a water-soluble ink, the ink dissolves in the water. As the water continues to move, the component substances in the ink are carried along. The different substances spread outward at different rates on the paper circle.

The rate of travel for a substance depends on two factors: the magnitude of the attraction between the particles of the substance and the particles of water, and the magnitude of the attraction between the particles of the substance and the paper. Because the attraction for each of the component substances is different, the pigments separate from one another as the water moves. Those substances with greatest attraction for the water move across the paper the most; those with greatest attraction for the paper move the least.

The process of separating the components of a mixture in this way is called paper chromatography. The resulting "flower" produced on the paper circle is called a chromatogram. There are types of chromatography other than paper chromatography, but all are used to separate mixtures.

Part 3: Lesson Extensions

Writing Extension

Figure 3

For this extension it would be wise to purchase many seed packets at the end of the planting season when the cost is minimal. You could also time this activity to correlate with spring and/or Mother's Day. Have each student take a seed packet, carefully cut off the top, and place the seeds in a small envelope. Then, have students cut off the bottom and right side and open the seed packet so it resembles a book cover. Have them staple small sheets of plain paper cut to the size of the seed packet to the inside of the cover to make a small book. (See Figure 3.) Have students tape the envelope containing the seeds to the inside back cover. Students can use the booklet as a science journal to record their observations about the science activity.

Math Extension

Collect a wide variety of seed catalogs. Have students working individually or in small groups cut out enough pictures of flowers from the catalogs to make a "rainbow garden" collage. At the same time, they should cut out or write down the price of each seed packet. Have students figure out how much it would cost to actually plant their rainbow gardens. Assign the students an imaginary amount of money and ask them to keep track of what plants or seeds they would buy and what change they would receive. Also, have them compare the cost of similar seeds and plants from different companies.

Cross-Cultural Integration

 This section is intended for teacher background. You may wish to use the information in this section to develop age-appropriate activities for your classroom.

People often react to colors in ways that match their traditional cultural significance. Often these reactions/beliefs stem from the history or myths of a particular culture. A color's meaning can vary in different parts of the world, or even within the same country. *When Blue Meant Yellow: How Colors Got Their Names* (See Additional Books) describes the origins of nearly 200 color names and also discusses how cultures around the world distinguish colors differently. Presented in the following paragraphs is just a tiny sampling of the fascinating historical and cultural information about color.

Red

Red is a color with many associations. In English, French, German, and Latin the word "red" stems from a root that probably meant "blood." As a result, red means physical life and energy. Red also signifies bloodshed and is the color of the planet and war god Mars. A victorious Roman general would paint his face red and ride through the streets proudly. Indian war chiefs painted their faces red in preparation for battle. Red is commonly seen as a symbol of power. Ancient kings often chose this color for their garments. The expression "roll out the red carpet" indicates an appropriate way to treat people of great importance.

Yellow

The color yellow has been connected with treachery. During the Spanish Inquisition, those condemned for heresy were dressed in yellow. In France, the doors of traitors were marked with yellow paint.

Green

Green is the color of vegetation, the renewal of life in the spring. The Green Man of British inn signs commemorates an important figure of old springtime activities. In England this man was called Jack in the Green or Jack in the Bush. Jack was the center of the May Day celebration. He was a man covered with ivy leaves, crowned with paper roses, and encased in a framework shaped like a bottle.

Green is for some unknown reason also the color of envy. Perhaps this is the reason for the old Scottish rule that if a girl married before her older sisters, she gave them green stockings.

Blue

The word "blue" comes from the Middle English word "blew" and the Old English word "blaw." The early Britons and modern Maori both tattooed themselves in blue, a sacrificial color. The Britons used a blue paint (woad) as war paint because going to war was considered to be a sacrifice.

Violet/Purple

Purple has become associated with royalty and wealth. Purple stems from the Greek word *porphura*, a species of shellfish that yielded the dye Tyrian purple. This dye, which actually was crimson, or at most a deep purplish red, was reserved for use on special cloth and garments. Emperors, military commanders, and other high officials wore "purple" robes. As late as the seventeenth century, the word "purple" still meant this crimson color, and was associated with ecclesiastical and royal mourning, as well as with royalty. Modern purple (a mixture of blue and red) remains associated with royalty.

Additional Information

Native American tribes such as the Cherokee, Pueblo, and Aztecs used colors to designate particular directions. For the Pueblo, white represented east, and blue or yellow represented south. The Cherokees equated red with east and the attribute success, blue referred to north and trouble, black referred to west and death, and white indicated south and happiness. The Aztecs spoke of four main colors—red, yellow, white, and black—which were the four main types of corn, the four cardinal directions, and the gods associated with them.

In Chinese theater, character was denoted by a complicated system of color symbolism: white for treachery, black for integrity, red for courage, and blue for ferocity. Demons and villains had predominantly green faces. Chinese robes and headdresses also had color symbolism indicating character and rank.

Part 4: For Further Study

Additional Books

Nonfiction

Title: *Science Book of Color*
Author: Neil Ardley
Publisher: Harcourt Brace Jovanovich   ISBN: 0-15-200576-5
Summary: Explains the principles of color and gives instructions for a variety of simple experiments.

Title: *When Blue Meant Yellow: How Colors Got Their Names*
Author: Jeanne Heifetz
Publisher: Holt   ISBN: 0-8050-3178-2
Summary: Describes the origins of nearly 200 color names. This book also discusses how cultures around the world distinguish colors differently.

References

"Chromatography Flowers," *Fun with Chemistry: A Guidebook of K–12 Activities;* Sarquis, M., Sarquis J., Eds.; Institute for Chemical Education: Madison, WI, 1993; Vol. 2, pp 23–28.
Sarquis, M.; Sarquis, J.; Williams, J. "Chromatography Color Burst;" *Teaching Chemistry with TOYS: Activities for Grades K–9;* McGraw-Hill: New York, 1995; pp 195–199.

Flip Cards

❶

Write your name lightly in pencil on one side of the paper circle.

Use the three colored markers to make a ring of small dots around the center of the paper circle.

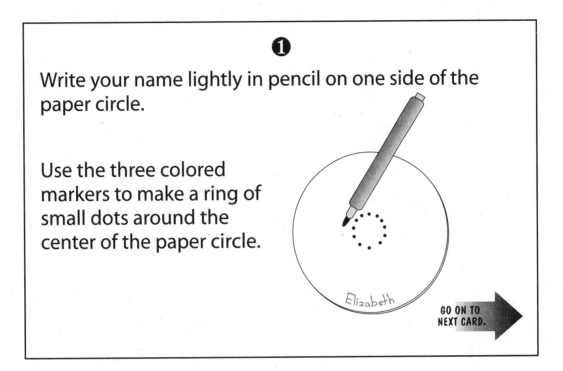

GO ON TO NEXT CARD.

❷

Put enough water in the cup so the bottom of the pipe cleaner will dip into the water.

GO ON TO NEXT CARD.

❸

Completely wet a piece of pipe cleaner and stick it in the center of the paper circle.

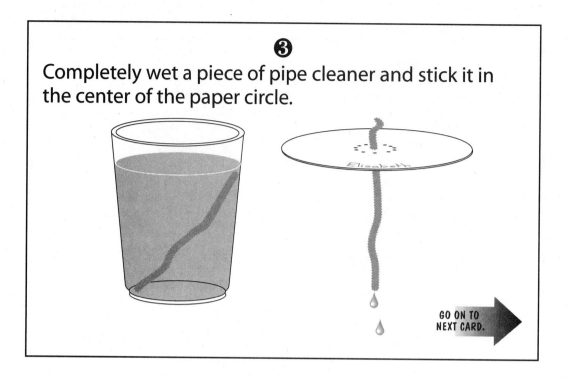

GO ON TO
NEXT CARD.

❹

Put the paper on top of the cup with the bottom of the pipe cleaner in the water.

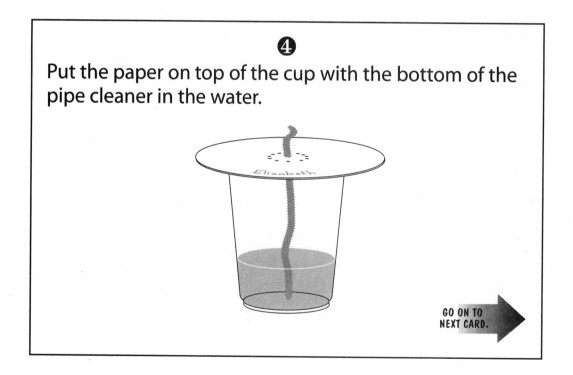

GO ON TO
NEXT CARD.

❺

When the water gets near the edge of the paper, remove the paper from the pipe cleaner. Set the paper aside to dry.

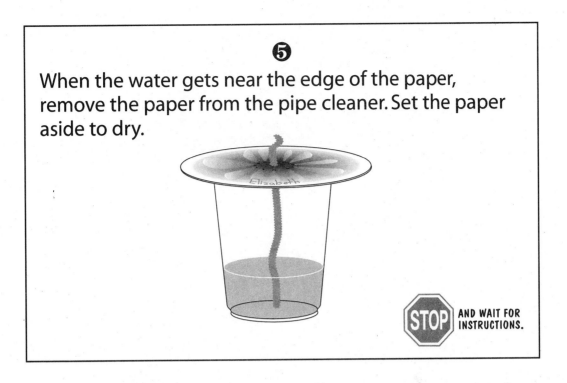

STOP AND WAIT FOR INSTRUCTIONS.

Kente Chromatography

SCIENCE CATEGORY: Properties of Objects and Materials
TOPICS: Mixtures, Chromatography
OBJECTIVE: Students learn that many black pigments are really mixtures of colors.

In this lesson, students explore cultural meanings of the word "black" and use chromatography to discover that there is more to many black pigments than meets the eye. Ideally, this activity should follow "Chromatography Garden."

- Prior to beginning the lesson, students write descriptions of a diverse collection of black objects.

- As a class, students discuss the objects they have observed and record observations on a science chart.

- After a chalk chromatography experiment is set up, students hear the story *The Black Snowman* and listen for different meanings of the word "black" in the story. After listening to the story they observe what has happened to the chalk and add observations to the science chart.

- Students use black markers, water, and chromatography to make colorful kente-like paper and cloth.

- To conclude the lesson, students write a letter to Jacob, telling him what they have learned about the color black and describing one of the chromatography activities, in case Jacob would like to try the activity.

Featured Fiction Book: *The Black Snowman*
Author: Phil Mendez
Illustrator: Carole Byard
Publisher: Scholastic, Inc.
ISBN: 0-590-44873-0
Summary: Jacob and his brother make a snowman from the dirty city snow. The boys wrap the snowman in a cloth they find. But the scrap is really a kente, an African storyteller's shawl, which has magical qualities the boys soon discover.

Part 1: Building Bridges

Building Student Knowledge and Motivation

Set up a classroom science center with a diverse collection of black objects or photographs of black objects. Make sure that some of the objects represent culturally positive images of black. Positive items could be a black belt in karate or a black tuxedo or other dressy black evening wear suitable for a "black tie" event. Some items should represent common culturally negative images of black, such as a cowboy or knight wearing black (the bad guy) or a bad witch wearing black and keeping a black cat. Other black items in the center could be culturally neutral. Have students visit the center and record the name and a brief description of each item. (Masters for several types of science journal pages are provided in the Using Science Journals section at the beginning of this book.)

Getting Ready to Read

Title a new science chart "The Color Black" and divide it into three columns: "Item," "Description," and "Feelings." Have students share their observations of each item and list words to describe feelings they would associate with each. Bring up the idea that a color itself can represent feelings, even when that color is not associated with a particular object.

Figure 1

Before reading the story, set up a simple demonstration: Use a water-soluble marker as described in Materials to draw a black ring around a piece of white, porous chalk, about 1 inch from the bottom of the chalk. (Make sure the chalk is not dustless.) Check the marker in advance to be sure it will produce a multicolored chromatograph. Add "black ring on chalk" to the list of items on the science chart, and record a description and any feelings the class suggests. Pour about ½ inch of water into a small, clear plastic cup. Ask students to predict what will happen when you put the chalk in the water. Stand the chalk on end in the water, ring side down. (See Figure 1.) Tell students that the class will look at the chalk in a little while.

Show students the cover of *The Black Snowman*. Ask students what they think the story is about. Tell students to listen for ideas about the color black as you read the story. Be sure to keep an eye on the chalk as you read, as you want to remove it from the water before all the color reaches the top. The story is rather long, and if the chalk is in the water too long the separate colors will recombine at the top of the chalk. When you see that the water has traveled up most of the length of the chalk, take it out of the water and set it aside for viewing after the story.

Bridging to the Science Activity

Through class discussion, add more items to the science chart based on what Jacob and the black snowman say about the color black in the story. Discuss and record the feelings the characters in the story associate with each item. Ask students if they feel the same as or differently than the characters.

Bring out the chalk from Getting Ready to Read. Ask students to describe it now, and add descriptions and any feelings the class suggests to the science chart. Ask students where they think the colors on the chalk came from, but do not elaborate at this time. Tell students they will be repeating the experiment with different materials to see if the results are similar.

Part 2: Science Activity

Materials

For the Procedure, Parts A and B

Per group

- black **water-soluble** marker

➤ *Water-soluble Vis-a-Vis® pens work well. Try markers in advance to be sure they provide the desired separation. Do not use water-soluble markers sold as "washable." They give poor results.*

For the Procedure, Part A

Per class

- hole punch
- (optional) piece of authentic kente cloth or cotton fabric printed to look like kente cloth

➤ *Kente cloth can be purchased from some stores that specialize in international imports. Cotton fabric printed to look like kente cloth is available in most fabric stores.*

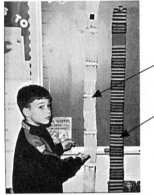

chromatography kente

real kente cloth

Per student

- piece of white blotter paper or heavy filter paper, about 3 inches x 5 inches
- clear plastic cup wide enough for narrow end of paper to rest on bottom
- piece of yarn about 2 feet long

Per pair of students

- clear plastic 32-ounce deep deli container or similar container
- ruler
- 4-inch x 10-inch strip of lightweight white 100% cotton cloth, such as lawn

➤ *Wash cloth to remove sizing before cutting the cloth into 4-inch x 10-inch strips.*

Per class

- paper towels
- needle and thread
- (optional) black cloth to line finished kente

Getting Ready

Part A:

1. Draw a horizontal pencil line about 1 inch above the bottom of each blotter paper piece. (The bottom is one of the 3-inch-across ends.)

2. Use a hole punch to make a hole near the top/center of each blotter paper piece.

Procedure

Part A: Mini Kente Chromatography

1. If available, show students a sample of kente cloth. Review the importance of the kente cloth in *The Black Snowman*. Tell students that they will be repeating the chalk experiment with heavy paper and at the same time making a mini kente to wear.

2. Have each student use a pencil to print his or her name in the 1-inch area below the pencil line on the piece of blotter paper. (See Getting Ready.) Then, have them use black water-soluble marker to trace along the pencil line. Ask students to predict what will happen when they put the paper in the water.

3. Add "black line on paper" to the list of items on the science chart, and record a description and any feelings the class suggests.

4. Tell students to pour about ½ inch of water into the cups.

5. Have each student carefully place the paper in the cup, black line down. (See Figure 2.)

When the paper is in the container, the marker line must be above the water level. If the line is not above the water level, the ink will run into the water. In this case, have the student discard the paper, rinse out the cup, and start over.

Figure 2: Place the paper strip in the water.

6. Have students observe the paper, the black line, and the water level. (As the water moves up the paper, the black line begins to separate, and the colors creep up the paper.)

7. When the water has moved up the paper almost to the top, have students remove the paper from the cup and lay it on paper towels to dry.

It will take about 45 minutes for the water to reach the upper edge of the paper.

8. Ask students to describe the paper now, and add descriptions and any feelings the class suggests to the science chart. Compare the results with paper to those with chalk. Ask students where they think the colors on the paper came from. How does the mini kente compare with real kente cloth?

9. Have each student string a length of yarn through the hole in the paper and tie it so that the students can wear their mini kentes like necklaces.

Part B: Class Kente Chromatography

1. Tell students that they will be repeating the experiment with fabric and at the same time making a class kente cloth.

2. Instruct each pair of students to draw a line with the black marker about 1 inch from each end of the cloth strip.

3. Add "black line on cloth" to the list of items on the science chart, and record a description and any feelings the class suggests.

4. Have each pair pour about ½ inch of water into the deli container and place the ruler across the top.

5. Tell students to drape the cloth strip over the ruler so that each end is hanging down and just touching the water. (See Figure 3.)

 When the cloth is in the container, the marker lines must be above the water level. If the lines are not above the water level, the ink will run into the water and a separation will not occur.

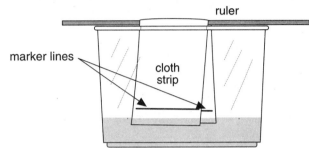

Figure 3: Place the ends of the cloth in the water.

6. Have students observe the cloth, the black lines, and the water. When the colors reach the ruler, students should remove the cloth and lay it on paper towels to dry.

7. Ask students to describe the cloth now, and add to the science chart descriptions and any feelings the class suggests. Compare the results with the fabric to those with the paper and the chalk. Ask students where they think the colors on the cloth came from.

8. Through class discussion, summarize students' observations and conclusions about the three activities, and bring out the idea that the colors on the chalk, paper, and fabric came from the black ink. Emphasize that although black ink looks like it's all one kind of thing, it is really a mixture of different colors of ink.

9. Turn to the part of *The Black Snowman* where the snowman changes colors. Reread those two paragraphs aloud to the class, and show the picture of the snowman with a rainbow-colored face. Ask, "How is this part of the story similar to our activity?"

10. Introduce the word "chromatography" and add information to the science chart about chromatography and mixtures as desired. (See the Science Explanation for background.)

11. Sew the fabric strips end to end to make a long kente. If desired, use black cloth to line the kente and give it a finished look. Ask, "How does the class kente compare with real kente cloth?" Students may be disappointed that their chromatography kente is not as bright as the real one, but explain that their kente is unique because it shows something special about the color black.

Part C: Class Discussion

The Black Snowman is a powerful story that brings up many important issues about being African-American and about cultural perceptions of the color black. During this lesson, your students have had an opportunity to reflect on their feelings about the story and their ideas about the color black from both cultural and scientific viewpoints. At this point in the lesson, involve students in a class discussion to help them summarize and synthesize these ideas.

Science Explanation

The following explanation is intended for the teacher's information. Modify the explanation for students as required.

Although black ink appears to be a single color, it is actually a mixture of different-colored pigments. As in "Chromatography Garden," this lesson uses a technique called chromatography to separate the various pigments contained in an ink mixture. Chromatography requires a stationary phase, such as blotter paper, and a mobile phase, such as water, to move the dissolved pigments. (See "Chromatography Garden" for more information on chromatography.) In this lesson, you use three different materials for the stationary phase: chalk, blotter paper, and cotton fabric. These materials all work well as a stationary phase because they are absorbent. Water moves through the chalk, paper, or fabric because of a phenomenon called capillary action. The small pores or capillaries found in these materials allow the water to move above the level of the liquid in the cup. The separation obtained through chromatography depends on an interaction between the pigments, the water, and the material used for the stationary phase. Your students may have observed differences in the results obtained with chalk, paper, and fabric.

In this activity we use chromatography to demonstrate that black ink is usually a mixture of many colors. But why do we see this mixture of colored pigments as black? Strictly speaking, black is not a color itself, but the absence of light. As discussed in "Whirling Colors," an object appears to be a particular color because of the color of light that bounces off it. For example, red light bounces off red ink; the other colors of light are absorbed. The red light reaches our eyes, and we see the ink as being the color red. In the case of black ink, nearly all the light that hits the ink is absorbed by the various colors of pigment present in the ink mixture. Very little light bounces back to our eyes, and we see the ink as black.

Part 3: Lesson Extensions

Writing Extensions

Figure 4

1. Have students write a letter to Jacob describing what they have learned about the color black and why black is such a special color. Have students include in the letter a description of how to repeat one of the activities, in case Jacob would like to see for himself. Mount the letters on large snowman shapes cut out of black paper. (See Figure 4.) If desired, students can make additional strips of paper chromatography to use as a chromatography kente on the snowman. Students can wear the class kente while sharing their letters with the class.

2. Have students find the meanings for English words and expressions using the word black (such as "blackmail," "in the black," "black eye," "black tie," and "black belt") and write sentences using these words and expressions.

Teaching Physical Science through Children's Literature

Cross-Cultural Integration

 This section is intended for teacher background. You may wish to use the information in this section to develop age-appropriate activities for your classroom.

The Color Black

Black is one of the oldest color words in English, from an Indo-European root that means "to shine," or "to gleam." Many cultures have words for different kinds of black: a group of people called the Naisoi (from the South Pacific) use one word for the kind of black that is "dark like a forest," and another word for black that is "dark like night." The Navajo have one word for the black of darkness and another for black objects. In English, "jet black" means the most intense black of all. The name "jet black" comes from fossilized driftwood called jet, which is formed when the wood becomes buried in the mud of the sea floor. Jet takes a very high polish, which makes it popular for jewelry.

The color black has different meanings in different cultures, and sometimes even within the same culture. To the Cherokees, black referred to west and death. The Aztecs spoke of four main colors—red, yellow, white, and black—which were the four main types of corn, the four cardinal directions, and the gods associated with them. In Chinese theater, black represented integrity, but in Chinese robes and headdresses, black was supposedly worn by disreputable people.

Negative associations with the color black are well known in western culture, such as "black magic" and "blackmail." However, it is important to remember that the color black is not always associated with evil or death. In heraldry, black represents constancy, prudence, and wisdom. Edward, Prince of Wales and the oldest son of Edward III, was referred to as the Black Prince, possibly because those virtues were attributed to him. The phrase of being "in the black" also has a good connotation, meaning being out of debt or showing a profit.

Kente Cloth

The Ashanti people of Ghana are known for their beautiful kente cloth. The traditional looms for making kente are very narrow and produce cloth only four inches wide, but as long as 30 feet. The designs are bright, colorful, and complicated. The narrow strips of fabric are artistically sewn into long wide pieces. Kente cloth became the formal dress of the Ashanti and is now the traditional dress of Ghana.

Kente designs have become so famous that they have been given names, and favorite proverbs are associated with them. One kente design is called Mamponhemaa. The word means "queen mother of Mampong." Another design is called Sikafuturo, which means gold dust. As the name implies, this cloth is very expensive, and only the rich can afford it. Ebusuaye Dom, the name of another design, means "a family is an army," a proverb that says there is strength in family unity.

Kente is now worn for all formal occasions such as meetings, weddings, and parties. A man's kente outfit is similar to a Roman toga. With it he wears a bright, handwoven cap and Roman-style sandals. A woman's kente dress looks very much like an Indian sari—a long garment that serves as formal dress and shawl combined. Modern kente weavers, who work on broad looms, use kente designs to make fabric for clothing as well as for other woven items such as bedspreads and table cloths.

Part 4: For Further Study

Additional Books

Fiction

Title: *Rainbow Crow*
Author: Nancy VanLaan   Illustrator: Beatriz Vidal
Publisher: Alfred A. Knopf   ISBN: 0-394-99577-5
Summary: An American Indian tale of Crow, who has beautiful feathers. He goes to the Sun God to get fire to break the cold winter and melt the snow. As he brings back the fire, his feathers are charred and blackened. In his sadness, he sees that his feathers are really tiny rainbows of color.

Title: *A Story-A Story: An African Tale*
Author and Illustrator: Gail Haley
Publisher: Atheneum   ISBN: 0-689-71201-4
Summary: This retold tale recounts how most African folk tales came to be called "Spider Stories."

Nonfiction

Title: *Ashanti to Zulu: African Traditions*
Author: Margaret Musgrove   Illustrators: Leo and Diane Dillon
Publisher: Dial Books for Young Readers
ISBN: 0-8037-0308-2
Summary: Describes the ceremonies, celebrations, and customs of 26 African tribes beginning with the letters from A to Z. It includes a mention of the Ashanti and kente cloth.

References

Ammer, C. *Seeing Red or Tickled Pink—Color Terms in Everyday Language;* Dutton: New York, 1992.

Heifetz, J. *When Blue Meant Yellow: How Colors Got Their Names;* Henry Holt: New York, 1994.

Searching for Empty Space

SCIENCE CATEGORY: Properties of Objects and Materials
TOPICS: Air Takes Up Space, Compressibility of Gases
OBJECTIVE: Students observe that air, although invisible, does take up space.

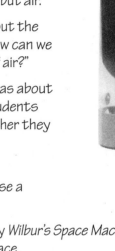

In this lesson, students use their observations to construct an alternative view to the common misconception that the space around us is "empty."

- Prior to beginning the lesson, the class plays a game of 20 questions to guess what is inside a sealed box that actually contains nothing but air.

- As a class, students discuss the 20 questions game and bring out the idea that air is not "nothing." They also discuss the question, "How can we demonstrate that something that looks empty is actually full of air?"

- Students hear the story *Wilbur's Space Machine* and listen for ideas about air and empty space in the story. Through a class discussion, students list the ideas about air they heard in the story and discuss whether they think those ideas are true or not.

- Students do several science center activities that give them opportunities to observe that air takes up space. They then devise a procedure of their own to demonstrate the same concept.

- To conclude the lesson, students write a new version of the story *Wilbur's Space Machine*, incorporating what they have observed about air and "empty" space.

Featured Fiction Book: *Wilbur's Space Machine*
Author and Illustrator: Lorna Balian
Publisher: Humbug Books
ISBN: 0-8234-0836-1
Summary: Wilbur constructs a machine to manufacture "empty space" because his house is too crowded. The "space" is contained in balloons and stored in his house. Soon there is no room left to live. When Wilbur ties the balloons to the house, it floats away.

Part 1: Building Bridges

Building Student Knowledge and Motivation

Several days before beginning the lesson, attractively decorate a sealed, "empty" box. Tell students that you want them to play a game of 20 questions to guess what is inside. Explain that they will not be able to touch or shake the box, and that you want them to ask thoughtful questions that will help the whole class collect information to solve the mystery. Tell them that you will answer their questions "yes," "no," or "sometimes." Give some examples of questions that don't help very much, like wild guesses such as "Is it an elephant?" when the box's dimensions are only 1 foot x 1 foot x 1 foot.

Conduct the game over a period of days, taking five or six student questions each day. Record the questions and your answers on a science chart for reference. When a student guesses the answer, or when the 20 questions are used up, show the inside of the box.

Getting Ready to Read

After the game is over, discuss the answer, "air." Students may protest that the box is empty and that "nothing" or "empty" should be the answer. Label a science chart with three columns: "How We Could Demonstrate," "How We Did Demonstrate," and "New Ideas." Discuss the observation that the box does look empty, and pose the question, "How can we demonstrate that something that looks empty is actually full—of air?" Chart all ideas in the "How We Could Demonstrate" column, but do not discuss further at this time.

Show students the cover of *Wilbur's Space Machine*. Ask them how they think the story relates to the "empty" box in the game of 20 questions. Tell students to listen for ideas about air and empty space in the story.

Bridging to the Science Activity

Through a class discussion, pose the question, "What is empty space?" Emphasize that you are not talking about outer space, but rather about the kind of space in an "empty" box or bag. Ask, "What do we mean when we say a box or container is 'empty'? What does it mean to fill it?" Reread the book or parts of the book, stopping at points that discuss space or the need for space. Look at Wilbur and Violet's home in the beginning of the story, when they have lots of "empty" space. Then look at the pictures showing how their "empty" space begins to dwindle. Discuss the differences between the pictures. Look at the pictures when Wilbur begins filling the house with empty space. Pay particular attention to the "Space Machine." Pose the question, "If Wilbur is filling the house with empty space, why is the house getting more and more crowded?" Look again at the Space Machine. Ask, "What do you think Wilbur is actually putting into all of the containers?"

Have students list the ideas about air and empty space they heard in the story and discuss whether they think those ideas are true or not. Refer to the class list of ideas about how to demonstrate that "empty" objects are full of air. Tell students that they will be using several methods to demonstrate that an "empty" container is filled with air and then designing their own methods to demonstrate this concept.

Part 2: Science Activity

Materials

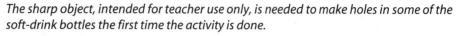

For Getting Ready only
- push pin, thumbtack, or nail

The sharp object, intended for teacher use only, is needed to make holes in some of the soft-drink bottles the first time the activity is done.

For Balloon in a Bottle
Per class
- two clear plastic 1-liter (L) soft-drink bottles

Although 1-L bottles work best, 2-L bottles can be substituted.

Per student
- balloon

For How Dry I Am
Per class
- tub or large bowl filled with water
- roll of paper towels
- tape
- clear 10-ounce plastic cup

Solo® makes a cup like this.

For Fill It Up
Per student
- business-sized envelope
- balloon

Safety and Disposal

For health reasons, use a clean balloon for each student. No special disposal procedures are required.

Getting Ready

1. Prepare a science center with three activities (Balloon in a Bottle, How Dry I Am, and Fill it Up):

    a. For Balloon in a Bottle, put a hole in one of the bottles by carefully pushing a push pin, thumbtack, or nail through the side. Put a number 1 on a bottle without a hole and a number 2 on the bottle with a hole. Put both bottles and a copy of the Question Sheet (provided) in the center.

b. For How Dry I Am, place a tub or large bowl filled with water, a plastic cup, the flip card instructions (provided), and a roll of paper towels in the center.

c. For Fill It Up, place the Instruction Sheet (provided) in the center. (You'll distribute materials for this activity to students.)

Procedure

Part A: Center Exploration

1. Divide students into groups and explain that each group will have a chance to visit a science center to do three science activities over the next few days: Balloon in a Bottle, How Dry I Am, and Fill It Up.

2. Emphasize that students should follow all instructions carefully and record their observations using words and/or pictures. (Masters for several types of science journal pages are provided in the Using Science Journals section.)

3. Distribute a balloon to each student for Balloon in a Bottle. Distribute a business-sized envelope and a balloon to each student for Fill It Up.

4. Over a period of several days, give students an opportunity to visit the center and record their observations.

Part B: Discussion

As students discuss their observations and ideas, add to the "How We Did Demonstrate" column of the science chart from Getting Ready to Read.

1. Have students share their observations of each activity. Ask, "What did all of the activities have in common?" *They showed that air takes up space.* Ask, "When you worked in the center, how could you tell that air took up space?" *We couldn't inflate the balloon when it was in the bottle without a hole, because the air inside took up space. The inflated balloon wouldn't fit back into the envelope, because the air inside the balloon took up space and made the balloon bigger. The paper towel in the bottom of the cup did not get wet when the cup was held straight down, because the air inside prevented the water from flowing into the cup.* Ask, "What does it mean for something to be 'empty?' Are things we often describe as 'empty' really empty?"

2. Bring out the idea that in students' everyday world, air fills the space that is not occupied by something else. An "empty" room is full of air, even though we can't see it. When we move, we push air aside; air moves out of our way and fills the space we just left.

3. Discuss what happens when an "empty" container, such as a box or balloon, is filled with something besides air. Ask, "If air takes up space, how can we put something else into the container?" *In order to put something else into the container, air must be able to flow out.* Relate this idea to the "Balloon in a Bottle" center. In Bottle 1, the balloon could not be inflated very much because the air filling the "empty" bottle could not flow out. Only when the air could flow out, as in Bottle 2, could the balloon be inflated in the bottle.

4. Refer back to *Wilbur's Space Machine.* Ask, "What is Wilbur's Space Machine filling the containers with?" *Air.* "Why is the house getting more crowded?" *The air-filled containers take up space.* Ask, "Do you think Wilbur's machine was really a space machine?"

Part C: Independent Exploration

1. Read *Air Is All Around You,* by Franklyn Branley. (See Additional Books).

2. Refer to the "How We Could Demonstrate" column of the science chart. Ask students if they have anything to change or add based on what they've learned.

3. Tell students that you would like each group to come up with an original plan for demonstrating that air takes up space. The plan should be different than the activities students have already done. Explain that this plan must include a list of materials needed, a drawing of the setup, and a set of steps for carrying out the plan.

4. Give groups time to develop their plans.

5. Have each group describe their plan to the class. List these plans in the "New Ideas" column of the science chart.

6. (optional) Bring in materials for groups to try out their ideas.

Science Explanation

The following explanation is intended for the teacher's information. Modify the explanation for students as required.

We live in an ocean of gas called the atmosphere. The air that makes up our atmosphere is a mixture of many gases; nitrogen and oxygen are the most abundant. Because air is invisible and constantly displaced by our movements, we scarcely notice it or think of it as taking up space. Like all gases, gases in the atmosphere flow and take the shape of their containers. Gases also expand to fill all available space.

Balloon in a Bottle

The Balloon in a Bottle activity demonstrates that it is difficult to fill something that is already full of air unless some of the air can escape. The air trapped inside the bottle prevents you from totally inflating the balloon. To blow up a balloon anywhere, you need to blow enough air into the balloon to provide enough pressure to stretch the rubber, and you need to apply enough pressure to push the air around the balloon out of the way. The former is observed by anyone who has ever blown up a new balloon. The latter is rarely noticed because it is typically so easy to displace air in the atmosphere that almost no extra pressure is required. However, the task becomes more difficult when the air around the balloon is not free to move away. Such is the case in this activity. Even though gases are compressible, it is impossible for most of us to blow forcefully enough to exert the pressure needed to compress the trapped air very much. Putting a hole in the bottle allows air initially inside the bottle to escape and thus makes room for the balloon to expand.

How Dry I Am

In the How Dry I Am activity, air is trapped in the cup when the cup is submerged. The air in the cup keeps water out, so the paper towel stays dry (unless the paper towel dislodges or slips downward). Some water will enter the open end of the cup because the air in the cup is slightly compressed as the cup is pushed into the water. Tilting the cup to the side underwater allows air in the cup to escape and rise through the more-dense water. Then water is able to enter the cup. If enough air escapes, water will wet the paper towel.

Fill It Up
In the Fill It Up activity, the balloon originally fits into the envelope because the balloon contains very little air. The uninflated balloon and the tiny bit of air fit easily into the envelope. But when the balloon is filled with air and the air is prevented from escaping, the balloon-air system takes up much more space and will not fit into the envelope.

Part 3: Lesson Extensions

Writing Extensions

1. Discuss the two science misconceptions in *Wilbur's Space Machine*. The balloons in the story would actually have been filled with air, not empty space. Also, balloons filled with room-temperature air don't float, so the house would not have floated away. This science activity challenges the first misconception. To challenge the second misconception, blow up a balloon, tie it off, and release it. Emphasize that *Wilbur's Space Machine* is not written as a science book—it is written for entertainment. Discuss why science misconceptions can make a book entertaining. Have the students use what they now know about air to write a realistic story about Wilbur.

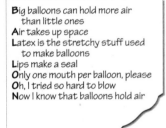

Big balloons can hold more air
  than little ones
Air takes up space
Latex is the stretchy stuff used
  to make balloons
Lips make a seal
Only one mouth per balloon, please
Oh, I tried so hard to blow
Now I know that balloons hold air

2. As a class, complete a science acrostic (acronym), referring back to journals or the science charts as necessary: Write the word "balloon" vertically on the board. Come up with a word, phrase, or sentence that begins with each letter of "balloon." Each word, phrase, or sentence must be related to balloons and to the science activity. An example is provided at left. If desired, follow up by having each student choose an appropriate word (air, space, invisible) and write an acrostic of his or her own.

Cross-Cultural Integration

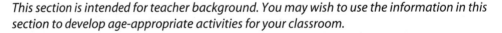

This section is intended for teacher background. You may wish to use the information in this section to develop age-appropriate activities for your classroom.

A diving bell is a good example of how air takes up space. Diving bells work on the same principle as the cup in the How Dry I Am activity: a hollow structure open at one end is lowered into water with the opening pointing downward, trapping a pocket of air that can be used for breathing by passengers. The earliest record of a diving bell appeared in the 1500s, but the forerunner of the modern diving bell was designed by Dr. Edmund Halley (for whom the famous comet is named) in 1690. Halley's diving bell was a large wooden cone. Lead weights on the cone were used to make it sink when placed in water. Divers could work underwater in the trapped air space. Diving bells were traditionally used for underwater observation or for recovering sunken wreckage. John Smeaton made the first modern diving bell, which was rectangular.

Today's diving bells are much more complex than early designs. Today they are much like tiny submarines, with motors, supplemental air supplies, technology for removing carbon dioxide and replacing it with oxygen, and communication equipment.

The bathysphere was a similar apparatus designed by Dr. William Beebe from New York. Beebe's construction was a 5,000-pound steel structure with observation windows. In 1934, he used his bathysphere to descend to a depth of 3,028 feet—the deepest anyone had gone at the time.

Part 4: For Further Study

Additional Books

Nonfiction
Title: *Air Is All Around You*
Author: Franklyn M. Branley   Illustrator: Holly Keller
Publisher: Harper Trophy   ISBN: 0-06-445048-1
Summary: Describes the various properties of air and shows how to demonstrate that air takes up space and that there is gas dissolved in water.

Title: *The Science Book of Air*
Author: Neil Ardley
Publisher: Harcourt Brace Jovanovich   ISBN: 0-15-200578-1
Summary: This book contains many simple experiments that demonstrate basic principles of air and flight.

References

"The Bottled Balloon," *SuperScience*. October 1991, 28–29.
Chamber's Encyclopedia; Pergamon: Oxford, 1967; p 68.
Ontario Science Center. *Scienceworks;* Addison-Wesley: Reading, MA, 1984; p 6.

Balloon in a Bottle

Be sure each of you has an opportunity to perform each step sometime during the lab period. Talk over each question before you record your answers. Have fun!

1. Push a deflated balloon into bottle 1 and stretch the open end of the balloon back over the mouth of the bottle. (See figure.) Be sure you each have your OWN balloon.

   Predict what will happen when you blow into the balloon.

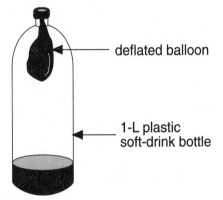

deflated balloon

1-L plastic
soft-drink bottle

2. Now blow into your balloon. What happened?

3. Take your balloon out of the bottle and blow it up. What happened?

4. Talk it over with your group. Can you explain the difference between what happened in Step 2 and Step 3?

5. Put your balloon in Bottle 2 (with hole). Predict what will happen this time when you blow into the balloon.

6. Now blow into your balloon. What happened? Can you explain this?

7. What did you learn from this experiment?

Fill It Up

1. Put the uninflated balloon in the envelope.

2. Take the balloon out of the envelope.

3. Blow up the balloon.

4. Without letting the air out of the balloon, does the balloon still fit into the envelope? Why or why not?

❶

How Dry I Am

Place a loop of tape in the bottom of a cup and stuff a paper towel into the cup. Turn the cup upside down and make sure the paper towel stays securely in place.

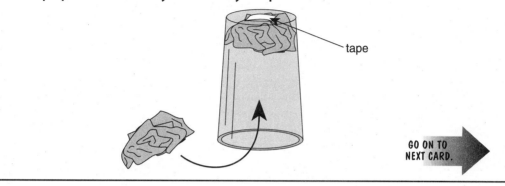

tape

GO ON TO
NEXT CARD.

❷

Keep the cup upside down and push it straight into the tub of water as far as it will go.

GO ON TO
NEXT CARD.

❸

Lift the cup straight up out of the water and then turn it right side up.

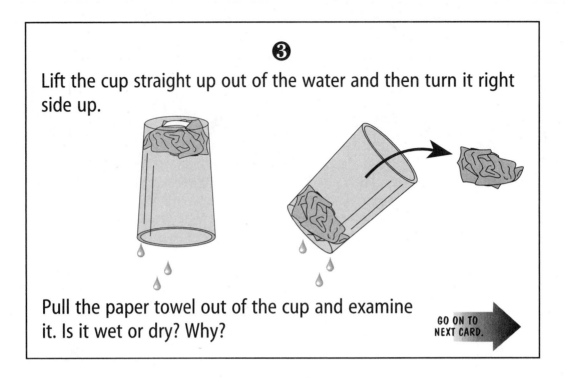

Pull the paper towel out of the cup and examine it. Is it wet or dry? Why?

GO ON TO NEXT CARD.

❹

Stuff the paper towel back in the cup. Turn the cup upside down and push it under the water again.

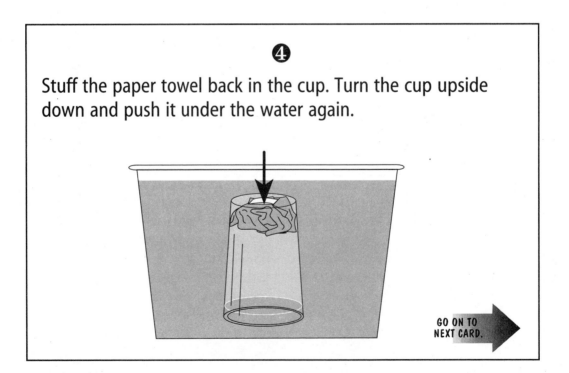

GO ON TO NEXT CARD.

❺

While the cup is under water, tip it a little bit. If nothing happens, keep tipping the cup until something happens. Describe what you see.

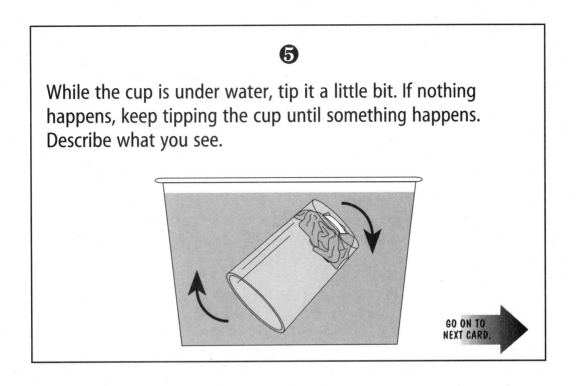

GO ON TO
NEXT CARD.

❻

Pull the cup out of the water and then turn it right side up.

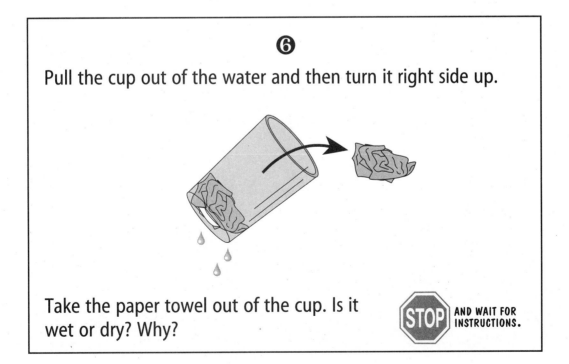

Take the paper towel out of the cup. Is it wet or dry? Why?

STOP AND WAIT FOR INSTRUCTIONS.

Glitter Wands

SCIENCE CATEGORY: Properties of Objects and Materials
TOPICS: States of Matter, Density
OBJECTIVE: Students observe examples of the three states of matter and identify matter in each of these states.

In this lesson, students make glitter wands that contain samples of the three states of matter and use these wands to observe the materials. You may wish to use this lesson after other lessons that focus on individual states of matter.

- Prior to beginning the lesson, students practice identifying the states of matter by examining fishbowls with various contents.

- As a class, students discuss their observations and the characteristics of matter in each state.

- Students hear the story *The Rainbow Fish* and look for examples of solids, liquids, and gases in the Rainbow Fish's environment.

- Students make glitter wands that contain examples of all three states of matter, including glitter and sequins that remind them of the Rainbow Fish's scales. They use these wands to observe some of the characteristics of matter in each state.

- To conclude the lesson, students examine their own environment to find solids, liquids, and gases and write descriptions of each in fish-shaped books.

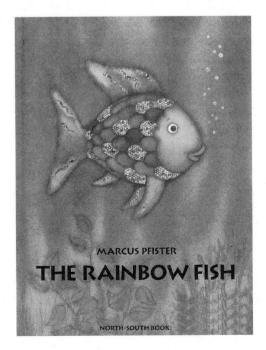

Featured Fiction Book: *The Rainbow Fish*
Author and Illustrator: Marcus Pfister
Publisher: North-South Books
ISBN: 1-55858-009-3
Summary: The Rainbow Fish, with his shimmering scales, is the most beautiful fish in the ocean. But he is proud and vain, and none of the other fish wants to be his friend—until he learns to give away some of his most prized possessions.

Part 1: Building Bridges

Building Student Knowledge and Motivation

Set out several fishbowls or other kinds of bowls containing matter in various states. For solids, use items from the glitter wands students will make, such as sequins, glitter, and/or small plastic shapes. For a liquid, use tap water. At least one bowl should be "empty"—containing only air. Some bowls should contain matter in more than one state. Have students identify the materials in each bowl as solid, liquid, and/or gas. Record responses on a class science chart. (See Figure 1.)

If students are confused by the "empty" bowl, blow bubbles into tap water and ask students what is inside the bubbles. Then point to the "empty" bowl and ask what it contains. If students still have problems identifying the bowl as containing air, try the following activity: Place a plastic bag over the mouth of a jar and secure it with a string or strong rubber band. (See Figure 2.) Have students try gently pushing the bag into the jar. The resistance felt is because air in the jar takes up space.

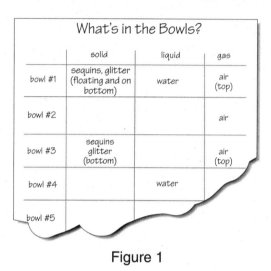

Figure 1

What's in the Bowls?

	solid	liquid	gas
bowl #1	sequins, glitter (floating and on bottom)	water	air (top)
bowl #2			air
bowl #3	sequins glitter (bottom)		air (top)
bowl #4		water	
bowl #5			

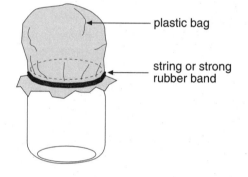

plastic bag

string or strong rubber band

Figure 2: Demonstrate that a jar contains air.

As a class, discuss where each item is in the bowl, especially in relationship to other items (including air) in the same bowl. For example, are solids on the bottom? Are they floating? Record observations on the class science chart.

Getting Ready to Read

Show students the cover of *The Rainbow Fish*. Have students point out examples of solids, liquids, and gases on the cover. Compare these examples to the class science chart filled out previously. How are the examples from the book and from the bowls similar? How are they different? Tell students to look for other examples of the three states of matter as you read the story.

Bridging to the Science Activity

Through a class discussion, have students describe the solids, liquids, and gases they observed in the Rainbow Fish's environment. Talk about where these states of matter usually appear in the pictures and what they usually look like. (For example, do they have a shape? A color?) Tell students they will be making toys that may remind them of the Rainbow Fish and his friends, and they should look for the three states of matter in their toys.

Teaching Physical Science through Children's Literature

Part 2: Science Activity

Materials

For the Procedure

Per class
- hot-melt glue gun and glue
- scissors
- (optional) washable marker

Per group
- paper or plastic funnel that will fit in ½-inch-diameter tubing
- assorted glitter, sequins, and/or small plastic objects, such as beads
- teaspoon

Per student
- 12-inch length of ½-inch-diameter, clear, rigid, plastic tubing

 This tubing can be purchased in 3-foot lengths at an aquarium supply store or hardware store and can be cut to appropriate lengths with scissors or a knife. Tubing with larger or smaller diameters may be difficult to fill or seal. Try substitutions in advance.

- water
- cork to fit tubing

Corks are available from Frey Scientific, 905 Hickory Lane, P.O. Box 8101, Mansfield, OH 44901-8101; 800/225-FREY; FAX 419/589-1522. Size 2, grade XX corks (#F02556) work well in ½-inch-diameter tubing.

For the Science Extensions

❶ All materials listed for the Procedure plus the following:
Per student
- ribbon, string, or keychain
- loop of wire or jeweler's loop
- (optional) clear plastic tube (about 4–4½ inches long) with screw-on cap

An appropriate tube with cap (#808) can be purchased from Creative Educational Surplus, 9801 James Circle, Suite C, Bloomington, MN 55431; 800/886-6428.

❷ All materials listed for the Procedure plus the following:
Per class
- light corn syrup (Karo®) or baby oil

Safety and Disposal

The teacher or an adult assistant should be the only ones to handle the hot-melt glue gun and glue. Use extreme caution as hot glue can cause serious burns.

Filter unwanted water/glitter mixtures through tissue paper, dispose of the solid in a trash can, and pour the water down the drain.

Getting Ready

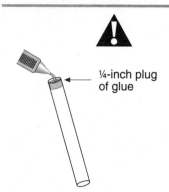

¼-inch plug of glue

Figure 2

Use caution when working with hot-melt glue. In addition, be careful when using this method so the plug doesn't slide too far into the tube.

1. For each piece of tubing, use a pair of scissors to cut a piece of unmelted glue stick approximately ¼ inch long. Insert this plug of glue into one end of the tubing and push it in until it is slightly below the opening of the tube. (See Figure 2.) Using a hot-melt glue gun, apply hot glue to the plugged end to completely seal it. Test sealed tubes for leaks before using in class. Reseal any tubes as needed.

2. For younger students, you may want to mark a line with washable marker on the tube at approximately the 1-teaspoon level to help students gauge how much glitter and sequins to use.

Procedure

1. Give each student a length of tubing with one end sealed. (See Getting Ready.)

2. Model the following steps for students:

   a. Use a funnel to add no more than 1 teaspoon glitter and sequins to the tube.
   Use sequins sparingly (perhaps about five per tube), because they tend to clump and prevent items in the wand from swirling freely.

   b. Fill the tube with water to about 6 centimeters (cm) below the rim of the tube. Leaving air in the tube will allow the glitter to move through the wand better.

   c. Cork the open end of the tube and invert the tube. Ask students to observe your wand. Does the wand have enough glitter? Does the glitter swirl freely?

Flip Cards

3. Have students make their own glitter wands using the flip card instructions (provided) as a reference. Tell students that if they are not satisfied with the result, they can add more glitter, pour out a little water to make room for more air, or discard the contents of the tube (See Safety and Disposal) and start over.

4. When students are satisfied with the results, have them bring the glitter wands to you or another adult. Remove the cork, replace it with a ¼-inch plug of unmelted hot-melt glue (as in Getting Ready, Step 1), and seal the top of the tube with the glue gun. (See Figure 3.) After the glue is cool, have students invert their wands to check for leaks. Reseal if needed.

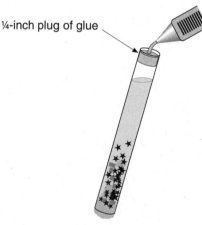

¼-inch plug of glue

Figure 3: When students are satisfied with the results, remove the cork and seal the open end of the tube.

Teaching Physical Science through Children's Literature

5. Have students play with their glitter wands and observe the positions of the solids, liquids, and gases. Ask, "Do the positions change? Where does the gas end up?"

Science Variations and Extensions

1. Make keychains or necklaces with shorter lengths of tubing that have been modified as shown in Figure 4. Alternatively, use short tubes with screw-on caps. (See Materials.)

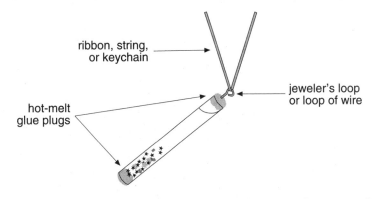

ribbon, string, or keychain

jeweler's loop or loop of wire

hot-melt glue plugs

Figure 4: Use shorter lengths of tubing that have been modified.

2. Instead of pure water, use baby oil or a 50/50 mixture of light corn syrup and water in the wand to create a slower rate of flow.

Science Explanation

The following explanation is intended for the teacher's information. Modify the explanation for students as required.

Wands (or batons), keychains, and necklaces similar to those made in this activity have become fashionable novelty items. If you examine some of the simpler ones, you can see that they contain a liquid (most often water), a small bubble of a gas (helpful for agitating the solids when the tube is inverted), and various small solid items (including glitter, sequins, small plastic stars, moons, and other shapes). When inverted, the materials in the tube shift and create a whirling, swirling motion that can mesmerize the observers. But what is the science behind these toys?

An important characteristic of matter is its state, or phase. The states of matter are commonly described as solid, liquid, and gas. Usually, we can determine the state of matter by looking at it. To better understand the differences between the states of matter, we must consider the nature of matter. Matter is made up of particles. In a solid, the particles touch and vibrate, but each remains in a fixed position relative to neighboring particles. In a liquid, particles touch but are able to move past one another; they are not in fixed positions relative to neighboring particles. In a gas, particles do not touch; each particle moves randomly and continuously, independently of adjacent particles. Substances can exist in all three states; the state depends on the temperature of the substance and the pressure applied to it. When we say a substance is a solid, liquid, or gas, we usually mean it occurs in that state at room temperature and atmospheric pressure (the pressure at sea level), unless otherwise specified. Changing the temperature and pressure can cause the matter to change to a different state.

The materials in the wands (air, water, and glitter) have different densities, which accounts for much of their behavior in the sealed tube. The air always floats to the top and the glitter tends to sink in most cases. Some of the solids in the tube may be less dense than water, and others may be more dense. The solids that are less dense will float in water. The more dense solids will sink in water.

Why do some of the more dense materials sometimes move to the top of the baton? The agitation of the solids by the air bubble and the movement of the wand creates currents in the water, which may momentarily carry some of the more dense materials to the top. The surface tension of the water may also allow small pieces of the more dense solids to float. However, with time these items will also settle. Other times, an air bubble adheres to a small solid. If the net density of the bubble plus the solid is less than the density of water, the bubble/solid floats up.

In Science Extension 2, students use a more viscous (thicker) liquid, which slows the flow of the solid pieces. The 50/50 mixture of corn syrup and water is also more dense than pure water, so that some solids that previously sank may now float.

Part 3: Lesson Extension

Writing Extension

In *The Rainbow Fish,* students saw that the fish had solids, liquids, and gases in their environment. As a family take-home activity, have students conduct a states of matter treasure hunt. Have each student pick a special place in his or her own environment (indoors or out) and list and/or describe the solids, liquids, and gases in that environment. Students may need help coming up with more than one gas. You might want to point out that air is not a pure substance, but a mixture of many gases, with nitrogen and oxygen being present in greatest amounts. Other gases students might be familiar with are helium (in helium balloons), steam (the gaseous form of water), or butane from a lighter.

Have students write their lists/descriptions in fish-shaped books: Draw a large fish outline on lined paper and photocopy. Give each student several sheets of the patterned paper and have them cut out as many fish shapes as they need. They will need at least three shapes: one each for solid, liquid, and gas. (See Figure 5.) Students can make covers for their books from construction paper and decorate with sequins or foil. Staple the books together. If desired, make a bulletin board about the states of matter. Draw a large fishbowl on the bulletin board and staple students' books in the bowl.

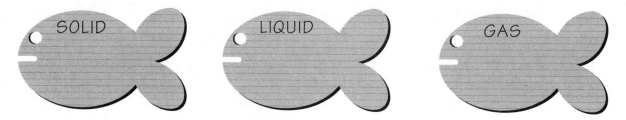

Figure 5: Have students write about solids, liquids, and gases in fish-shaped books.

Flip Cards

❶

Add no more than 1 teaspoon glitter and a few sequins to the tube.

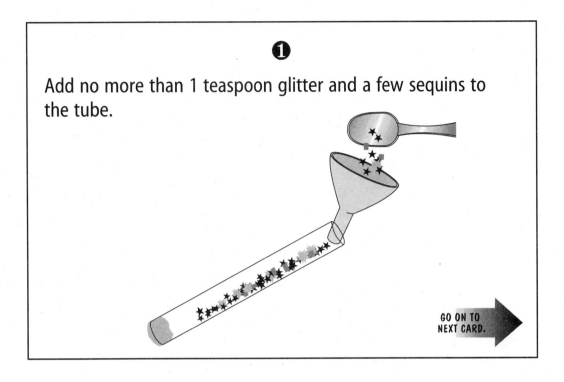

GO ON TO NEXT CARD.

❷

Fill the tubing with water to about 6 centimeters below the rim of the tube.

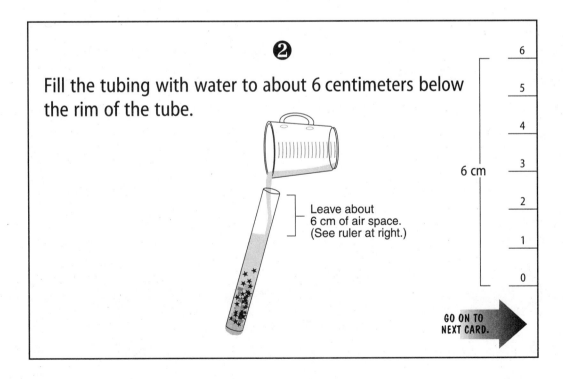

Leave about
6 cm of air space.
(See ruler at right.)

6 cm

6
5
4
3
2
1
0

GO ON TO NEXT CARD.

❸

Cork the open end of the tube. Turn the baton upside down and observe. Does the glitter swirl freely? Where does the gas bubble go?

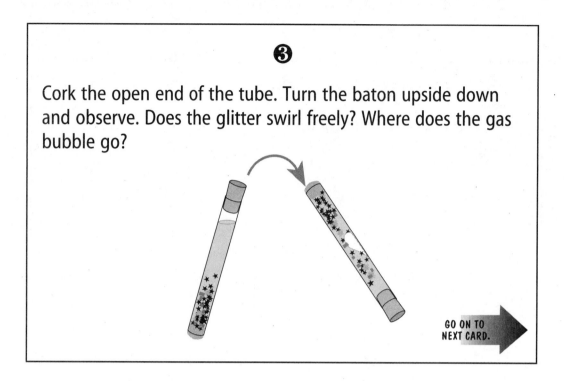

GO ON TO NEXT CARD.

❹

When you are satisfied with your result, bring the baton to an adult to be glued.

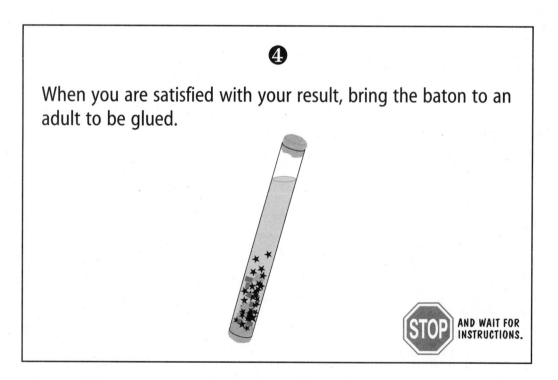

STOP AND WAIT FOR INSTRUCTIONS.

Making Clouds and Rain

SCIENCE CATEGORY: Properties of Objects and Materials
TOPICS: Weather, Water Cycle, Changes of State, Effect of Temperature on Matter
OBJECTIVE: Students learn what clouds are and why rain comes from clouds.

In this lesson, students make a cloud and a model of a water cycle and discuss the importance of rain to living things.

- For at least a week prior to beginning the lesson, students chart daily weather observations using symbols representing sun, clouds, rain, wind, and snow. They also have access to a variety of written materials relating to weather.

- Through a class discussion, students produce a weather web to summarize their daily weather observations. They discuss what would happen if it never rained.

- Students hear the story *Bringing the Rain to Kapiti Plain* about a Nandi herdsman who brings rain to the drought-plagued African plain. They compare the illustrations in the book to the descriptions in their weather web and add descriptive words to their web to reflect the weather in the story.

- Students make cloud bottles and water cycle models and learn how clouds form and rain falls.

- To conclude the lesson, students listen to an excerpt from the nonfiction book *Drought* and add new information to their weather web. Finally, they write and illustrate a "before rain" and "after rain" book to share their ideas about "Why do we need rain?"

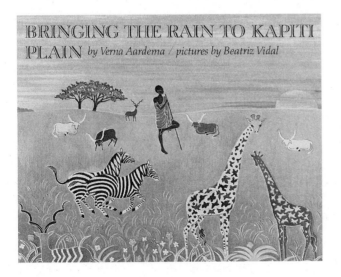

Featured Fiction Book: *Bringing the Rain to Kapiti Plain*
Author: Verna Aardema
Illustrator: Beatriz Vidal
Publisher: Pied Piper Books
ISBN: 0-14-054616-2
Summary: The story is a retelling of a tale from a Nandi village in Kenya, Africa. In the tale, a young shepherd brings rain during a drought by shooting an arrow into the clouds.

Part 1: Building Bridges

Building Student Knowledge and Motivation

For at least a week prior to beginning this lesson, have students chart daily weather on a blank calendar using symbols representing major weather categories, such as clouds, rain, snow, sun, and wind. During this same period of time, begin bringing in newspaper and magazine articles, nonfiction books, and pictures relating to weather. Leave these materials in a reading center for students to read and look at, but do not particularly discuss the materials at this time.

Getting Ready to Read

Turn to a clean sheet on your science chart. Involve the students in creating a weather web chart. Write "weather" in the middle of the chart. Talk about the different kinds of weather conditions students observed in the past week and web these categories out from "weather." (See Figure 1.) Ask, "How do you know when it is sunny? What do you feel, smell, see, and hear?" Encourage students to think of descriptive words and write these on the web as appropriate. (Save the web chart to use later.)

Read the title *Bringing the Rain to Kapiti Plain*. Ask "Which kind of weather will this book focus on?" *Rain*. Ask, "Why do we need rain? Why can't it be sunny all the time?" As appropriate, list or chart the students' ideas about the need for rain. Tell students to listen for weather words as you read the story aloud.

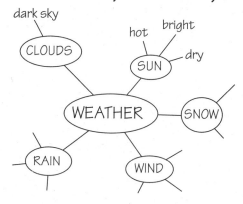

Figure 1: Weather web chart

Bridging to the Science Activity

Have students describe the weather conditions in the story. Ask, "When did the weather change? What other changes did you see in the story?" Have students compare the illustrations in the book to the descriptions on their weather web. Does their web describe weather like that described and illustrated in the story? Have students add descriptive words about the weather in the story to their web. Ask students, "Where does rain come from?" *Clouds*. Ask, "Where do clouds come from?" Let students suggest a variety of answers, but don't discuss at this time. Tell students that they will be making clouds and rain and trying to figure out what is needed for clouds to form.

Part 2: Science Activity

Materials

For the Procedure, Parts A and B

For both methods, per class
- matches
- (optional) dark background

For Method 1, per class
- wide-mouthed, clear glass jar at least 15 centimeters (cm) tall with a lid
- large balloon that inflates to at least 11 inches
- strong rubber band

For Method 2, per group
- clear and colorless plastic 2-L soft-drink bottle with cap

For the Procedure, Part C

Per group
- 2 clear and colorless plastic 2-L soft-drink bottles
- 2–3 ice cubes
- very warm water

Safety and Disposal

Standard safety measures should be used when working with matches or open flames. No special disposal procedures are required.

Getting Ready

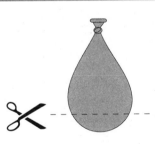

Figure 2

For Part A, Method 1 of the Procedure, knot the balloon and cut off the opposite end. You will use the knotted part of the balloon in the activity. (See Figure 2.) For Part C of the Procedure, cut off the top two-thirds of one of the 2-L bottles. Then cut off the top third of the other bottle so the smaller bottom can be suspended inside the larger bottom. (See Figure 3.)

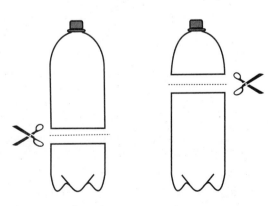

Figure 3: Cut off the 2-L bottles for Part C of the Procedure.

Part A: Make a Cloud

1. Ask students to watch carefully and be prepared to describe what they see. Tell students to think about what is needed for a cloud to form. Let the students know they will not see a fluffy white cloud like they see in the sky. Rather, the inside of the jar or bottle will look foggy or cloudy.

If you choose to use both cloud bottle methods in Part A, your students will have a greater opportunity to see a pattern. In Part B, student groups should repeat only Method 2. The glass jar used for Method 1 is too easily broken.

2. Moisten the inside of the jar or bottle by swirling some room-temperature water around in it and pouring out the excess.

3. (optional) Place the jar or bottle against a dark background.

The teacher should be the only one to handle the match.

4. Light two matches and blow them out near the opening of the inverted jar or bottle. Quickly move the tips of the smoking matches into the container to fill the jar with smoke. (See Figure 4.)

Figure 4

5. Select and do at least one of the following methods to change the air pressure:

The first step of each method is to quickly cover the jar or bottle. If you do not do this quickly, the smoke will escape.

Method 1: Balloon/Jar Method

a. Quickly cover the jar with a large knotted piece of a balloon. Tightly fasten the balloon around the mouth of the jar with a rubber band.

b. Quickly and firmly pull up on the balloon, being careful not to tear it or poke a hole in it. (See Figure 5.) The cloud will form in the jar. Push the balloon down into the container, and the cloud will disappear. (You may want someone else to hold the jar steady and help prevent it from falling.)

Figure 5

Method 2: Bottle Method

a. Quickly twist the cap onto the 2-L bottle.

b. Squeeze the bottle, then release. (See Figure 6.) As you release, a misty cloud will form inside the bottle. The change is subtle.

6. Repeat the process several times, having students look for the change that occurs. To help them see the change, have them squeeze and release the bottle in front of a dark background or person wearing dark clothes.

Figure 6

Part B: Exploring with the Cloud Bottles

1. Have students repeat the Bottle Method cloud demonstration in their own groups.

2. Discuss what a cloud is. A cloud is not made of water vapor—water vapor is an invisible gas. A cloud is actually a collection of tiny drops of water.

3. Have each group repeat the Bottle Method, leaving out one element that is required for the cloud to form. That is, one group leave out smoke, another leave out water (They may need a fresh, dry bottle), and a third leave out the air pressure change (by not squeezing the bottle).

4. Through a facilitated discussion, lead students to conclude that the cloud cannot form without all of these factors being present. Explain to students that the pressure change causes the air in the bottle to get cooler and allows the cloud to form. Tell them that they will now use this idea about cooling the air to make clouds and rain form in a cup.

5. Ask students if the clouds they made looked like clouds they see in the sky. Discuss the differences. Ask, "Why are rain clouds dark?" *Because they are holding so much water that sunlight does not pass through as in other clouds.*

6. Leave the cloud bottles out at a center for further exploration. (The cloud bottles will continue to work for a while without adding more smoke. Instruct students to come to you to handle the matches when more smoke is needed.)

Part C: Water Cycle Model

1. Model the water cycle in a bottle for the students as follows:

    a. Place warm water to a depth of about 2 inches in the larger cut-off bottom of a 2-L bottle. Immediately place the smaller cut-off bottom inside the larger bottom.

    b. Put the ice cubes in the top bottle. (See Figure 7.)

2. Have each group of students make a water cycle model of their own using the flip card instructions (provided) as a reference.

3. Give students time to observe their water cycles, draw the changes they see, and answer these questions: Where did the tiny mist of water on the bottom of the ice container come from? Where did the drops of "rain" come from?

Initially the condensation on the sides of the bottom 2-L bottle may make it difficult to see drops forming on the cool upper surface. Most of this condensation will clear within ½ hour. The water cycles may take some time to "rain" depending on the room temperature and temperature of the water. You may want to put them in a visible location and have students check periodically for changes over the next few hours.

4. Have groups share their drawings and observations. Bring out students' observations of the series of changes that occurred. How did the water cycle model look right away? How did it look later? Through a class discussion, trace the route of a drop of water in the water cycle. Make sure students understand the water drops formed inside the bottle and did not come from the ice on top of the water cycle. Discuss why the water drops finally fell from the top as "rain." *They became so large and heavy that they fell.* Relate this model to real clouds and rain. (See the Science Explanation.)

5. Have students look again at the pictures in *Bringing the Rain to Kapiti Plain.* Ask, "Where is the water at the beginning of the story?" *In the cloud.* Discuss where the water in the cloud might have come from originally. Ask, "In the story, why did it finally rain?" *Because Ki-pat shot an arrow into the cloud.* Discuss the differences between the story's explanation for rain and the reason for rain in their water cycle cups.

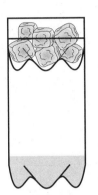

Figure 7

Flip
Cards

Science Explanation

> *The following explanation is intended for the teacher's information. Modify the explanation for students as required.*

Water vapor is water in the gas phase. When water vapor is cooled, it can condense into liquid water. That is why water drops condense on the outside of a glass containing an ice-cold beverage. Eyeglass wearers have experienced this phenomenon if their glasses have "fogged up" upon walking from a cold area to a warm, humid one. This process was evident in Part C of the activity.

While refrigeration is one means by which water vapor is cooled, this activity illustrates another: expansion of the vapor. This is the basis of the observations in Parts A and B of the activity. The jar or bottle contains very small suspended smoke particles, a small amount of liquid water you can see, and water vapor and air you cannot see. When you pull out on the balloon piece or when you release the bottle, the gas expands (increases in volume) and therefore cools. The cooling causes some of the water vapor to condense on the smoke particles, making a cloud visible. In contrast, when you push in the balloon piece or squeeze the bottle, the volume of the air decreases, providing enough heat to revaporize the water droplets and make the cloud disappear.

In nature, most clouds form through a process similar to the one demonstrated in this activity. As air containing water vapor rises, it expands and cools. Tiny particles in the atmosphere (such as the smoke particles in the jar) serve as sites for condensation of the cooled vapor. Thus, water droplets form on the particles, making a cloud. When these droplets become so heavy and large that the cloud cannot hold them, they drop to the earth as rain.

The same process happens in the water cycle model. Warm air containing water vapor rises from the warm water in the bottom bottle. This warm moist air eventually rises to the ice-cold surface of the top bottle. At this point, water droplets form on this cold surface and become visible. Eventually, the droplets fall like rain back into the warm water.

Part 3: Lesson Extensions

Writing Extension

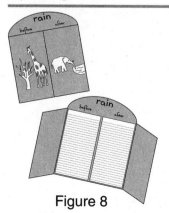

Figure 8

Discuss what might have happened if the rains had not come to Kapiti Plain. Read pages 7–9 of *Drought* (See Additional Books) and discuss a "world without rain." Show the pictures of the Sahel region of northern Africa on pages 24–27. Introduce the term "drought." As a class, look at the weather web and add new information as desired. Leave the web chart out as a reference. Have students make a "before rain" and "after rain" book to compare and contrast in words and drawings what plants, animals, people, and the earth are like before and after rain. (See Figure 8 for a sample book design.) Remind students to look at the weather web if they need ideas for words.

Cross-Cultural Integration

In east Africa, where Kapiti Plain lies, the official language is Swahili. Share *Moja Means One* and *Jambo Means Hello* (See Additional Books) with the students and allow them to try to pronounce the words. The illustrations provide a good opportunity to compare the East African lifestyle to their own. Also, try cooking some east-African-type foods. *Cooking the African Way* (See Additional Books) has easy recipes that can be adapted to classroom use. Chapatis (recipe provided here), rice pancakes, plantain, and ground nut sauce could be made in a classroom setting using an electric skillet, toaster oven, and crock pot. The following is a recipe for chapatis, an east African dish. In Africa, chapatis are considered a luxury because they are made with imported flour, which is expensive. They can be served with stew or eaten as a snack with butter or sugar.

Chapatis (makes six)

½ teaspoon salt   3 cups unbleached all-purpose flour
¾ to 1 cup water   ¾ cup plus 1 to 3 tablespoons vegetable oil

In a large bowl, combine salt and 2½ cups flour. Add ¾ cup oil and mix well. Add water little by little, stirring after each addition, until dough is soft. Knead dough in bowl for 5–10 minutes. Sprinkle about ¼ cup flour on a flat surface. Take a 2-inch ball of dough and, with a floured rolling pin, roll out into a ⅛-inch-thick circle the size of a saucer. Repeat with remaining dough, sprinkling flat surface with flour if dough sticks. Heat 1 tablespoon oil over medium-high heat for 1 minute. Fry chapati 3–5 minutes per side or until brown. Remove from pan and let drain on paper towels. Fry remaining chapatis, adding more oil if necessary. Serve immediately or place in a covered container until ready to serve.

Part 4: For Further Study

Additional Books

Nonfiction

Title: *Drought*
Author: Christopher Lampton
Publisher: Millbrook Press   ISBN: 1-878841-91-2
Summary: This book investigates the causes and disastrous effects of drought, giving the history of some of the severest droughts on record in the United States and elsewhere.

Title: *The Cloud Book*
Author: Tomie dePaola
Publisher: Holiday House   ISBN: 0-8234-0531-1
Summary: This book introduces the 10 most common types of clouds, the myths that have been inspired by their shapes, and what they can tell about coming weather.

Title: *Cooking the African Way*
Authors: Constance Nabwire and Bertha Vining Montgomery
Publisher: Lerner Publications   ISBN: 0-8225-9564-8
Summary: This book provides an introduction to the cooking of East and West Africa with information on the land and people of this area of the giant continent. Recipes are included.

Title: *Jambo Means Hello: Swahili Alphabet Book*
Author: Muriel Feelings   Illustrator: Tom Feelings
Publisher: Puffin Pied Piper   ISBN: 0-8037-4428-5
Summary: This book presents a word, with English translation, for each of the 24 letters in the Swahili alphabet. A brief explanation of each word introduces an East African custom.

Title: *Moja Means One: Swahili Counting Book*
Author: Muriel Feelings   Illustrator: Tom Feelings
Publisher: Penguin Group   ISBN: 0-14-055296-0
Summary: The numbers one through 10 in Swahili accompany two-page illustrations of various aspects of East African life.

Title: *The Science Book of Weather*
Author: Neil Ardley
Publisher: Harcourt Brace Jovanovich   ISBN: 0-15-200624-9
Summary: Simple experiments demonstrate the different forces that cause different kinds of weather.

References

Ardley, N. *The Science Book of Weather;* Harcourt Brace Jovanovich: San Diego, 1992.
Brandwein, P.F.; et al. *Matter: An Earth Science;* Harcourt Brace Jovanovich: New York, 1980.
"Cloud in a Jar;" *Fun With Chemistry: A Guidebook for K–12 Activities;* Sarquis, M., Sarquis J., Eds.; Institute for Chemical Education: Madison, WI, 1993; Vol. 2, pp 329–332.
Foolproof, Failsafe Seasonal Science; Dalheim, M., Ed.; Instructor Books: New York, 1982.

Flip Cards

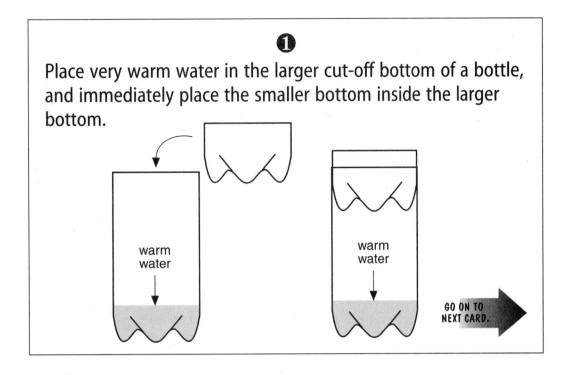

❶

Place very warm water in the larger cut-off bottom of a bottle, and immediately place the smaller bottom inside the larger bottom.

warm water

warm water

GO ON TO NEXT CARD.

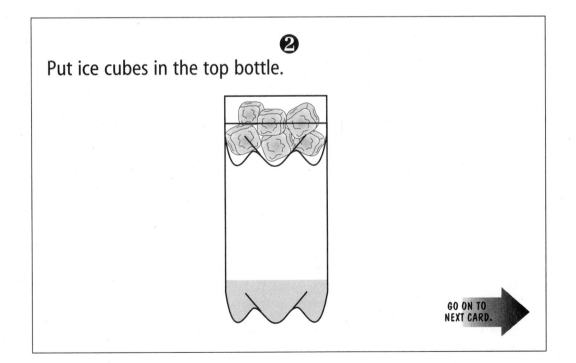

❷

Put ice cubes in the top bottle.

GO ON TO NEXT CARD.

❸

Observe the changes in your water cycle model.

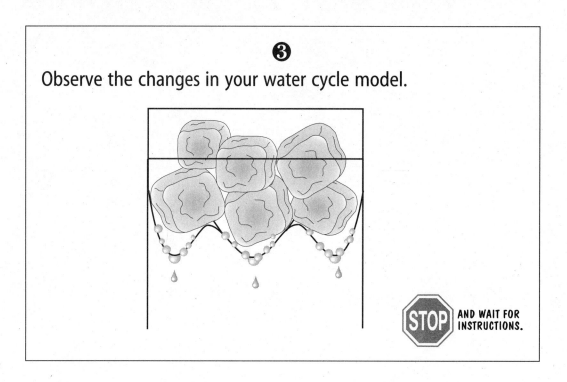

STOP AND WAIT FOR INSTRUCTIONS.

Weather Forecasters

SCIENCE CATEGORY: Properties of Objects and Materials
TOPICS: Weather, Forces
OBJECTIVE: Students become familiar with some weather forecasting tools and techniques.

In this lesson, students use barometers, humidity indicators, thermometers, and other tools to observe and predict the weather. Ideally, this lesson should follow "Making Clouds and Rain."

- Prior to beginning the lesson, students watch videotaped weather forecasts from local news. They also have access to written materials relating to weather forecasting.

- Through a class discussion, students brainstorm a list of words they have heard or read in weather forecasts. After hearing excerpts from *Weather Forecasting* by Gail Gibbons, students add to the brainstorming list and discuss what clues meteorologists use to predict weather.

- Students hear the story *The Rains Are Coming* and look for weather clues used to predict the rains in the story.

- With a variety of homemade scientific weather instruments, students collect their own weather predicting "clues" (such as changes in atmospheric pressure, humidity, and temperature) and compare these to the kinds of clues broadcast in the TV weather reports and written in *The Rains Are Coming*.

- To conclude the lesson, students use data they have gathered from the classroom weather station to write or record a weather forecast to be posted outside the classroom or broadcast to the school.

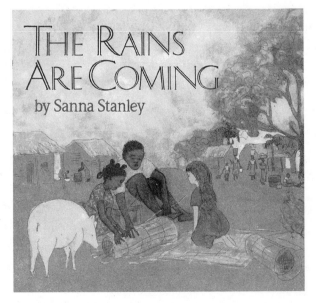

Featured Fiction Book: *The Rains Are Coming*
Author and Illustrator: Sanna Stanley
Publisher: Greenwillow Books
ISBN: 0-688-10948-9
Summary: Aimee keeps expecting rain, but it never comes. On her birthday, the picnic table is set, and Aimee runs through the village to get her friends. But as she runs, wherever she goes, she hears "Zimvula zeti kwiza"— "The rains are coming."

Part 1: Building Bridges

Building Student Knowledge and Motivation

For about a week prior to beginning the lesson, play a videotape of a television weather forecast each day. While watching each weather forecast, have students write down weather terms they hear, such as "cold front," "high pressure," and "humidity." Students do not need to know what these words mean. During this same time period, begin bringing in newspaper and magazine articles, nonfiction books such as *Weather Forecasting* (See Additional Books), and pictures relating to weather forecasting. (The daily weather maps in *USA Today* are large and colorful.) Leave these in a reading center for students to read and look at. Encourage students to use these materials to add words to their weather word lists.

Getting Ready to Read

Ask students, "Did you ever have your plans spoiled by bad weather?" Inquire if students knew that such bad weather was coming. If no one mentions television or newspaper weather forecasts, bring them into the discussion. Bring up the point that a forecast is not a wild guess; it is a prediction based on clues. Turn to a clean sheet on your science chart. Draw three columns on the chart. Label the first column "Weather Forecasting Clues from TV and Newspapers." Have students take out their individual weather word lists. Tell the students that the words on their lists describe some of the clues used by weather forecasters. As a class, compile the words from the individual lists into a class list in the first column of the chart. Read all or part of the book *Weather Forecasting,* by Gail Gibbons. Be sure to include the parts about the immediate weather forecaster and the long-range or extended weather forecaster.

Show students the cover of *The Rains Are Coming.* Ask them how they think this book relates to weather forecasting. Tell students that the people in this story might not have had access to television or newspaper weather forecasts. Ask students to listen for weather clues that the villagers of Zaire in the story use to predict that "the rains are coming." Tell students to also listen for "Zimvula zeti kwiza," which means "the rains are coming" in Kikongo, one of the languages spoken in Zaire. As you read the book, pause each time someone says this sentence to Aimee so the class can recite together, "Zimvula zeti kwiza."

Bridging to the Science Activity

Label the second column on the chart "Weather Forecasting Clues in *The Rains Are Coming.*" Ask students to list these clues from the story. (A clue such as "small clouds moving across the sky" or "The sky had turned a heavy gray" appears on nearly every page of the story.)

Label the third column on the chart "Weather Forecasting in Our Classroom." Tell students that the class will be making some weather instruments to gather weather clues for their own immediate and long-range weather forecasts.

Teaching Physical Science through Children's Literature

Part 2: Science Activity

Materials

For the Procedure, Part A
Per class
- large balloon (that inflates to at least 11 inches)
- scissors
- quart-sized or larger wide-mouthed jar
- heavy rubber band
- 2 plastic drinking straws
- Superglue or low-temperature hot glue gun and glue
- 2 straight pins, different lengths and extra long if possible
- shallow cardboard box, about 15 inches x 10 inches x 2 inches
- paint and paintbrush or markers

For the Procedure, Part B
Per student
- 4-inch x 7-inch piece of white blotter paper presprayed with cobalt chloride solution ($CoCl_2$) and dried (See Getting Ready.)

➤ *Blotter paper can be ordered from most office supply stores.*

- scissors
- small piece of a magnetic strip
- (optional) white glue

Per class
- 25–50 milliliters (mL) of 10% aqueous cobalt chloride solution (See Getting Ready.)

➤ *Cobalt chloride hexahydrate crystals (#C0225) are available from Flinn Scientific, P.O. Box 219, Batavia, IL 60510; 800/452-1261.*

- containers for measuring and mixing solution
- spray bottle for cobalt chloride solution
- waxed paper or aluminum foil
- shallow container such as a plastic tub
- tongs or tweezers
- (optional) spray bottle of water
- (optional) hair dryer
- goggles

For the Procedure, Part C
Per class
- (optional) additional weather station instruments, such as thermometer, wind sock, weather vane, anemometer (wind meter), rain gauge, and nephoscope (instrument for determining the direction in which clouds are moving)

For the Procedure, Part D
- permanent black marker

Safety and Disposal

Cobalt chloride ($CoCl_2$) is harmful if swallowed; remind students not to taste it. Cobalt chloride is also a possible skin irritant; be sure to wash your hands after treating the blotter paper and instruct students to wash well if skin contact occurs or after handling the treated blotter paper. Goggles must be worn while making, handling, and spraying the cobalt chloride solution. Spraying should be done in a shallow container, such as a plastic tub or a box, and away from observers. Unused solution may be stored for future use.

Only the teacher should handle the Superglue or glue gun and the cobalt chloride solution.

Getting Ready

For the Procedure, Part B

Students should not be allowed to do these steps. Eye protection must be worn while making and using the cobalt chloride solution. Avoid touching the solution or wet treated paper. If spraying, be sure to aim into a shallow container, such as a plastic tub, and away from observers. Be sure to wash your hands after completing the following steps. See Safety and Disposal for additional cautions.

1. Prepare a 10% cobalt chloride solution ($CoCl_2$) by dissolving 5 grams (about 1 teaspoon) cobalt chloride hexahydrate crystals ($CoCl_2 \cdot 6H_2O$) in 50 mL (about ⅕ cup) water.

2. Treat the blotter paper with the 10% $CoCl_2$ solution in one of the following ways:

   a. Spray the solution onto strips of paper in a shallow container, taking care not to direct the spray toward any bystanders. Use a pair of tongs or tweezers to handle the treated paper.

   b. Pour the solution into a shallow container and use a pair of tongs or tweezers to handle the paper while dipping and removing it from the solution.

3. Place the blotter paper on waxed paper or aluminum foil to air dry overnight.

Procedure

Part A: Making a Barometer

Make the barometer as a demonstration.

1. Cut off the neck of the balloon and stretch the balloon over the neck of the jar. Pull the balloon tight so there are no bubbles or dimples in the surface. Secure the balloon to the neck of the jar with a large rubber band.

2. Cut a 5-inch length of one of the straws. Cut two 1-inch-long slits opposite each other on one end of the straw piece. Bend the slit ends to form a base for the straw. (See Figure 1.) Slit the other end of the straw piece in the same way to form a resting place for the second straw.

3. Glue the bent base of the straw to the center of the balloon with Superglue or low-temperature hot glue. (See Figure 2.) While the glue is drying, trim one end of the other straw to a point. This will be the pointer of the barometer.

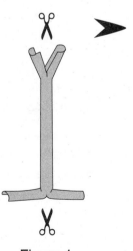

Figure 1

4. After the glue is completely dry, place the second straw sideways through the notched end of the upright straw piece. The pointer end should be on the right. Hold this straw in place with the shorter pin. (See Figure 2.)

5. Remove any flaps from a shallow cardboard box and decorate with paint or markers. Stand the jar apparatus in front of the box. (See Figure 2.) With the top straw in a level position, stick the second pin through the straw about 1 inch to the right of the first pin as shown in Figure 2. Stick this second pin all the way through the straw so that the pin sticks into the box, loosely holding the straw to the box. (You will have to push the jar as close as possible to the box. Even so, the upright straw may slant slightly inward. There should still be about 1 inch of pin between the straw and the box.)

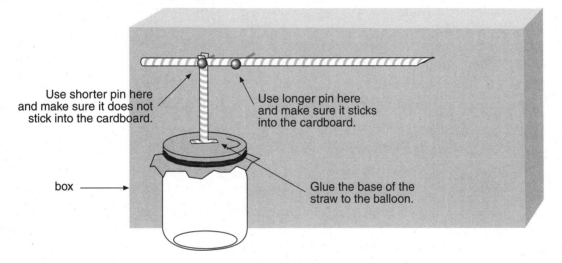

Use shorter pin here and make sure it does not stick into the cardboard.

Use longer pin here and make sure it sticks into the cardboard.

box →

Glue the base of the straw to the balloon.

Figure 2: Barometer setup

Part B: Making a Humidity Detector

For students in grades K–1, the teacher should make and handle the humidity detector, since students might be tempted to put the detectors in their mouths. Avoid ingestion of the cobalt chloride. Be sure to wash hands after making the humidity detectors, and wear goggles when preparing or using the solution.

1. Have each student draw a shape on the presprayed and dried piece of blotter paper and cut the shape out.

2. Have students decorate the figures as desired and glue or stick a magnetic strip onto the back of the figure (so that it can be attached to a refrigerator).

3. (optional) Spray the figures with a fine mist of water and observe what happens. Use a hair dryer to dry the paper and observe.

Part C: Additional Weather Instruments (optional)

Make or gather additional weather station instruments so that students can gather a greater variety of data, see several scientific instruments at work, and develop a better picture of the weather conditions. Examples include a thermometer, a wind sock, a weather vane, an anemometer (wind meter), a rain gauge, and a nephoscope (instrument for determining the direction in which clouds are moving). Easy-to-make versions of many of these instruments can be found in *The Science Book of Weather* and *Science Crafts for Kids.* (See Additional Books.)

Part D: Making Observations

1. Divide students into weather-watching groups and tell them that they will be using their senses (like the people in *The Rains Are Coming*) as well as the weather instruments in the classroom to gather weather information. Have them record their daily observations of the instrument readings and the weather. (Masters for several types of science journal pages are provided in the Using Science Journals section at the beginning of the book.)

2. Place the barometer where it will be out of direct sunlight. Tell students they will observe the pointer straw each day and compare its location as the weather changes: Each day one group will use a marker to mark the position of the pointer and the date on the cardboard box behind the barometer. All groups will record whether the marker is higher or lower than it was the previous day.

3. Tell each group to place the humidity indicator figures in different locations inside the school. If your school is air conditioned, have students take a humidity indicator outside once a day for about 5 minutes. Have groups observe the figures for several days and record observations.

4. Review the use of any other available weather instruments and tell students to make and record daily observations with them.

5. After a few days, have groups share their observations. Through a facilitated discussion, help students begin to see some relationship between the data gathered on one day and the weather recorded on that same day as well as the next day. Review the idea of the immediate forecast (how data collected in the morning pertains to the afternoon weather) and the extended forecast (how data collected on one day pertains to weather in following days). Discuss what weather clues they have gathered. Would some clues help more with the immediate forecast? Would other clues be useful for an extended forecast? Record these different clues on the "Weather Forecasting in Our Classroom" part of the chart.

Science Explanation

The following explanation is intended for the teacher's information. Modify the explanation for students as required.

Barometer

A barometer is an instrument that measures atmospheric pressure. Because the amount of air and the temperature of the air inside the barometer jar stay relatively constant, the pressure inside the jar can be assumed to be about constant. The atmospheric pressure however, does change with movements of weather fronts. The change in atmospheric pressure causes the pointer of the homemade barometer to move.

The homemade barometer works like a seesaw where the longer pin sticking into the box is the pivot point. Initially, the pressure inside the jar is equal to the pressure outside the jar. (See Figure 3a.) The balloon is flat and the pointer points horizontally. When the air pressure outside the jar increases, the pressure of the air outside the jar is greater than that on the inside. This excess pressure on the outside pushes down on the surface of the stretched balloon, lowering the surface of the balloon and the attached support straw. (See Figure 3b.) The non-pointer end of the second straw is pulled down, the straw pivots, and the pointer rises. When the air pressure outside the jar decreases, the pressure of the air trapped inside the jar is greater and pushes up on the balloon, raising the surface of the balloon and the attached support straw. (See Figure 3c.) The non-pointer end of the second straw is pushed up, the straw pivots, and the pointer falls. You can show the relationship between pointer position and outside air pressure by collecting data over several weeks or a month. Get the barometric pressure daily from a weather station and read and record the position of the homemade barometer's pointer relative to the previous day's position. The higher the barometric pressure, the higher the position of the pointer.

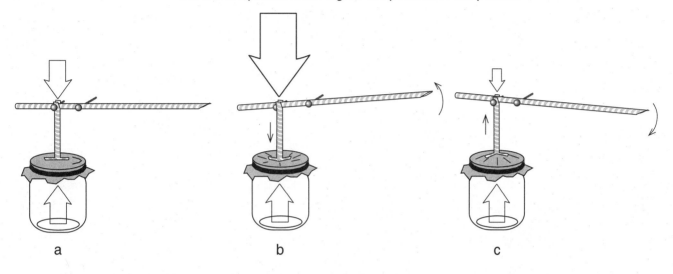

a   b   c

Figure 3: The barometer made in this activity works like a seesaw. Note that under constant temperature, the pressure of the air trapped inside the jar stays about constant.

Why does air pressure change? One variable that affects air pressure is altitude. You could measure this effect if you carried a barometer from sea level to the mountains. The gas particles that make up the atmosphere exert force on the surface below, and at sea level, there are more gas particles above you than there are at higher altitudes. Thus, the air pressure is greater at sea level. As you go to higher elevations, there are fewer gas molecules above you, so the pressure is less.

However, you probably aren't hiking from the sea to the mountains with your barometer during this activity—you stay at the same altitude. At a given altitude, air pressure changes with the movement of air masses, the edges of which are called fronts. As you know from listening to weather reports, when fronts move, the weather usually changes. Typically, high pressure means the incoming air is cool and dry, and low pressure means that the incoming air is warm and moist, which usually brings precipitation.

It is important to note that the homemade barometer built in this activity is also affected by changes in temperature. Temperature changes can cause the trapped air inside the jar to expand or contract. An increase in temperature causes the volume of the gas to increase, while decreasing the temperature causes the volume to decrease. When the volume increases, the rubber is stretched above the mouth of the jar, and the pointer drops. When the volume decreases, the rubber is stretched below the mouth of the jar, and the pointer rises. Thus, if the temperature in the room changes frequently, your pressure data may not correlate with the weather report data.

Humidity Detector

A humidity indicator measures how much moisture is present in the air. The colors observed are a result of the loss or gain of water. Anhydrous (without water) cobalt chloride ($CoCl_2$) is blue while cobalt chloride hexahydrate ($CoCl_2 \bullet 6H_2O$) is pink. The blue cobalt chloride is observed when little or no water is present (for example, in very dry or heated air). The pink color is observed when the amount of water present is great (for example, in humid air or aqueous solutions). A purple color represents a combination of the anhydrous and hydrated forms and indicates the presence of a moderate level of moisture. The chemical reaction of cobalt chloride and water is shown in Figure 4. This reversible reaction provides a method for observing changes in the humidity—pink indicates humid days and blue indicates dry days.

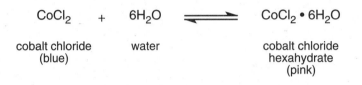

$$CoCl_2 \quad + \quad 6H_2O \quad \rightleftharpoons \quad CoCl_2 \bullet 6H_2O$$

cobalt chloride   water   cobalt chloride
(blue)   hexahydrate
(pink)

Figure 4: The reaction of cobalt chloride and water

Part 3: Lesson Extensions

Writing Extensions

- After groups have used the weather station to make weather observations for several days, assign each group a specific day about which to write a weather forecast. The forecast should include both an immediate forecast that describes current conditions as well as a long-term forecast that is based on weather clues gathered with the weather station. After writing the forecast, students can either illustrate it and post it outside the classroom for others to check or record their forecast and play it over the school's loudspeaker system.

- Have students write stories about a child who made a "weather machine" in order to control the weather. Ask the students to describe what the machine was made of, how it looked, and whether or not it worked. Have the students illustrate their stories.

Cross-Cultural Integration

This section is intended for teacher background. You may wish to use the information in this section to develop age-appropriate activities for your classroom.

The Republic of Zaire, which is about the size of the part of the United States east of the Mississippi River, is the second largest country in central western Africa. The country straddles the equator, and the northern third of Zaire has a dry season from early November to late March. The dry season of the northern third occurs during the rainy season of the two-thirds of Zaire that are south of the equator. Some places on either side of the equator have two rainy seasons and two dry seasons. The average rainfall ranges from 1,000 to 2,200 millimeters (39 to 87 inches). Parts of southeastern Zaire are characterized by long four-month to five-month dry seasons and occasional drought.

The *Rains Are Coming* is set in the lower western area of Zaire. This area is slightly below the equator and has two major seasons each year: a rainy season when it is hottest and a dry season when it is coldest. The following activities can help students relate to life in western Africa.

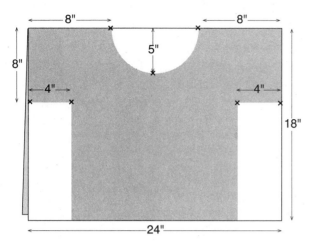

Figure 5: Dashiki pattern

- Dashikis (African shirts) are worn in West Africa. Your students can make paper dashikis. Give each student a 36-inch x 24-inch piece of sheet paper or white butcher paper. You could use bags for very small students. Have each student do the following: Fold the sheet of paper in half to make a rectangle 18 inches x 24 inches. (See Figure 5.) Measure along the fold two points that are 8 inches in from each side and mark these two points. Start at a point halfway between these two, measure 5 inches in from the fold, and mark this point. Draw a curve through these three points and cut along this curve (through both thicknesses of paper) to make a neck hole.

Mark a point 8 inches below the fold along each 18-inch side. Then measure and mark new points 4 inches into the sheet of paper from each of those points. Draw rectangles from the 8-inch points to the 4-inch points down to the unfolded edge of the sheet of paper and cut out these rectangles.

Use colored markers or fabric markers to decorate the fronts and backs of the shirts. Draw colorful patterns or pictures of things that appear in *The Rains Are Coming.* Use scissors or a hole punch to make holes every 2 inches along the sides and under the armholes. Tie 6-inch lengths of yarn through the holes to "sew" the dashikis together. The dashikis can be slipped on over the head. Wear the dashikis to read African stories, play African games, or enjoy African foods.

- Many of the illustrations in *The Rains Are Coming* show people with baskets and other items being carried on their heads. Students could bring baskets and stuffed animals from home to see how much they can keep balanced on their heads and how far they can walk while balancing.

- A popular candy in western Africa is a peanut mixture called *kanya, kayan, or kanyan.* It can be made with fresh roasted peanuts or peanut butter, and is usually sold by child peddlers. It can be made in class easily using the following recipe, which yields about 15 pieces:

Kanyan
- ½ cup smooth peanut butter
- ½ cup sugar
- ½ cup uncooked cream of rice cereal, more or less, as needed

Put peanut butter and sugar in a mortar or a small mixing bowl. Using a pestle or the back of a mixing spoon, beat the peanut butter and sugar together until well mixed. Slowly add cream of rice, stirring continually and adding more cream of rice if necessary to make a firm dough. Put the dough in a loaf pan and, using the back of a spoon or clean hands, press the dough evenly to cover the bottom. Chill in a refrigerator to set. Cut into small rectangular bars to serve.

Part 4: For Further Study

Additional Books

Nonfiction

Title: *Weather Forecasting*
Author: Gail Gibbons
Publisher: Aladdin Books   ISBN: 0-689-71683-4
Summary: Describes forecasters at work in a weather station as they use sophisticated equipment to track and gauge the constant changes in the weather.

Title: *Africa Dream*
Author: Eloise Greenfield   Illustrator: Carole Byard
Publisher: John Day   ISBN: 0-06-443277-7
Summary: Gives a basic background to the diversity of Africa.

Title: *Ashanti to Zulu: African Traditions*
Author: Margaret Musgrove   Illustrators: Leo and Diane Dillon
Publisher: Dial Books for Young Readers   ISBN: 0-8037-0308-2
Summary: Describes traditions from all over Africa.

Title: *The Science Book of Weather*
Author: Neil Ardley
Publisher: Harcourt Brace Jovanovich   ISBN: 0-15-200624-9
Summary: Simple experiments demonstrate the different forces that cause different kinds of weather.

Title: *Science Crafts for Kids*
Authors: Gwen Diehn and Terry Krautwurst
Publisher: Sterling   ISBN: 0-8069-0283-3
Summary: Kids learn about scientific principles while doing hands-on science projects.

References

Albyn, C.L. *The Multicultural Cookbook for Students;* Oryx: Phoenix, 1993; p 38.

Caney, S. *Steven Caney's Toy Book;* Workman: New York, 1972.

Diehn, G.; Krautwurst, T. "Barometer;" *Science Crafts for Kids;* Sterling: New York, 1994; pp 64–65.

Sarquis, M.; Sarquis, J.; Williams, J. "Under Pressure;" *Teaching Chemistry with TOYS: Activities for Grades K–9;* McGraw Hill: New York, 1995; pp 115–122.

Zaire: A Country Study; Meditz, S.W., Merrill, T., Eds.; U.S. Government Printing Office: Washington, D.C., 1994; pp 63–69.

Shrinky Plastic

SCIENCE CATEGORY: Properties of Objects and Materials
TOPICS: Effects of Temperature on Matter, Polymers, Heat
OBJECTIVE: Students become familiar with objects made of various plastics and some of their properties and observe the effect of heat on shrinkable polystyrene.

In this lesson, students observe polystyrene (the plastic used to make Shrinky Dinks®) shrinking when heated. Students explore the idea that different materials have different properties.

- Prior to beginning the lesson, students examine a variety of plastic objects and describe their different properties. Among those objects are two identical drawings of George (from *George Shrinks*) on shrinkable polystyrene, one heated (and shrunk) and one not.

- As a class, students summarize on a science chart their observations of the plastic items, including the full-sized and shrunken polystyrene.

- Students hear the story *George Shrinks* and discuss how the story relates to the shrunken plastic.

- Students make and observe shrinkable polystyrene objects of their own, including a self-portrait.

- To conclude the lesson, students use their shrunken self-portrait in a story book.

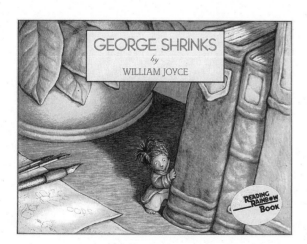

Featured Fiction Book: *George Shrinks*
Author and Illustrator: William Joyce
Publisher: Harper & Row
ISBN: 0-06-443129-0
Summary: While George's parents are out, George dreams he is small. When he wakes up, he finds that his dream has come true.

Part 1: Building Bridges

Building Student Knowledge and Motivation

Set up a center that includes a variety of plastic objects. Make sure that many different observable characteristics are represented by the set of objects, such as transparent, opaque, stiff, flexible, hard, rubbery, soft, and crumbly. Possible items include clear and opaque food containers, Styrofoam™ cups and packing peanuts, plastic wrap, super balls, toothpaste tubes, a rain slicker, a beach ball, and scraps of vinyl upholstery. Include among these objects two identical drawings of George (from *George Shrinks*) on shrinkable polystyrene, one heated and shrunken and one not. (Because the pictures of George in the book are small, enlarge a picture of George and then trace it onto two same-sized pieces of polystyrene. Shrink one of these according to the directions provided in the Procedure.) Over a period of several days, give groups of students time to examine the objects and record their observations. (Masters for several types of science journal pages are provided in the Using Science Journals section at the beginning of the book.)

Getting Ready to Read

Title a new sheet of chart paper "Look at Plastics (Observations)" and label two columns: "Object" and "Description." Have students share their observations of the plastic items and record these on the science chart. Ask, "Do you think all these objects are made of exactly the same kind of plastic? Why?" Bring out the idea that different kinds of plastic can have different characteristics or properties.

Show the two drawings of George on shrinkable polystyrene, and have students discuss the similarities and differences. Hold up the book *George Shrinks*. Ask students to think about what these two plastic pieces have to do with the story as you read aloud.

Bridging to the Science Activity

Again show the two drawings of George on shrinkable polystyrene and discuss how they relate to the story. Discuss the similarities and differences between the two pieces. Tell students that they are made from exactly the same kind of plastic, but that one piece shrunk. Explain that the appearance of a material can sometimes change; for example, this kind of plastic shrinks when heated.

Ask students if they think they could actually shrink like George. Discuss the idea that the materials that make up our bodies are very different than the material that makes the shrinkable plastic. Tell students that you want them to have a chance to observe shrinkable plastic more carefully and that they will be making their own shrunken figures.

Part 2: Science Activity

Materials

For the Procedure
Per student
- 2 pieces of any of the following types of shrinkable polystyrene plastic (Look for recycle code #6 and/or the letters PS):
  - clear plastic salad box ("clamshell" style)
  - clear portion of a lid from a Dannon® yogurt single-serving container
  - commercial shrinkable plastic such as Shrinky Dinks

➤ *You may wish to have each student bring in at least two pieces of clear, clean polystyrene. You may also be able to get donations from a deli. Make sure all are marked with recycle code #6. Do not use the rims of clear yogurt cup lids—cut off and discard. Blank sheets of "frosted" shrinkable polystyrene are available in quantity from K & B Innovations, 141 Cottonwood Avenue, Hartland, WI 53029-2014; 414/367-8266. The frosted texture allows students to use colored pencils instead of markers to decorate the plastic. Colored pencils will not work on the unfrosted polystyrene. The company has a special wholesale price for school orders.*

Per group of 3–4 students
- scissors
- graph paper with ¼-inch rules
- several different-colored, fine- or medium-point permanent markers and/or colored pencils

➤ *Markette and Sanford brands of permanent markers work very well. Colored pencils can be used only for frosted commercial "Shrinky Dink" material.*

Per class
- hot pad or oven mitt
- piece of brown paper grocery bag
- cookie sheet or metal tray
- smooth item such as a board or cardboard
- double-pan balance
- conventional oven or toaster oven (Microwave ovens will not work.)
- piece of paper
- tape
- (optional) sandpaper
- (optional) an assortment of cookie cutters

For the Science Extension
All materials listed for the Procedure except
- substitute foamed vegetable trays of more than one color for the clear polystyrene containers

Safety and Disposal

Allow the shrunken polystyrene designs to cool before handling. An adult must operate the oven. You may want to use sandpaper to smooth points or sharp edges on the shrunken pieces. No special disposal procedures are required.

1. If using recycled polystyrene, trim as needed to make flat, square pieces. If using commercial shrinkable plastic, cut into squares.

    The shrunken object will be less than one-fourth the size of the original plastic. Size the squares accordingly.

2. Since oven temperatures can vary, test the oven you plan to use in advance to determine the best baking time. A toaster oven may take less time (a minute or less at 325°F) than a conventional oven (about 3 minutes at 325°F). Avoid using an institution-sized oven if it has a large internal fan that could blow the plastic pieces around.

Procedure

Part A: Making the Shrinkable Figures

1. Model the following steps for students:

    a. Use permanent markers or colored pencils to create a design on polystyrene. If desired, have simple-shaped cookie cutters available for students to trace and decorate.

    Colors will be more intense on the shrunken design. Be sure the polystyrene is free of dust, since dust particles are more noticeable after shrinking. Remember, colored pencils will work only on the frosted polystyrene.

    b. Cut out the design.

    Tell students that if their design is complicated, they can just cut around it in an oval or other simple shape.

    c. Place the shape on a blank sheet of graph paper, trace around its edge, and label the tracing "before heating."

    d. Cut out the traced shape.

    e. Put your initials on the back of the polystyrene shape.

2. Have students make their own shrinkable figures using flip cards 1 and 2 (provided) as a reference.

Part B: Heating the Shrinkable Figures

1. Preheat the oven to 325°F.

2. Lay a sheet of brown paper from a grocery bag on a cookie sheet or metal tray and place the students' plastic figures on the paper.

3. Use an oven mitt or hot pad to place the tray in the oven and heat the plastic figures until they stop shrinking. If possible, have students observe what is happening.

    Adult supervision is required during heating, removing the hot objects, and handling immediately after.

4. Use an oven mitt or hot pad to remove the hot tray from the oven.

    Because oven temperatures can vary, watch shrinking time carefully. Pieces of polystyrene will typically first curl and then lie flat as they shrink. (If the curled edges touch, they may stick. Should this happen, using extreme caution, pull them apart while still warm, and reheat as needed to flatten.) The plastic might need to be flattened while still warm with a smooth item such as a board or cardboard.

5. After the shrunken plastic figures have cooled, remove them from the cookie sheet.

6. Model the following steps for students and have them repeat using flip cards 3 and 4 as a reference:

   a. Place the shrunken figure on a sheet of graph paper, trace around its edge, and label it "after heating."

   b. Cut out the traced shape.

   c. Count the number of complete squares in each traced shape and write the numbers on the shapes. Are there more complete squares in the "before heating" or "after heating" figure?

7. Put the graph paper shapes on the bulletin board.

8. Using a double-pan balance, compare the masses of the two "Georges" you used in Part 1: Building Bridges. Ask, "How can the smaller one have a mass equal to the bigger one?" Have students carefully observe. If they do not notice, point out that the shrunken George is much thicker.

Part C: Making Shrunken Self-Portraits

1. Give each student a new, unshrunk piece of polystyrene. Model the following steps for students:

   a. Draw a rectangle on a piece of paper the size of your piece of polystyrene.

   b. Draw a self-portrait within the rectangle on the paper.

   c. Put the polystyrene exactly over the rectangle and tape on one edge.

   d. Use permanent markers or colored pencils to trace your self-portrait onto the polystyrene, cut out the design, and put your initials on the back of the plastic portrait.

2. Have students make shrinking self-portraits using flip cards 5 and 6 (provided) as a reference.

3. Repeat Steps 1–5 from Part B.

Science Extension

Have students repeat Parts A and B of the Procedure using foam vegetable trays. How are the results similar? Different?

Science Explanation

The following explanation is intended for the teacher's information. Modify the explanation for students as required.

Commercial Shrinky Dinks and the shrinkable figures in this activity are made of a plastic called polystyrene, a common polymer. A polymer is a large, chain-like molecule made by combining many smaller molecules called monomers. (Poly = many, mono = one, mer = unit.) To visualize this, imagine a very, very long string of pop-beads. Polymers can be natural or synthetic. Living things or the materials produced by living things are nearly entirely composed of natural polymers. Natural polymers include collagen, keratins, enzymes, certain hormones, hemoglobin, DNA, starch, cellulose, cotton, wool, wood, flax, latex, rubber, silk, and paper. Synthetic polymers are used to make nearly every kind of product imaginable, including synthetic fabrics (such as nylon and polyester), construction materials, food packaging, toys, and vehicles.

Scientists are able to develop polymers with a wide range of properties. Polymers can be flexible or rigid, transparent or opaque, heat resistant or not, waterproof or water-soluble, electrical insulators or conductors, hard or soft, elastic or stiff. These many properties are possible because polymers can be made from different kinds of monomers, and the monomers can be put together in many different repeating patterns.

Polystyrene and certain other polymers can have the ability to shrink when heated, a somewhat unusual property. Most common solids, when heated, either expand before they melt into liquids (for example, metals) or decompose into different materials (for example, wood into charcoal). The shrinking nature of polystyrene and other shrinkable plastics is the result of the way they are manufactured. As they are produced, these plastics are heated, stretched out into a film, then quickly cooled. The sudden cooling "freezes" the molecules of the polymer in their stretched-out configuration. To visualize this "freezing," imagine how a person might appear if suddenly asked to freeze while doing jumping jacks. When the plastics are heated once again, the molecules within them are released from their "frozen" configurations; they return to their original dimensions, resulting in the observed shrinkage. Depending on how the polystyrene was stretched during manufacturing, it may not shrink uniformly when heated. For example, a circle may turn out to be an oval after shrinking. The commercial Shrinky Dink material is manufactured in such a way that it shrinks very uniformly.

Part 3: Lesson Extensions

Writing Extension

Figure 1: Cut out an area so that the student's self-portrait shows through the front cover and every page.

Have students use the shrunken self-portraits they created in Part C of the Procedure to make their own books patterned after *George Shrinks*. (See Figure 1.) Have each student make a cover with two pieces of construction paper. Have them glue the self-portrait on the inside back cover and cut out a circle on the front cover so that the self-portrait is visible through the front cover. Have them make see-through pages by tracing the cut-out circle from the cover onto each page, then cutting the circles out. Bind the book along one side. (The reader should be able to see the self-portrait through every page.) The title of the book will be *[Student's name] Shrinks*. The book will begin with the student waking up one morning to find that he or she has shrunk. Allow students to tell what happens to them next.

The illustrations should be centered around the shrunken self-portrait, which will appear on every page. You may want to make a template cover and first page, leaving blanks for students to fill in their names.

Part 4: For Further Study

Additional Books

Fiction

Title: *Alice in Wonderland* (any version)
Author: Lewis Carroll
Summary: Alice eats a magic food and shrinks.

Title: *Flat Stanley*
Author: Jeff Brown
Publisher: Trophy   ISBN: 0-06-440293-2
Summary: A boy becomes flat and can slip easily under doors.

Title: *Harry and the Terrible Whatzit*
Author and Illustrator: Dick Gackenbach
Publisher: Clarion   ISBN: 0-89919-223-8
Summary: Harry is afraid to go down into the cellar. His mother goes down to get
   some pickles and doesn't return. (She goes out to the garden.) Harry decides to
   rescue her and runs into a double-headed, three-clawed, six-toed, long-horned
   Whatzit. As Harry's fear of this creature diminishes, so does the creature's size
   until it shrinks to the size of a peanut.

References

Modern Plastics Encyclopedia; McGraw-Hill: New York, 1983; Vol. 60, No. 10A, pp 72–74, 224–226.
Rodriguez, F. "Classroom Demonstrations of Polymer Principles," *Journal of Chemical Education.*
   1990, 67(9), 784–788.
Sarquis, M.; Sarquis, J.; Williams, J. "Shape Shifters;" *Teaching Chemistry with TOYS: Activities for
   Grades K–9;* McGraw-Hill: New York, 1995; pp 151–156.
"Shrinkable Plastics;" *Fun with Chemistry: A Guidebook of K–12 Activities;* Sarquis, M., Sarquis, J.,
   Eds.; Institute for Chemical Education: Madison, WI, 1991; Vol. 1, pp 101–105.

Flip Cards

❶
Shrinking Figures

Color and cut out a design. Put your initials on the back of your design.

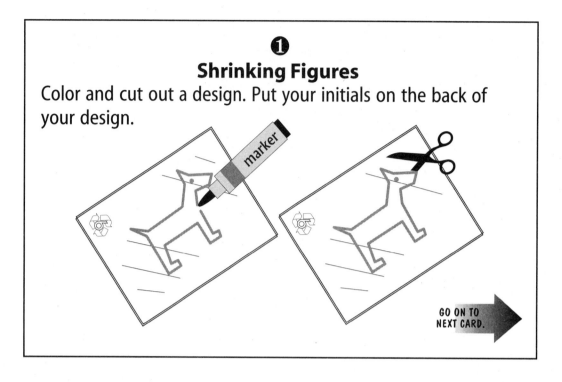

GO ON TO
NEXT CARD.

❷

Lay the shape on a sheet of graph paper and trace around it. Label the graph paper shape "before heating" and cut it out. Give the plastic shape to an adult to heat in the oven.

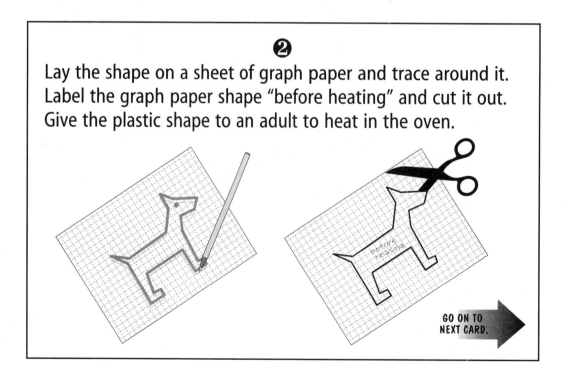

GO ON TO
NEXT CARD.

❸

Lay the shrunken figure on a sheet of graph paper and trace around it. Label the graph paper shape "after heating" and cut it out.

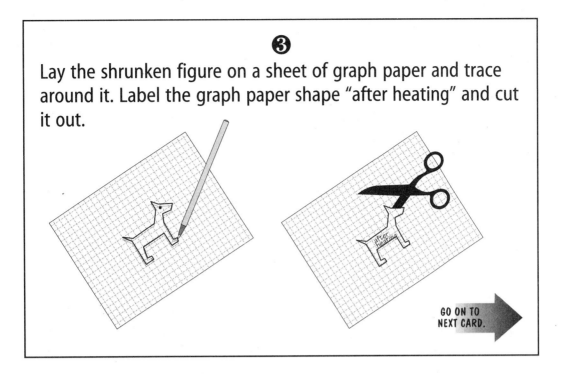

GO ON TO
NEXT CARD.

❹

Count the number of complete squares in each traced shape and write the numbers on the shapes. Are there more complete squares in the "before heating" or "after heating" figure?

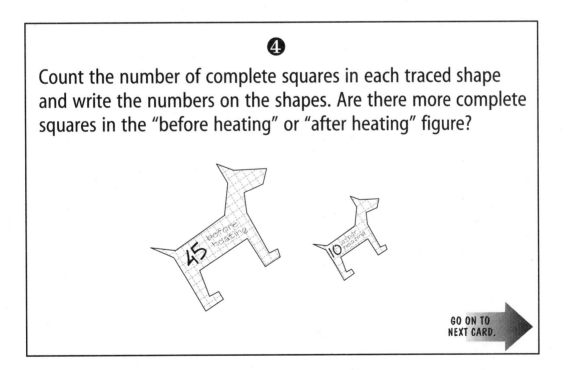

GO ON TO
NEXT CARD.

❺

Shrunken Self-Portraits

Trace your polystyrene rectangle on a piece of paper. Use colored markers to draw a self-portrait within the rectangle on the paper.

GO ON TO
NEXT CARD.

❻

Put the polystyrene exactly over the rectangle and tape on one edge. Trace your self-portrait onto the polystyrene.

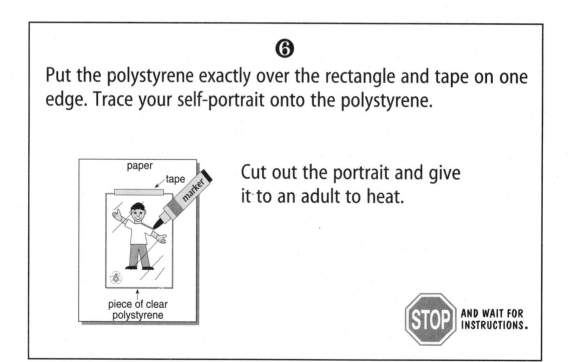

Cut out the portrait and give it to an adult to heat.

STOP AND WAIT FOR INSTRUCTIONS.

Growing Gators

SCIENCE CATEGORY: Properties of Objects and Materials
TOPICS: Properties of Polymers, Physical Changes, Scientific Experimentation
OBJECTIVE: Students use a scientific experiment to answer a question and become familiar with the properties of a type of polymer.

In this lesson, students observe polymer alligators that expand in water and experiment to determine the effect of salt on the growing process. Students predict, observe, measure, and graph the growth of these grow alligators.

- Prior to beginning the lesson, a grow alligator is placed in a jar on the teacher's desk for a few days with no explanation or discussion.

- Students hear the story of *Zack's Alligator*, pausing to predict what will happen at key points in the plot.

- After the story, students compare and contrast Bridget from *Zack's Alligator* with the grow alligator in the jar.

- Students are presented with an imaginary dilemma based on characters in *Zack's Alligator*: Zack soaks Bridget in salt water, but she doesn't grow. What did he do wrong? Zack wonders if salt water might be the problem, but how can he find out? Students conduct an experiment to answer Zack's question and continue by designing additional experiments of their own using other superabsorbent polymer products, such as those used in diapers.

- To conclude the lesson, students write to Zack, explaining what they did to test his idea and what they found out.

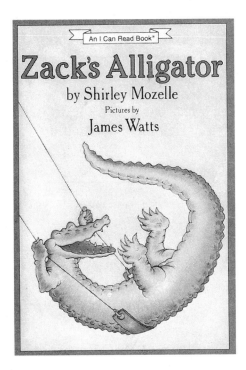

Featured Fiction Book: *Zack's Alligator*
Author: Shirley Mozelle
Illustrator: James Watts
Publisher: HarperCollins
ISBN: 0-06-444186-5
Summary: When Zack soaks his new alligator keychain in water, it grows into a full-sized and fun-loving alligator.

Part 1: Building Bridges

Building Student Knowledge and Motivation

A few days before beginning the lesson, put a Magic Animal grow alligator (See Materials) in a large empty jar on your desk. (Do not add any water to the jar at this time.) If students ask questions about the alligator, allow them to discuss the alligator, but do not offer any reason why the alligator is there.

Getting Ready to Read

Show students the cover of *Zack's Alligator* and ask students what they think the story will be about. Read through page 7, where Zack opens the second box (but has not yet looked inside), then pause and ask students to predict what will be inside the box. After reading page 9, where Zack puts Bridget in the sink and turns on the water, ask students to predict what will happen to Bridget.

Bridging to the Science Activity

After completing the story, hold up the Magic Animal alligator from your desk. Ask, "Has anyone noticed this alligator on my desk? Is it similar to anything in the story?" Have students compare and contrast the toy alligator with Bridget in the story. Then tell students that you have a story to tell them about another event that happened to Zack and Bridget.

One day, Zack took Bridget to the seashore because he thought she would have plenty of room to grow there. Since the day was warm and sunny, Zack decided to make Bridget grow so they could play. He put her in the ocean water, but nothing happened—Bridget stayed the same size. Zack picked her up again and shook off the salty water. He was puzzled. "Why didn't Bridget grow?" he thought. "Is something different about seawater? Hmm, it has salt in it. Maybe that's the reason. But how can I be sure?" (If needed, review the idea that ocean water is salty.)

Explain to students that sometimes we think we know the cause for an effect we have observed, but we aren't sure. Tell them that a scientific experiment is a good way to find out if the suspected cause really produces the observed effect. Explain that students will be doing an experiment for Zack to help him decide if the salt in the water prevented Bridget from growing. Discuss how to graph and record data and explain the importance of being accurate. Explain to students that they will grow their own alligators like Zack did.

Part 2: Science Activity

Materials

For the Procedure
Per group
- 3 cups tap water
- quart-sized, zipper-type freezer bag

- Magic Animal alligator

➤ *Magic Animal alligators are available from World of Science stores. For the location nearest you, call 716/475-0100. Alternatively, smaller dinosaur-shaped grow creatures are available from the Allen-Lewis Company, P.O. Box 16546, Denver, CO 80216; 800/525-6658. Allen-Lewis may offer special arrangements for classroom teachers for a reduction in the minimum order requirement. Mention Terrific Science Programs at Miami University when ordering. Both the alligators and the dinosaurs are reusable.*

Per class
- table salt (sodium chloride, NaCl)
- teaspoon

For the Science Extensions

❶ All materials listed for the Procedure plus the following:
Per class
- graph paper

❷ All materials listed for the Procedure plus the following:
Per class
- balance

❸ All materials listed for the Procedure plus the following:
Per group
- large container, such as a pickle jar from the cafeteria

❹ Per group
- superabsorbent disposable diaper

Safety and Disposal

No special safety or disposal procedures are required.

Getting Ready

1. The variable in this experiment is the amount of salt in the water used to "grow" the alligator. To set up this variable, prepare a bag for each group that contains one of the following: 3 teaspoons salt, 2 teaspoons salt, 1 teaspoon salt, or no salt. Label the bags appropriately. Try to have at least two teams testing each amount of salt.

2. Copy and tape together the two sheets of the Grow Alligator Measuring Chart (provided). Students will use the chart to measure the alligators twice each day for several days. Decide on a time frame for measuring, for example 9:00 a.m. and 1:00 p.m. Plan to begin the experiment at the time you have chosen for the morning measurement.

Procedure

Part A: Answering Zack's Question

1. Tell students to trace the alligator on the Data Sheet. Next, have students place the alligator on the bar labeled "Day 1, AM" on the Grow Alligator Measuring Chart. Make sure students orient the alligator so that the longest dimension lies along the column. Color in the number of squares covered by the alligator. Tell students to count the number of squares they colored and record this number on the Data Sheet.

2. Instruct each group to look at their bag, read the label, and answer Question 2 on the Data Sheet. Explain that different groups have different amounts of salt (or no salt) in the bag. Through a facilitated discussion, introduce the role of a variable in an experiment. Emphasize that in an experiment, only one thing changes (the variable). Explain that the amount of salt is the variable in this experiment.

3. When everyone is ready, have one representative of each group bring their bag to the front of the room. Measure 3 cups of water into the zipper-type bag, place the alligator in the bag, and seal.

4. Have groups set the bags aside until time for the afternoon measurement.

5. At the decided-upon time, have each group measure their alligator by laying the bag containing the alligator on top of the Measuring Chart. Instruct students to gently turn the bag and/or move the alligator until it is resting in the proper orientation on the second bar of the chart. Have students color in the number of squares covered by the alligator and record this number on the Data Sheet.

6. Have groups repeat Step 5 twice a day for two or more days.
   If the alligators get too big to stretch out in the bags, students may need to take them out, dry them off, measure them, and put them back into the bags.

7. Label a graph as shown in Figure 1.

8. Record each group's final measurement on the science chart and discuss results. Ask, "Which alligator grew the most? The least?" Ask students if they can see a relationship between the amount of salt and the amount of growth. They should be able to conclude that the more salt in the water, the less the alligators grow.

9. Continue the discussion, making sure that students realize that the only difference in experimental setups among groups was the amount of salt in each group's water: "Did each bag hold the same amount of water?" *Yes.* "Did each alligator stay in the water for the same amount of time?" *Yes.* "Then why did the alligators grow different amounts?" *The different amounts of salt must have caused a difference in the amount of growth.*

10. Challenge students to figure out how to shrink the alligators. Have groups make and record observations and measurements, including how many days it takes the alligators to shrink back to original size.

11. Discuss the material the alligator is made of and give examples of everyday uses, such as in some disposable diapers, the toy called G.U.T.S., and a water-retaining soil additive for plants (such as Soil Moist™).

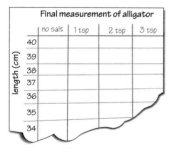

Figure 1

Part B: Experimenting with Other Variables

1. Have the class list variables besides salt that could affect the growth of grow alligators. *Water temperature; amount of time; another substance, such as sugar, dissolved in the water.*

2. Have each group choose one variable to test (from an approved list, for safety reasons), keeping all other variables constant. Record results on another graph similar to the one shown in Figure 1.

Science Extensions

1. Have students measure the area of the grow alligator by taking it out of the bag, patting it dry with a paper towel, setting it on graph paper, tracing the outline of the alligator, and counting boxes. Record the number counted. Measure the change in area over the same three-day period.

2. Have students measure the mass of the alligator before, during, and after soaking.

3. In a large container (such as a pickle jar from the cafeteria), have students measure by water displacement the volume change of the alligator. Before the alligator starts growing, place it in the container and mark the water level. Then after full growth is attained, put the alligator back into the same jar with the same starting amount of water; mark the new water level after the grow alligator is dunked.

4. Have students experiment with the water-absorbing properties of a superabsorbent disposable diaper. (Different manufacturers make diapers containing superabsorbers; the diapers are identified by a variety of terms such as "ultra dry" and "extra dry.") Have students predict how many cups of water a diaper will hold. After the diaper is saturated, cut it open and allow students to see the superabsorbent polymer inside.

Science Explanation

The following explanation is intended for the teacher's information. Modify the explanation for students as required.

The grow alligators in this activity contain two different polymers; the hydrophilic ("water-loving") polymer that is responsible for the absorption of water and a second polymer that is hydrophobic ("water-hating"). (See "Shrinky Plastic" for more information on polymers.) The hydrophilic polymer in the alligator is a superabsorber. Superabsorbers are found in diapers and toys (such as grow alligators and G.U.T.S.). These polymers can absorb large amounts of water. The hydrophobic polymer forms the framework of the alligator, enabling it to grow without losing its original shape.

When the hydrophilic polymer comes in contact with water, a gel forms that has many times the volume of the dry polymer. Less water is absorbed when salt is present. As the concentration of salt increases, the amount of water absorbed by the hydrophilic polymer is decreased. As a result, the grow alligator in water containing three teaspoons salt per three cups water has the smallest change, while the grow alligator in tap water with no added salt has the greatest change. When the grow alligator is removed from water, the water slowly evaporates and the grow alligator shrinks back to its original size.

Part 3: Lesson Extensions

Writing Extensions

1. Remind students that Zack wants to know why Bridget did not grow when placed in seawater, and that an important part of any experiment is describing the procedure and results to others. Have students write letters to Zack describing what they did to test his theory and what they found out. Encourage them to write and draw pictures to communicate their findings clearly.

2. Have the class write an "alligator tall tale," with one student writing the first sentence on a sheet of paper, another student writing the next sentence on a new sheet of paper, and so on until every student has written at least one sentence and the story has ended. Tape the sheets of paper together and fold accordion-style. Tape a cut-out alligator head to the free end of the first sentence and a tail to the free end of the last sentence. (See Figure 2.) Unfold the story to make the alligator grow.

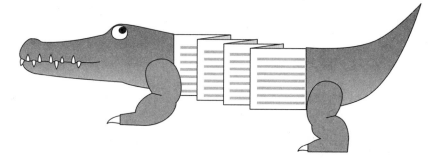

Figure 2: Make an "alligator tall tale" book by taping all of the pages together in a chain and taping an alligator head and tail to the ends.

Math Extension

Have the students use their data to answer the following questions: How much did your grow alligator grow between the first and last measurements? Between which two measurements was there the greatest growth?

Part 4: For Further Study

Additional Books

Fiction

Title: *The Secret in the Matchbox*
Author: Val Willis
Illustrator: John Shelley
Publisher: Farrar, Straus and Giroux
ISBN: 0-374-46593-2
Summary: A boy takes a special matchbox to school. When the matchbox is opened, a tiny dragon emerges and grows larger and larger. The dragon threatens to terrorize the classroom, but the boy eventually gets the dragon safely back in the matchbox.

References

Chem Fax! Publication Numbers 755.10, Flinn Scientific: Batavia, IL.

Polymers: Linking Chemistry and Fun, developed by Marie Sherman, Ursuline Academy, St. Louis, MO.

Sarquis, M., Sarquis J., Williams, J. "Salt Solutions and Grow Creatures;" *Teaching Chemistry with TOYS: Activities for Grades K–9;* McGraw-Hill: New York, 1995; pp 221–228.

"Superabsorbent Polymer;" *Fun with Chemistry: A Guidebook of K–12 Activities;* Sarquis, M., Sarquis, J., Eds.; Institute for Chemical Education: Madison, WI, 1993; Vol. 2, pp 95–99.

Woodward, L. "Super Slurper;" *Polymers All Around You;* Terrific Science: Middletown, OH, 1992; pp 19–21.

Names _____ _____

_____ _____

Data Sheet

Growing Gators

1. Trace your grow alligator below and show where it is longest.

2. Which of the following is in your bag?

   ❑ no salt   ❑ 1 teaspoon of salt   ❑ 2 teaspoons of salt   ❑ 3 teaspoons of salt

3. Use your Grow Alligator Measuring Chart to fill in this table.

Time of Measurement	Day 1, AM	Day 1, PM	Day 2, AM	Day 2, PM	Day 3, AM	Day 3, PM
Number of Squares (centimeters)						

104

Grow Alligator Measuring Chart

Number of Squares (centimeters)

40						
39						
38						
37						
36						
35						
35						
34						
33						
32						
31						
30						
29						
28						
27						
26						
25						
24						
23						
22						
21						

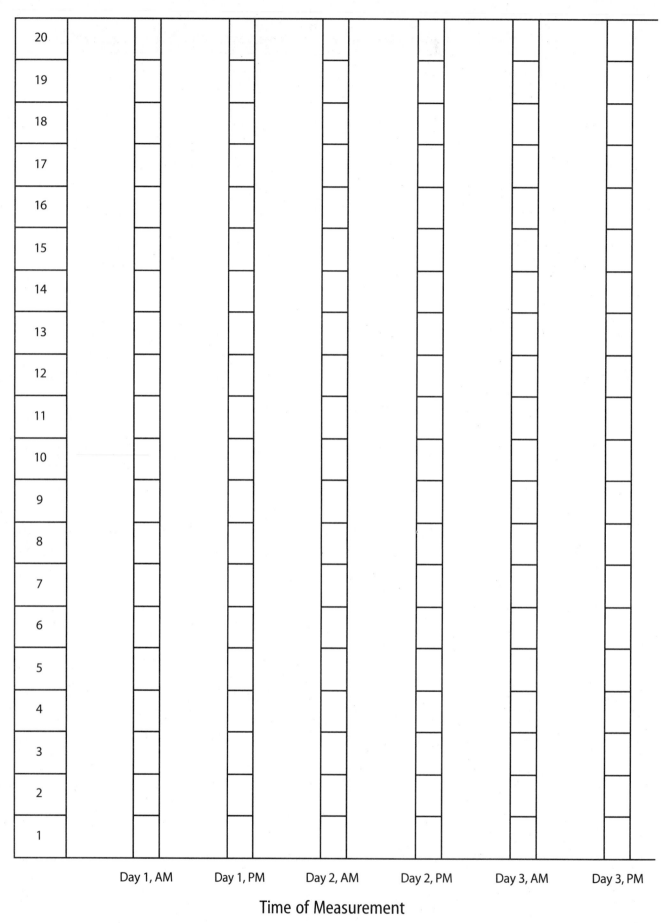

Time of Measurement

Iron for Breakfast

SCIENCE CATEGORY: Properties of Objects and Materials
TOPICS: Nutrition, Magnetic Properties of Iron
OBJECTIVE: Students gain experience with using a magnet as a tool to determine the presence of iron in food.

In this lesson, students use magnets to extract food-grade iron filings from iron-fortified food, discuss the reasons why food manufacturers add iron to food, and review good nutrition practices.

- To introduce the lesson, students collect magazine pictures of what they consider to be "good foods." As a class, they use these pictures to construct their idea of a food pyramid.

- As a class, students discuss the food pyramid and what constitutes "good food" according to nutritionists as well as what they might consider "good food." They rearrange their food pyramid as necessary and make a class chart of various people's ideas of a good breakfast.

- Students hear the story *Gregory, the Terrible Eater* and listen to discover what Gregory and his parents think is "good food." Through class discussion, they add to the "good food" chart.

- Students learn about "good foods" from around the world and add to the science chart as they listen to an excerpt from *Good Morning, Let's Eat!*

- Students use magnets to extract food-grade iron filings from iron-fortified food.

- Students use package labels to evaluate the nutritional value, including iron content, of snack foods and make bar graphs of nutritional information.

- To conclude the lesson, students write a letter from Gregory to his parents telling them what "good food" he would like in his lunch bag.

Featured Fiction Book: *Gregory, the Terrible Eater*
Author: Mitchell Sharmat
Illustrators: Jose Aruego and Ariane Dewey
Publisher: Scholastic, Inc.
ISBN: 0-590-43350-4
Summary: Gregory's parents are very concerned when Gregory prefers fruits, vegetables, fish, and cereal to tin cans, boxes, and bottle caps. Dr. Ram helps Mother and Father Goat find a cure for Gregory's "terrible" eating habits.

Part 1: Building Bridges

Building Student Knowledge and Motivation

Make sure students know that iron is attracted to magnets. If students are not already familiar with this concept, set up opportunities for them to learn.

Tell the class that you have a delicious food to show them. Bring out and pretend to eat an iron object, such as a frying pan or barbell, acting as though the item were quite delicious. (Do not use a small iron item that students might actually try to ingest, such as a nail.) Students will probably respond with comments such as "ooh," and "yuck." Tell them that if they don't think your choice is a good one, then they will need to show you some of their ideas about good food. Give students the assignment to find and (with permission) cut out two or three small to medium-sized magazine pictures of good food. Tell them to bring the pictures in any time over the next few days. Also leave a few magazines out in the classroom for students who do not bring pictures from home. At this time, do not elaborate on what "good food" might mean.

Set up a classroom bulletin board as shown in Figure 1. As students bring in their food pictures from home, tell them to tack the pictures onto the food pyramid chart where they think they belong. If they don't know where to put the pictures, have them tack them in the "Don't Know Where" section. If one or more of the food pyramid sections gets filled up, have students with foods from those categories put their pictures in the "No More Room" section.

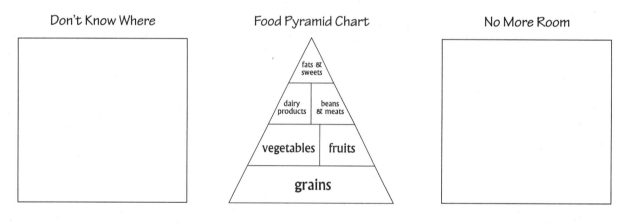

Figure 1: Set up a classroom bulletin board.

Getting Ready to Read

After all the pictures are in place, tell students that the food pyramid is the standard of "good food" recommended by nutritionists as healthful—good **for** you. Explain that the foods you should eat the most of go on the bottom of the pyramid (That's why this section has the most space), and that the foods you should eat the least of go on the top. (That's why this section has the least space.) As a class, review the pictures on the bulletin board. Move around any pictures that may have ended up in the wrong place, and figure out where the "Don't Know Where" pictures belong. Discuss what kinds of foods ended up in the "No More Room" section. (These are probably foods that belong at the top of the pyramid, such as candy and potato

Teaching Physical Science through Children's Literature

chips.) Ask students, "Did you each bring the same pictures for the bulletin board?" Discuss the idea that in choosing pictures of "good foods," students may have chosen pictures of foods that "taste good," are "good for you," or both, and that people's opinions about these differ.

Label a new sheet of chart paper "What Is a Good Breakfast?" and divide it into four columns: "Nutritionists," "Gregory" (Divide this column into "beginning of story" and "end of story"), "Gregory's Parents" (Divide this column into "beginning of story" and "end of story"), and "Around the World." As a class, list foods in the Nutritionists column as appropriate, based on the foods from the bulletin board.

Show students the cover of *Gregory, the Terrible Eater.* Ask students what they think the book has to do with nutrition and food pyramids. Tell students to listen for examples of "good food" for breakfast from the characters' points of view as you read the story.

Bridging to the Science Activity

Bring out the "What Is a Good Breakfast?" chart and ask students for examples of what Gregory and his parents thought was "good food" for breakfast at the beginning of the story and at the end. List these as appropriate on the science chart. (For purposes of later discussion, make sure that some metal items are listed.) Ask, "Why did they change their opinions?"

Show students the book *Good Morning, Let's Eat!* Read page 4, "What Is This Thing Called Breakfast?" as well as other excerpts as desired. (The book is illustrated with photographs from around the world and discusses cultural differences about what is considered "good food" for breakfast.) After reading, have students give examples of good breakfast food from other cultures and list these on the science chart. Discuss the idea of "good food" and its many possible meanings. Ask, "Does everyone agree what good food is? Who decides?"

Compare the good food lists from the chart. Ask students, "Did you ever eat anything on the food list for Gregory or his parents?" After some discussion, specifically ask students if they ever ate anything like some of the metal objects Gregory ate. Bring out the iron object you pretended to eat earlier. Tell students that they probably have eaten iron metal (like the iron in your "delicious" object from Building Student Knowledge and Motivation) for breakfast for much of their lives without realizing it. Ask, "Would you consider iron metal a good food? Would Gregory's parents consider that a good food?" Bring out the idea that both Gregory and his parents would like iron-fortified food—Gregory would like the food, and his parents would like the iron (a metal). Tell student that they are going to see some of that metal for themselves.

Part 2: Science Activity

Materials

For the Procedure, Part A
Per group
- nonmetallic container, about 500 milliliters (2 cups) in volume
- new, unsharpened pencil

- ceramic ring-shaped or U-shaped magnet, rumen magnet (sometimes called a cow magnet), or romax magnet (segmented cow magnet)

> *Rumen and romax magnets are much more expensive than ceramic magnets, but they are also much stronger and can extract more iron from the food. Depending on the food you use, you may need the stronger magnets to extract the iron. Test in advance. Inexpensive ceramic ring-shaped magnets are available at Radio Shack stores. Delta Education (P.O. Box 3000, Nashua, NH 03061-3000; 800/442-5444) sells U-shaped ceramic magnets (#80-130-0463), rumen (cow) magnets (#80-130-4632), and romax (segmented cow) magnets (#80-130-7052). Rumen and romax magnets are also available more cheaply from slaughterhouses and agricultural suppliers such as Jeffers mail-order catalog, 800/533-3377.*

- plastic bag
- magnifying lens
- 2 twist ties or rubber bands
- piece of white paper
- about 3 tablespoons enriched Farina™ listing iron as an ingredient or other iron-fortified food that lists iron or reduced iron as an ingredient, such as Carnation® Instant Breakfast or iron-fortified grits

> *Most iron-fortified foods list iron compounds such as ferric phosphate as an ingredient; these will not work. Read the labels carefully and test in advance.*

Per class
- sturdy zipper-type plastic bag
- about 3 tablespoons enriched Farina listing iron as an ingredient or other iron-fortified food that lists iron or reduced iron as an ingredient
- very strong magnet, such as a rumen (cow) or romax (segmented cow) magnet

For the Procedure, Part B
Per student
- small photo of student
- 60-mm-diameter (2¼-inch-diameter) petri dish

> *Petri dishes of this size are available from Frey Scientific (#F07445), 905 Hickory Lane, P.O. Box 8101, Mansfield, OH 44901-8101; 800/225-FREY.*

- small magnet
- ¹⁄₁₆ teaspoon iron filings

> *Iron filings (#80-060-0313) are available from Delta Education.*

Per class
- hot-melt glue gun and glue
- (optional) commercial iron filing toys similar to those made in Part B
- rubber cement

Safety and Disposal

You or an adult assistant should be the only one to handle the glue gun. Use caution, as hot glue can cause serious burns. No special disposal procedures are required.

Getting Ready

Figure 2

1. Test the iron-fortified food and magnets you will be using to make sure the iron can be extracted.

2. For each group, attach a magnet to a pencil with a twist tie or rubber band. This assembly is referred to as a stirrer. Insert each stirrer into a plastic bag and fasten with another tie. (See Figure 2.)

3. For Part B, cut the student photos into circles that will fit the bottom of the wider half of the petri dishes. (See Figure 3.)

Procedure

Part A: Analyzing Iron-Fortified Food

1. Show students the container of iron-fortified food to be tested.

2. The box may say "fortified" or "iron fortified." Discuss what "iron fortified" means. Ask, "Do you think we can see the iron in the food?"

3. Explain to students that you have not added anything to the food, pointing out the unopened container as proof.

4. Pour about 3 tablespoons of the food into each group's non-metallic container and have students observe the food carefully. Ask, "Can you see anything that might be iron?" Ask, "How could we find out if there is iron in the food?" Through a facilitated discussion, lead students to conclude that a magnet would be a good tool for finding iron.

5. Model the following steps for students:

   a. Use the plastic bag-covered stirrer to stir the food in the container.

   b. Remove the bag-covered stirrer from the container and use the magnifying lens to observe the iron filings clinging to the bag.

   c. Undo the tie from the bag and pull the stirrer out of the bag, allowing the iron filings to fall onto the piece of white paper.

   Do not let the magnet directly touch the iron filings, because once in contact with the magnet, the filings are extremely difficult to remove.

   d. Place the magnet under the paper and move it around, observing the magnetic behavior of the filings.

6. Have students follow the modeled steps to check their food for iron, using flip cards (provided) as a reference.

7. Have each group discuss their observations and share with the class.

8. Ask, "What is this iron you saw? People talk about 'pumping iron' with barbells at the gym. Do you think the iron in the food is the same substance the iron barbells are made of?" Explain that the food does actually have food-grade iron filings added to it by the manufacturer. Discuss the nutritional importance of iron.

9. Set up a learning center with a sturdy zipper-type plastic bag (zipped and taped closed) containing Farina or another iron-fortified food (as described in the Materials), a strong magnet, and the flip card (provided). Have students

move the magnet all around the surface of the bag. The magnet will collect iron filings from the food, forming a visible black spot on the inside of the bag. Also include in the center the book *Gregory, the Terrible Eater* and several nonfiction books on food and nutrition.

Part B: Making Iron Filing Toys

To help your students observe the magnetic property of iron filings, provide some commercial iron-filing toys and/or make iron filing toys as follows:

1. Adhere the student photos face up on the bottom of the wider half of the petri dish as shown in Figure 3.

2. Put about 1⁄16 teaspoon iron filings in the middle of the petri dish lid. Put the bottom of the petri dish into the lid.

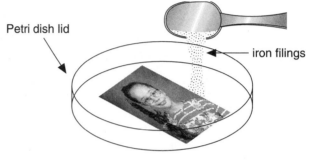

Figure 3: Pour the iron filings into the petri dish.

Use caution when working with hot-melt glue.

3. Seal the petri dish by placing the tip of the hot-melt glue gun directly on the seam between the lid and base of the dish, pulling the trigger, and slowly rotating the dish so that glue drizzles down into the seam. (See Figure 4.) Work slowly so that the seam is completely filled with no gaps in the glue.

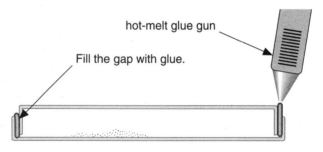

Figure 4: Seal the petri dish.

4. Have your students try to put a beard on their own picture by holding the dish flat and dragging a small magnet across the bottom of the toy.

Science Explanation

The following explanation is intended for the teacher's information. Modify the explanation for students as required.

Many of us have had opportunities to observe that iron is attracted to magnets. We were able to use this property in this activity to extract the food-grade iron filings from the food.

Teaching Physical Science through Children's Literature

Iron (Fe) is an essential element. Every molecule of hemoglobin (the compound in red blood cells that carries oxygen from the lungs to the tissues) has four iron ions in it. An iron-deficient diet results in fatigue, reduced resistance to disease, and increased heart and respiratory rate. If all of the iron from your body were extracted and converted into elemental iron, you would have enough iron to make up only two small nails. This amount is about 5–7 grams (g).

A healthy adult needs about 18 milligrams (mg) of iron each day. Dietary iron is found in large amounts in organ meats such as liver, kidney, and heart. It is also present naturally in egg yolks, some vegetables, and shellfish. In these foods iron is typically present as iron(III) $\{Fe^{3+}\}$ ions. Our bodies absorb iron in the small intestine in the form of iron(III), which is then reduced to iron(II) $\{Fe^{2+}\}$. Under normal conditions our bodies absorb only 5–15% of the iron in the foods that we eat. Vitamin C can increase the amount of iron absorbed into the body. To ensure that we have adequate iron in our diets, many foods are iron fortified. In some cases, foods are fortified with iron compounds such as ferric phosphate; in other cases (such as in Farina), foods are fortified with food-grade iron filings.

Part 3: Lesson Extensions

Math Extension

After discussing your students' favorite foods and why parents are so concerned that children eat "good" foods (as Gregory's parents were), tell students that they will be evaluating a variety of snack foods for nutritious components:

- Bring in food labels from several snacks that provide nutrition information. Choose items with a wide range of fat and Calorie values per serving. Also choose items with various amounts of iron. You can also have students bring in additional labels from their favorite foods. Discuss how food labels communicate important information that helps us select foods.
- Label the x- and y-axes for three large bar graphs for fat, Calories, and iron.
- Have students take turns reading the food labels and graphing the values by drawing and coloring the bars on the graphs appropriately.
- Once all the information has been compiled, discuss the following questions:
  - What would you eat to get some iron in your diet?
  - If you wanted to eat more low-fat foods, which would be good choices?
  - If you wanted to limit Calories, what would you pick?
  - Do the foods with the most Calories have the most fat?
  - Why are fruits and vegetables considered healthy snacks?

Writing Extension

Have students write a letter from Gregory to his parents telling what he would like in his lunch bag. The letter should explain that many of Gregory's favorite foods contain iron—a metal—and describe how he could demonstrate this to his parents. The request should include one food and one "thing," and at least one of the items requested should contain iron. Then have students write a letter from Mother and Father to Gregory telling him what they packed in his lunch. Use these letters to decorate each side of a lunch bag as shown in Figure 5. Have students make paper food to put in the lunch bags as though Mother and Father had packed Gregory's lunch.

Figure 5: Have each student decorate a lunch bag with letters from Gregory and his parents.

Cross-Cultural Integration

 This section is intended for teacher background. You may wish to use the information in this section to develop age-appropriate activities for your classroom.

After discussing what strange foods goats eat in the story and what real goats eat, introduce the idea that foods eaten and enjoyed by people around the world might seem strange and even unappetizing to us but are perfectly delicious "good food" to those who grow up with them. Today people travel frequently and widely, bringing cultures closer together. Not long ago, most Americans could not have imagined themselves eating raw fish; this trendy food is now available at sushi bars across the country. Ask students if any have parents, grandparents, or great-grandparents who grew up in another country. Explain that they may have special foods in their own families that come from other cultures.

Sometimes strange-seeming dishes are part of the culinary cuisine of a small section of society. Hedgehogs, for example, are said to taste much like a suckling pig and are much appreciated by gypsies in Britain. They are baked in clay or roasted. Sugar ants are regarded as quite a treat in Australia by the Aborigines. Kangaroo tail provides Australians with another tasty dish. In the Outback of Australia, the kangaroo legs are boiled or roasted.

Camel meat has always been a popular dish with Arabs. The hump and the feet are the most chosen parts. Rooster cockscombs are served in French restaurants stuffed, plain, or breaded and grilled. Truffles, a fungus similar to mushrooms, grows underground and is a delicacy of Britain. Pigs are used to help hunt the truffles because they have a special fondness for these treats.

Part 4: For Further Study

Additional Books

Nonfiction

Title: *Good Morning, Let's Eat!*
Author: Karin Luisa Badt
Publisher: Childrens Press   ISBN: 0-516-48190-8
Summary: Describes breakfast foods and breakfast customs from around the world and includes many photographs.

Title: *Food*
Author: Terry Jennings
Publisher: Childrens Press   ISBN: 0-516-48402-8
Summary: An introduction to food and nutrition with accompanying study questions, activities, and experiments.

Title: *Food: Feasts, Cooks, and Kitchens*
Author: Richard Tames
Publisher: Franklin Watts   ISBN: 0-531-15711-3
Summary: Traces the history of food around the world, from the first farmers to the first canners, to today's fast food, and beyond to future farms at the bottom of the sea.

Title: *Multicultural Cookbook for Students*
Author: Carole Albyn
Publisher: Oryx Press   ISBN: 0-89774-735-6
Summary: Contains recipes for foods from many cultures.

Flip Cards

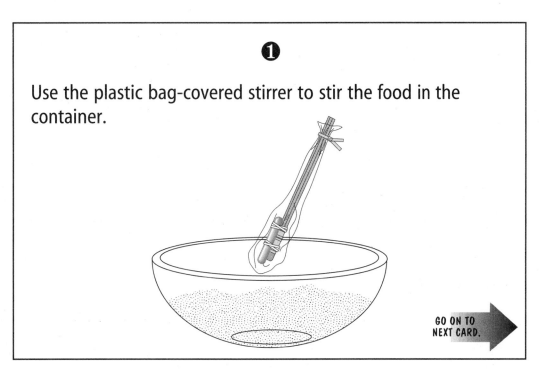

❶

Use the plastic bag-covered stirrer to stir the food in the container.

GO ON TO NEXT CARD.

❷

Remove the bag-covered stirrer from the container and observe the iron filings clinging to the bag.

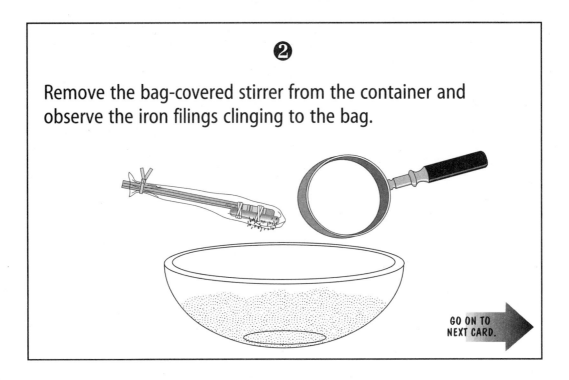

GO ON TO NEXT CARD.

❸

Undo the tie from the bag and pull the stirrer out of the bag, allowing the iron filings to fall on the piece of white paper.

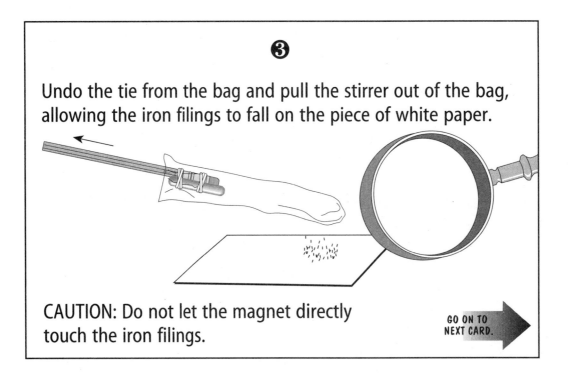

CAUTION: Do not let the magnet directly touch the iron filings.

GO ON TO NEXT CARD.

4

Place the magnet under the paper and move it around, observing the magnetic behavior of the filings.

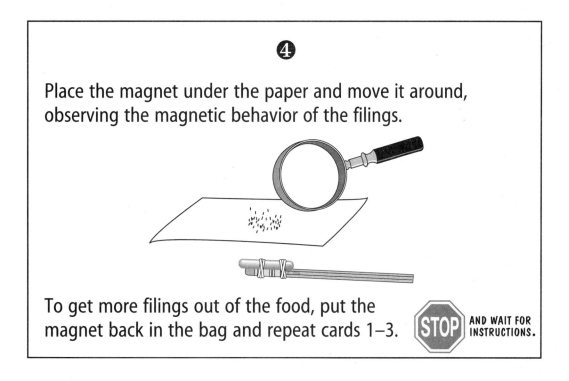

To get more filings out of the food, put the magnet back in the bag and repeat cards 1–3. [STOP] **AND WAIT FOR INSTRUCTIONS.**

Learning Center

Move the magnet all around the surface of the bag. Observe the iron filings that collect near the magnet on the inside of the bag.

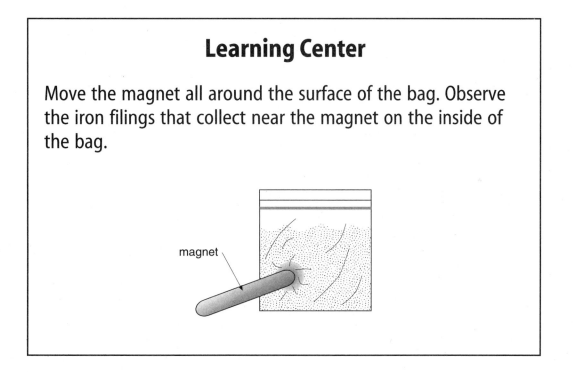

magnet

Babushka's Eggs'periment

SCIENCE CATEGORY: Properties of Objects and Materials
TOPICS: Egg Dyeing, Scientific Experimentation, Cause and Effect
OBJECTIVE: Students learn about cause-and-effect relationships and that eggs dye better when vinegar is added to the dye bath.

In this lesson, students do a scientific experiment to investigate the role of vinegar in the coloring of eggs. They also explore other cause-and-effect relationships by designing experiments of their own to test other variables (such as soaking time) that might affect egg dyeing results.

- Prior to beginning the lesson, students explore a variety of cause-and-effect situations and practice identifying both the cause and the effect.

- In a class discussion, students draw on their experiences to compile a class list of causes and effects and explain why they think that one makes the other happen.

- Students hear the story *Rechenka's Eggs* and listen for examples of cause and effect in the story.

- Students are presented with an imaginary dilemma based on characters in *Rechenka's Eggs*: Babushka decided to dye some eggs, but the colors didn't turn out very bright. What did she do wrong? Babushka has a hunch about what caused the problem. But is she right? Students conduct an experiment to answer Babushka's question and continue by designing additional experiments of their own.

- To conclude the lesson, students write to Babushka, explaining what they did to test her idea and what they found out.

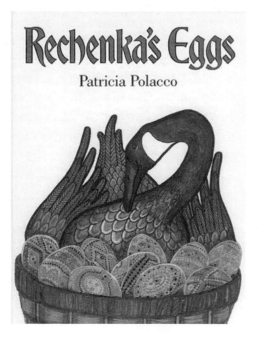

Featured Fiction Book: *Rechenka's Eggs*
Author and Illustrator: Patricia Polacco
Publisher: Philomel Books
ISBN: 0-399-21501-8
Summary: Babushka is known throughout her village for her beautifully painted eggs. One day she befriends an injured goose, names her Rechenka, and nurses her back to health. After the goose accidentally knocks over a basket of Babushka's painted eggs, she begins laying eggs that are magically painted.

Part 1: Building Bridges

Building Student Knowledge and Motivation

During the week prior to beginning the lesson, give small groups of students an opportunity to explore several cause-and-effect relationships at a science center. You can use a wide variety of items, such as a toy car (Push it and it moves), flashlight (Push the switch and it lights), water and dry sponge (Pour water on the sponge and it gets soft), and many others. Instruct students to record all of the causes and effects they can find. (Masters for several types of science journal pages are provided in the Using Science Journals section at the beginning of the book.)

Getting Ready to Read

Turn to a new page in your science chart and divide it into three columns. Label these columns "Cause," "Effect," and "Why do you think so?" Through a class discussion, compile a class list of cause-and-effect observations from the center and from everyday life and record these on the chart. For each cause-and-effect relationship listed, discuss why students think that one makes the other happen.

Show students the cover of *Rechenka's Eggs*. Ask them what they think the story is about. Ask the students to listen for cause-and-effect relationships in the story as you read aloud.

Bridging to the Science Activity

After reading the story, discuss the cause-and-effect relationships that the students found in the story and add these to the chart. Then tell students that you have a story to tell them about events that happened to Babushka after Rechenka left:

One day, Babushka wanted to dye a batch of eggs a nice dark red before she painted designs on them. She had done this many times before and knew the ingredients by heart: water, food color, and vinegar. She went to the cupboard and found the food color. She had water from the sink. But she was nearly out of vinegar. Only a drop was left in the bottle. She usually used more. "Oh well, I'll dye the eggs anyway. How much difference could the amount of vinegar make?" Babushka went on to dye her eggs. When the eggs were done, every one was a pale, pale pink. Not at all the dark red Babushka expected. "What caused this to happen?" Babushka wondered. "I have a hunch it has something to do with the vinegar, but how can I be sure?"

Explain to students that sometimes we think we know the cause for an effect we have observed, but we aren't sure. Tell them that a scientific experiment is a good way to find out if the suspected cause really produces the observed effect. Explain that the students will be doing an experiment for Babushka to help her decide if the missing vinegar really caused the eggs to come out pink instead of red.

Part 2: Science Activity

Materials

For Getting Ready
Per class
- large piece of eggshell

For the Procedure
Per group
- 1½ teaspoons red food color
- 1½ cups water
- measuring cup
- teaspoon
- 2 tablespoons vinegar
- beaker, bucket, or pan of water to rinse eggshell
- 3 plastic cups (9- to 10-ounce) or beakers
- 3 large pieces of eggshell
- 3 egg-shaped pieces of paper
- labels or masking tape
- transparent tape
- white glue
- paper towels
- (optional) rubber gloves to protect hands from the dye

For the Science Extension
Per student
- wax crayon or egg-dyeing kit containing beeswax

 Commercial kits containing beeswax, dyes, and tools to make dyed eggs like those in Rechenka's Eggs *are available from Hearthsong, 6519 N. Galena Rd., Peoria, IL 61614; 800/779-2211.*

Safety and Disposal

No special safety procedures are required. You may wish to have students wear rubber gloves to protect their hands from the dye. All solutions used in this activity can be disposed of by flushing them down the drain with water.

Getting Ready

Prepare 1½ cups dye solution for each group as follows: mix 1½ teaspoons red food color with enough water to make a total of 1½ cups of solution.

Using some of the dye solution without adding any vinegar, dye one large piece of eggshell a pale pink to represent the eggs that Babushka dyed.

Procedure

Part A: Varying the Amount of Vinegar

1. Label a science chart as shown in Figure 1. Tape the piece of pale pink eggshell on a piece of egg-shaped paper and tape the paper next to the title of the chart. Explain that this is a sample of the eggshell that Babushka dyed pink. Tell students that they will be mounting their dyed eggshell pieces on the chart to see which ones look most like Babushka's.

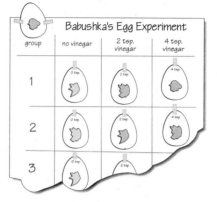

Figure 1: Label a science chart.

2. Model the following steps for students.

   a. Using labels or tape, label three different cups or beakers with the different amounts of vinegar to be studied: 0, 2, and 4 teaspoons.

   b. Measure ½ cup of the dye solution into each labeled container.

   c. Add to each container the amount of vinegar specified on the label and stir.

   d. Write the amount of vinegar in each container on an egg-shaped piece of paper and place the papers in front of the appropriate containers.

3. Have students work in cooperative groups to set up the experiment as modeled in Step 2 using flip cards 1–3 (provided) as a reference and then complete the experiment as described in cards 4–6.

4. Have groups mount their eggshell pieces on the chart and discuss results. Ask, "Which one is most like Babushka's?" Ask students if they can see a pattern. They should be able to point out that the more vinegar, the darker the color.

5. Continue the discussion, making sure that students realize that nothing changed in the experimental setup except the amounts of vinegar: "Did each cup have the same amount of red dye?" *Yes.* "Did each egg stay in the dye for the same amount of time?" *Yes.* "Then why are the shells different shades of red?" *The different amounts of vinegar must have caused a change in the color.*

6. Turn back to the cause-and-effect chart page from Getting Ready to Read. Ask students what they can add to the chart based on their experiment.

Part B: Experimenting with New Variables

1. As a class, list factors other than vinegar that students could vary to determine what effect these factors might have on the intensity of the color. *Water temperature, amount of food color in the dye solution, and amount of time.*

Teaching Physical Science through Children's Literature

2. Have each group choose one factor to vary, keeping the vinegar and the other variables constant. Mount the results on charts similar to the one used in Part A and discuss.

Science Extension

Have students use wax crayons to draw on the eggs before dyeing them and observe how wax resists the dye. (Ukrainian eggs are often decorated in a similar way. See Cross-Cultural Integration.)

Science Explanation

 The following explanation is intended for the teacher's information. Modify the explanation for students as required.

Vinegar or another acid is necessary when dyeing eggs due to the chemical nature of the shell. The main shell is primarily composed of calcite (calcium carbonate, $CaCO_3$). Over this is an outer layer called the cuticle, which is more than 90% protein. The structure of the cuticle varies as its environment becomes more acidic or basic. Under relatively acidic conditions (such as the vinegar-dye solution in the experiment), areas of the cuticle take on a positive charge. As the acid concentration of the solution increases, more areas of positive charge occur on the cuticle.

Although the exact makeup of a food color may vary slightly with brand, only seven dyes are approved for use in foods in the United States. Each contains at least one negative charge. This negative charge is the key to the way the dyes work. The negative charge on the dye is attracted to the positive charge on the cuticle. The greater the number of positive charges available on the surface of the eggshell, the more dye adheres, and the more intense the shell color becomes. When no vinegar (or other acid) is present, the cuticle protein has fewer positive charges. As a result, the shell is dyed only slightly.

The attraction between the positive and negative charges, which links the dye molecule with the cuticle of the eggshell, forms gradually over a period of minutes. Therefore, eggs dyed for increasing lengths of time should have deeper colors because more reactions with the dye were made. Effects from varying the temperature of the dye solution are much more difficult to predict. Cooling the solution should decrease the rate of reactions that occur in the dyeing process and result in paler eggs. Similarly, increasing the temperature of the solution should increase the rate of reactions and result in eggs with a more intense color. However, the attractions that bind the dye to the cuticle are disrupted at higher temperatures, and the dye may not adhere to the surface of the egg as well as expected.

Varying the concentration of food color in the dye solution will also have an effect on dyeing eggs. When the dye solution is more dilute, there are fewer negative charges to adhere to the positively charged shell, resulting in slightly colored shells. Conversely, when the dye solution is more concentrated, more negative charges can adhere to the shell, resulting in a deeper-colored egg.

Part 3: Lesson Extensions

Writing Extensions

1. Explain to students that an important part of science is describing your experiment and its results to others. Remind them that Babushka is anxious to find out why her eggs came out pink. Have students write to Babushka, explaining what they did to test her idea about the eggs and what they found out. Encourage them to write, draw, and include samples so that Babushka will really understand what happened.

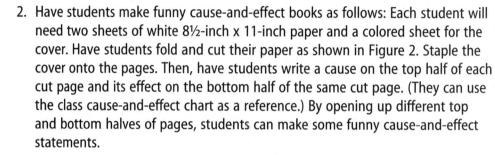

Figure 2

2. Have students make funny cause-and-effect books as follows: Each student will need two sheets of white 8½-inch x 11-inch paper and a colored sheet for the cover. Have students fold and cut their paper as shown in Figure 2. Staple the cover onto the pages. Then, have students write a cause on the top half of each cut page and its effect on the bottom half of the same cut page. (They can use the class cause-and-effect chart as a reference.) By opening up different top and bottom halves of pages, students can make some funny cause-and-effect statements.

Cross-Cultural Integration

> *This section is intended for teacher background. You may wish to use the information in this section to develop age-appropriate activities for your classroom.*

Ukrainians decorate eggs in a special way called *pysanky*. The artist draws a beautiful design on an egg with melted beeswax, using a tool dipped in or containing the wax. The traditional tool, called a kistka, has a funnel at the bottom that holds the melted wax and the artist allows the wax to flow from the funnel as he/she draws onto the egg. After painting the basic wax design on the egg, the artist dips the egg into dye, then draws additional designs on the egg and redips it into other colors of dye. The artist may repeat this process up to six or eight times until the entire design is drawn and all colors have been used. Black dye is often used for the last color. After the final dipping, the artist carefully holds the egg over a candle flame and melts the wax off, then applies a layer of varnish to give the egg a clear shine.

Ukrainian egg designs are very delicate and complicated. The patterns for the designs are passed down from parents to children over the years. Often a family will have a design that belongs to them much as a crest or a seal belongs to families in western European culture.

Part 4: For Further Study

Additional Books

Fiction

Title: *The Most Wonderful Egg in the World*
Author and Illustrator: Helme Heine
Publisher: Macmillan   ISBN: 0-689-50280-X
Summary: Three quarrelsome chickens compete to see who will lay the most beautiful egg.

Nonfiction

Title: *Ukrainian Easter Egg Design Book*
Author: Luba Perchyshyn
Publisher: Ukrainian Gift Shop   ISBN: 0-960-25024-7
Summary: Discusses the Ukrainian tradition of decorating eggs.

References

Baker, J.R.; Balch, D.A. "A Study of the Organic Material of Hen's Eggshell," *Biochemical Journal.* 1962, 82, 352.

Marmion, D.M. *Handbook of U.S. Colorants for Foods, Drugs and Cosmetics;* Wiley-Interscience: New York, 1979.

Mebane, R.C.; Rybolt, T.R. "Chemistry in the Dyeing of Eggs," *Journal of Chemical Education.* 1987, 64, 291–293.

"The Need for Vinegar;" "Time and Temperature;" *Fun with Chemistry: A Guidebook of K–12 Activities;* Sarquis, M., Sarquis, J., Eds.; Institute for Chemical Education: Madison, WI, 1993; Vol. 2, pp 39–42, 55–59.

Flip Cards

❶

Label three cups with the different amounts of vinegar to be studied: 0, 2, and 4 teaspoons.

Measure ½ cup of the dye solution into each labeled container.

GO ON TO NEXT CARD.

❷

Add the amount of vinegar specified on the label and stir.

GO ON TO NEXT CARD.

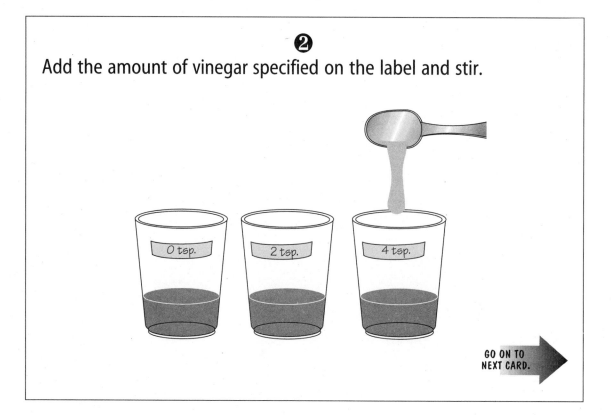

❸

Write the amount of vinegar in each cup on an egg-shaped piece of paper and place each paper in front of the appropriate cup.

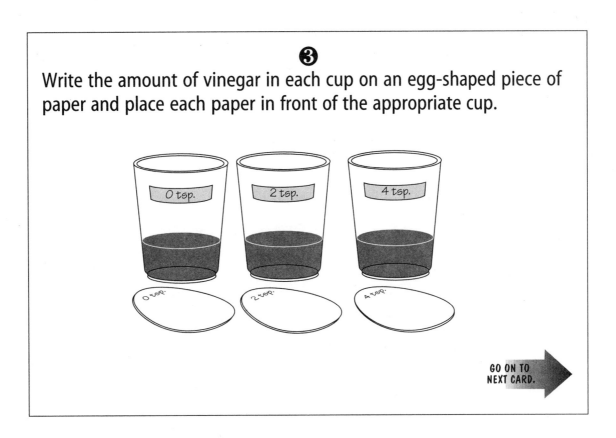

GO ON TO
NEXT CARD.

❹

Put your eggshell pieces in the dye for 5 minutes. Then take them out.

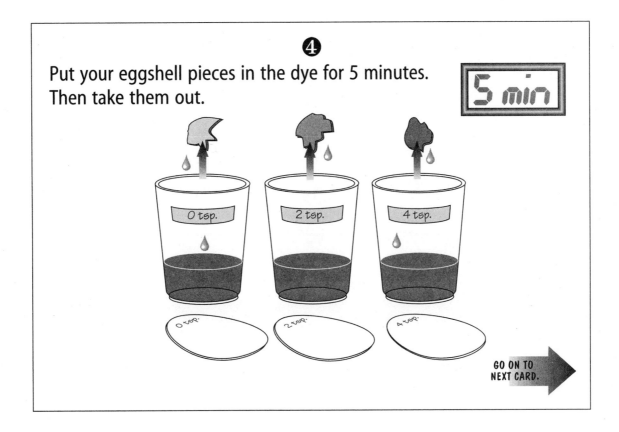

GO ON TO
NEXT CARD.

❺

Dip each eggshell in water five times to rinse and place it on a paper towel to dry.

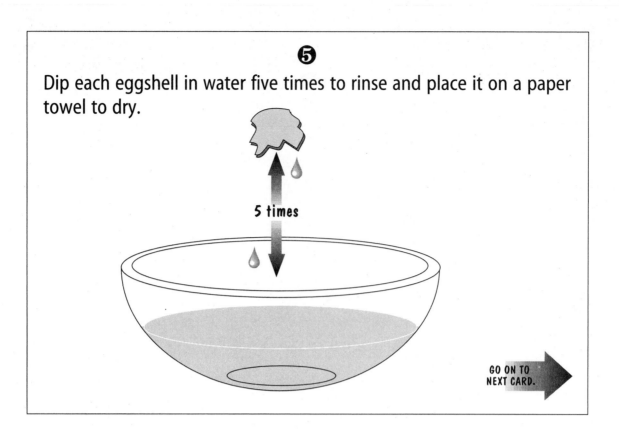

5 times

GO ON TO NEXT CARD.

❻

Glue each eggshell to the appropriate piece of paper.

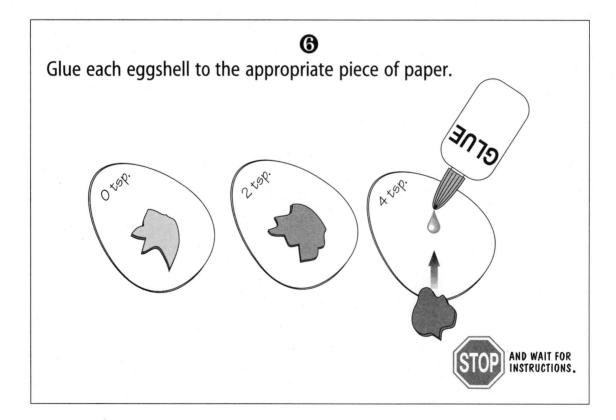

0 tsp.

2 tsp.

4 tsp.

GLUE

STOP AND WAIT FOR INSTRUCTIONS.

Teaching Physical Science through Children's Literature

Section 2:
Light, Heat, Electricity, and Magnetism

 # Colors of the Rainbow

SCIENCE CATEGORY: Light, Heat, Electricity, and Magnetism
TOPICS: Rainbows, Light, Prisms
OBJECTIVE: Students learn that white light is a combination of all colors and that white light can split into its component colors and form a rainbow.

In this lesson, students use prisms, water, and mirrors to create rainbows. Through class discussion, they compare different methods to decide what factors must be present for rainbows to form.

- Prior to beginning the lesson, students observe faceted lead crystal ornaments and have access to nonfiction books about light and colors of light.

- As a class, students discuss what they feel they know about light and begin a Know-Wonder-Learn (KWL) science chart.

- Students hear the story *The River that Gave Gifts* and listen to discover how the river gave the gift of a rainbow.

- Students use prisms, water, and mirrors to observe rainbows and record their observations.

- To conclude the lesson, students write a story in which rainbows appear, and include as part of the story an explanation of what a rainbow is and why the rainbow forms under the conditions in the story.

Featured Fiction Book: *The River that Gave Gifts*
Author and Illustrator: Margo Humphrey
Publisher: Children's Book Press
ISBN: 0-89239-027-1
Summary: Four children each make their own special gift to the beloved elder woman of the town.

Part 1: Building Bridges

Building Student Knowledge and Motivation

Several days prior to beginning the lesson, hang one or more faceted lead crystal ornaments in classroom windows. Also set out several nonfiction books about light and colors of light. Over a period of several days, give students an opportunity to look at the books and to notice any rainbows formed by the crystals.

Getting Ready to Read

Create a Know-Wonder-Learn (KWL) chart: Label a new sheet on the science chart "Colors of Light" and divide it into three columns labeled "Know," "Wonder," and "Learn." Have students share what they feel they know about light through experience, reading, and observations of the crystals, and record these ideas in the "Know" column. If no one suggests it, bring out the idea that a name for the colors they saw through the crystals is "rainbow." Ask students what they would like to know about light, and add this to the chart in the "Wonder" column. Student responses would ideally include "How a rainbow forms."

Show the students the cover of *The River that Gave Gifts.* Lead the class in a discussion to brainstorm different gifts that rivers might give us (for example, water to drink, fish to eat, water for crops, recreation, transportation). Ask students if they think a river could give us a rainbow. Brainstorm suggestions for how a river could do so, but do not indicate if any answers are right or wrong or elaborate beyond what students suggest. Tell them that in the story the river does give a gift of a rainbow. When you read the story to the class, tell students to listen carefully for clues about whether the rainbow in the story can be explained by science or whether this is a make-believe story.

Bridging to the Science Activity

Ask students to describe how the river gave a gift of a rainbow in the story. Have students think about the following question: Could rainbows really form as described in the story? Rather than elaborate here, have students think about this question and gather information to discuss later. (See Class Discussion.) Tell students that they will be trying several ways to make rainbows of their own and thinking about the scientific explanations for rainbows.

Part 2: Science Activity

Materials

For the Procedure
Per class
- overhead projector
- 1 or more prisms

Unbreakable acrylic prisms (#553-160-5130) are available from Delta Education, P.O. Box 3000, Nashua, NH 03061-9913; 800/442-5444. The rainbows produced by acrylic prisms may not be as clear as those produced by glass prisms, but acrylic is safer and less expensive.

- (optional) Giant Prism

The Giant Prism is a prism-shaped Plexiglas™ container that you fill with water. It is also available from Delta Education (#80-160-7847).

- flashlight

The brighter the flashlight, the better. For best results, use a flashlight with a krypton or halogen bulb.

- large bowl filled with water
- glass of water
- 8½-inch x 11-inch sheet of white paper
- unbreakable mirror small enough to fit inside the bowl

Break-resistant 3-inch x 5-inch mirrors are available from Delta Education (#80-130-2113). Mylar or foil mirrors will also work.

For the Science Extensions
- fine-mist spray bottle
- room that can be darkened
- garden hose
- krypton or halogen lantern flashlight that uses 4 D batteries

Only an extremely bright flashlight will work.

Safety and Disposal

If you use glass prisms, caution students to handle them with care. No special disposal procedures are required.

Getting Ready

Prepare a classroom science center with materials for three activities (Rainbows from Prisms, Rainbows from Water, and Water Prism) as follows:

- For Rainbows from Prisms, place the prisms (including a Giant Prism if desired), overhead projector, and flip cards 1 and 2 (provided) in the center. Tape two sheets of paper over the surface of the overhead projector, leaving only a tiny slit so that a narrow beam of light is projected.

- For Rainbows from Water, place a large bowl filled with water, an unbreakable mirror, a flashlight, and flip card 3 in the center.

- For Water Prisms, place a glass of water and a blank sheet of white 8½-inch x 11-inch paper in the center with flip card 4.

Procedure

Be aware that rainbows can be difficult to make, and these procedures may not work the first time. A strong source of white light is a crucial component for successful rainbows. Also keep in mind that there is a component of luck in getting just the right angle of light to produce good rainbows. Be patient and keep trying!

1. Divide students into groups and explain that each group will have a chance to visit a center to do three activities over the next few days: Rainbows from Prisms, Rainbows from Water, and Water Prisms.

Flip
Cards

2. Emphasize that students should follow all instructions on the flip cards carefully and record their observations using words and/or pictures. (Masters for several types of science journal pages are provided in the Using Science Journals section at the beginning of the book.) Ask students to particularly note what colors they see and in what order the colors appear. Tell students that it is not always easy to make rainbows and that they should be patient and keep trying.

3. Over a period of several days, give students opportunities to visit the center and record their observations. Keep the KWL science chart available for students to write new questions in the "Wonder" column.

Class Discussion

SCIENCE
CHART

Add to the KWL chart as appropriate as students discuss their observations and ideas.

1. Give groups an opportunity to share their observations. Ask, "What did you make in the center?" *Rainbows.* "Did you notice anything about the order of the colors in the rainbows?" Bring out the idea that "rainbow" is an everyday name for what scientists call the visible spectrum of light. The rainbow or visible spectrum has a specific order of colors. Explain that the spectrum is a continuous band of thousands of colors, blending from red through orange and yellow, all the way to violet. However, to make things simpler, we usually say that the colors of the rainbow are the seven colors named 300 years ago by a scientist named Isaac Newton: red, orange, yellow, green, blue, indigo, violet. Explain that the acronym ROYGBIV is often used to help people remember the order of these colors (Pronounce ROYGBIV like a person's name: "Roy G. Biv"), but that some scientists now leave out indigo when naming the colors of the spectrum. (You will probably need to explain that indigo is a shade of blue like dark blue jeans.) Ask students what colors they saw in their rainbows. Did they see any colors that fall in between the ROYGBIV colors, such as red-orange?

2. Discuss the different ways students made rainbows in the centers and the similarities and differences between the methods.

3. Through discussion, bring out the idea that in each center white light from the sun, a flashlight, or an overhead projector was shining through something. Explain that when white light passes through some objects, the light is bent (or refracted) and separated into a rainbow (the visible spectrum of light). Tell students that Isaac Newton did experiments with sunlight and prisms over 300 years ago and was the first person to show that white light from the sun was a mixture of all the colors of the rainbow. If desired, read pages 28–29 from *Light,* by David Burnie. (See Additional Books.)

4. Ask, "What has usually just happened when we see rainbows in the sky?" *Rain.* Pose this question to the students: "Since a rainbow is a result of white light passing through something, bending, and separating into colors, how do rainbows form in the sky?" Tell students you want them to think about this question for a while.

5. Ask students to think about the story *The River that Gave Gifts* again. Reread parts of the book appropriate to the discussion. Then, as a class discuss the following:

   • The river Yanava sits by is described as sparkling in the sun. From your observations in the center, what do you think sun and water have to do

Teaching Physical Science through Children's Literature

with rainbows? *Rainbows can form when white light such as sunlight passes through water and bends.*

- When Yanava wakes up from her nap by the river, it is night. She sees rays of light flying from her fingers. Is this make-believe or could it really happen? *It is make-believe.*

- Yanava makes her first rainbow in the dark. Is this really possible? *No, light is needed to make a rainbow.*

- When Yanava holds out her hands to make her first rainbow, colors stream from hand to hand. The book names the color that comes from each finger. How many colors does the book name? *Five.* Are these the colors of a real rainbow (the visible spectrum)? Are they in the right order? *The story leaves out orange and indigo, but the other colors are in the right order.*

- In the illustration where Yanava makes her first rainbow, how many colors are shown in the rainbow in her hands? *Six.* Are these the colors of a real rainbow? Are they in the right order? *Yes, they are the colors of a real rainbow and they are in the right order. In this picture, indigo is not shown.*

- When the children come to give their gifts to Neema, the room is dim. Yanava makes another rainbow with her hands. Is this real or make-believe? *Make-believe.* Why? *Because more light would be needed to make a rainbow.*

- Why do you think the author wrote a story about a rainbow forming from someone's hands in the dark? *To make the story interesting.* Would an author who was trying to present a scientific view of rainbows have written the story in the same way? *Probably not.*

6. Leave a number of nonfiction books about light along with rainbow-making items (prisms, flashlights, etc.) at a science center. If desired, include the Giant Water Prism and its accompanying book of experiments. After students have had a chance to read from the books and work with rainbows, return to the question from Step 4 and discuss. Do the Science Extensions if desired. Add to the "Learn" column of the science chart as desired.

Science Extensions

Make rainbows much like the ones that form in the sky:

Inside
Completely darken the room. You may wish to take small groups of students into a room that can easily be darkened. A windowless room will work well. Shine the

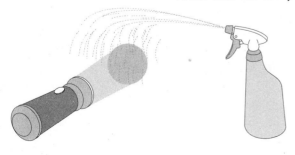

flashlight beam slightly upward. Set the spray bottle for the finest spray possible. Aim the nozzle slightly *above* the flashlight beam and squirt a spray of water. (See Figure 1.) As the droplets fall through the light beam, faint rainbow colors will appear for a moment. The effect is subtle. This will only be visible from one angle, so turn as you spray so that all students have a chance to see the rainbow.

Figure 1: Spray a mist of water slightly above the flashlight beam.

Outside

With the sun at your back, point a garden hose forward and upward and spray a mist of water. You will see a rainbow. Keep spraying to keep the rainbow visible. Students may need to view the light from different angles to see the rainbow. (Caution students not to look directly at the sun.)

Science Explanation

➤ *The following explanation is intended for the teacher's information. Modify the explanation for students as required.*

In everyday language we use the word "rainbow" in a variety of ways. We may use the word to describe a bright display of colorful flags, the shimmering colors we see in a soap bubble, or the flashes of color visible on the silvery side of a music or computer CD. We also use it to describe the bands of color that are sometimes visible in the sky after a rain.

This activity focuses on the scientific meaning of the word "rainbow:" the visible spectrum of light seen in the sky or indoors when white light (such as light from the sun) passes through a material (such as water or glass) that causes the light rays to bend. This bending of light is called refraction. The spectrum becomes visible because each color (wavelength) of light bends at a slightly different angle as it passes through the material, spreading the light out like a fan. Once the wavelengths are separated, the individual colors of the spectrum become visible to us. A rainbow in the sky is an atmospheric phenomenon produced when sunlight shining through raindrops is refracted and separated into the visible spectrum. The raindrops act like the water and mirror in the "Rainbows from Water" portion of this activity. Raindrops and prisms are similar in that they both refract light. But unlike prisms, the raindrops also reflect the light back in the direction of the light source. Thus, an atmospheric rainbow is seen on the same side of the raindrops as the light source. The rainbow created by a prism is seen on the opposite side of the prism from the light source.

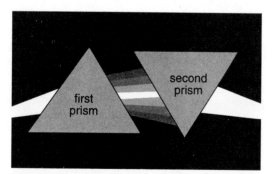
Figure 2: Newton's two-prism experiment

The prevalence of rainbow myths indicates that rainbows have been of interest to human observers for many thousands of years. But not until Isaac Newton reported on his prism experiments of 1666 were scientists presented with evidence that sunlight was composed of all the colors in the spectrum. Newton's most famous prism experiment consisted of passing sunlight through two triangular prisms. Passage through the first prism created a spectrum; passage through the second prism recombined the spectrum into white light. (See Figure 2.) This experiment demonstrated that the colors in the spectrum are a property of the light itself, not the prism.

As stated earlier, we might describe the colors on the surface of a bubble or on a CD as rainbows. However, since these colors are not a result of refracted light, they are not rainbows as we have defined them here. The colors on a surface of a bubble are a result of a phenomenon called thin film interference or iridescence. In thin film interference, some light bounces off the top layer of the film and some light passes through the top layer and bounces off the bottom of the film. Light waves that have traveled these two different paths interfere with each other, producing a rainbow-like effect. The rainbow-like colors on a CD are also a result of light interference, produced in this case by the pattern of tiny grooves on the CD's surface.

Part 3: Lesson Extensions

Writing Extensions

Colorful stripes
Beautiful archway
Magnificent pathway
Divided sunlight
Smiling face
A rainbow

Figure 3

1. Have students write a story about a place where a rainbow can be seen. Their stories can be imaginary or about something they have experienced; they can contain imaginary or real characters or no characters at all. Be sure students demonstrate in their stories that they understand what a rainbow is and why one would appear in the settings they've written about.

2. As a class or in small groups, have students write a simple poem using the adjective-noun pattern to describe a rainbow. Encourage students to include statements about the science behind rainbows. A sample poem is shown at left.

3. Give each student strips of construction paper corresponding with the colors of the spectrum. If desired, use the acronym ROYGBIV to emphasize the order of the colors, but remember that some scientists no longer specifically name indigo as one of the rainbow colors. Have students work individually or in groups to write a simple simile on each piece of paper that is appropriate for the color. Some examples of similes are "Her eyes are as green as emeralds," or "Her cheeks are as red as roses." After all students have completed their similes, put a brad through the paper strips to make a fan for each student. (See Figure 3.)

Cross-Cultural Integration

➤ *This section is intended for teacher background. You may wish to use the information in this section to develop age-appropriate activities for your classroom.*

Before the scientific reason for a rainbow's appearance was understood, rainbows were a common image in mythology.

*   The Greeks feared the rainbow and considered it a symbol of evil or an omen sent by Zeus as a warning. In mythology the rainbow was the bow that a sky deity used to fight against storm demons, as well as a bridge between heaven and earth. In folklore it was a symbol of divine peace, resurrection, and victory.

- Christian philosophers of the Middle Ages compared the seven rays of the rainbow to the seven gifts of the Holy Spirit.

- In Greek mythology, the goddess Iris is a personification of the rainbow. She, like the rainbow, comes and goes without warning. Because of her speed of movement and association with rainbows across the heavens, she holds a position as a messenger for the gods.

- In Norse mythology, Freyja (meaning "most renowned of the goddesses" or "most gently born") possesses a wonderful necklace that is the envy of all others. Freyja is the heaven goddess, and the necklace is said to represent the rainbow, as well as the moon, morning and evening, stars, and a red dawn.

- The Ifugao people in the Philippines say that the rainbow was made from the heart of a child born to a mortal man and a sky-maiden. The child had to be cut in half so the mother could return to the sky. The father, unable to restore life to his half, discarded it, but the mother returned and created all manner of animals from the child, as well as the rainbow from its heart.

- The Iroquois believe the rainbow to be the wife of Hino the Thunderer, who is guardian of the heavens. Hino destroys all things noxious, including the serpent of the waters, which was devouring humanity.

Our current understanding of the science behind rainbows is due in large part to Sir Isaac Newton. However, it is important to realize that prisms and rainbows made from prisms were well-known prior to Newton's experiments. What makes Newton's experiments important is the data he gathered and the conclusions he drew from that data. In his earliest report on the experiment (1671), Newton writes in the *Philosophical Transactions of the Royal Society of London:* "In the beginning of the Year 1666…I procured me a Triangular glass-Prisme, to try therewith the celebrated *Phenomena of Colors….* And in order thereto having darkened my window-shuts, to let in a convenient quantity of the Suns light, I placed my Prisme at its entrance, that it might be thereby refracted to the opposite wall." Newton continues to describe the series of experiments and his conclusions as well as new questions at each step.

Reading Newton's words is a glimpse into the mind of someone who has been called "the perfect scientific man." For older students, Newton's descriptions of his own experiments might serve as a real-life example of why recording their own observations is so important. You may also want your students to know that when Newton published this article in 1671, a somewhat hostile debate began between Newton and Robert Hooke about the validity of Newton's theory. In 1675, Newton complained, "I was so persecuted with discussions arising out of my theory of light that I blamed my own imprudence for parting with so substantial a blessing as my quiet to run after a shadow." As revered as Newton's work is today, it is easy to forget that what we consider to be the most basic scientific facts were often disputed when first proposed.

Part 4: For Further Study

Additional Books

Fiction

Title: *Arrow to the Sun*
Author and Illustrator: Gerald McDermott
Publisher: Viking   ISBN: 0-670-13369-8
Summary: *Arrow to the Sun* is a Pueblo Indian myth that explains that the rainbow is used to bring the spirit of the Lord of the Sun to the world of people.

Title: *Rainbow Rider*
Author: Jane Yolen   Illustrator: Michael Foreman
Publisher: Crowell   ISBN: 0-690-00301-3
Summary: Saddened to discover that sand, tumbleweed, and cactus are not suitable friends, the Rainbow Rider flings his tears to the sky, and something special happens.

Nonfiction

Title: *The Science Book of Light*
Author: Neil Ardley
Publisher: Harcourt Brace Jovanovich   ISBN: 0-15-200577-3
Summary: Simple experiments demonstrate the basic principles of light.

Title: *Fun with Light*
Author: Maria Gordon
Publisher: Thomson Learning   ISBN: 1-56847-308-7
Summary: Includes simple science experiments with light.

Title: *Light* (part of the Eyewitness Science series)
Author: David Burnie
Publisher: Dorling Kindersley   ISBN: 1-879431-79-3
Summary: This book is a guide to the origins, principles, and historical study of light.

References

Man, Myth, and Magic: An Illustrated Encyclopedia of the Supernatural; Cavendish, R., Ed.; Marshall Cavendish: New York, 1970; Vol. 1, p 296; Vol. 2, pp 494–496; Vol. 5, p 1173; Vol. 9, pp 2341–2342.

Primary Sources: Selected Writings on Color from Aristotle to Albers; Sloane, P., Ed.; Design: New York, 1991; pp 12–19.

Flip Cards

---

❶

Rainbows from Prisms

Look at the prisms and describe their shapes and sizes. Look through them and describe what you see.

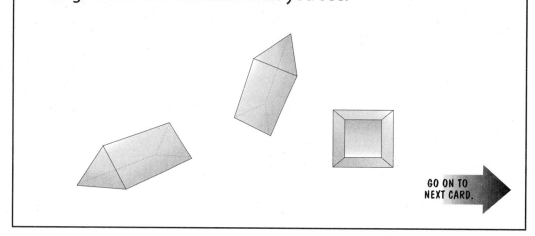

GO ON TO
NEXT CARD.

---

❷

Hold the prism in the narrow beam of light projected by the overhead projector. Twist and turn the prism until you see a rainbow. It may be on a wall or ceiling. Be patient and keep trying.

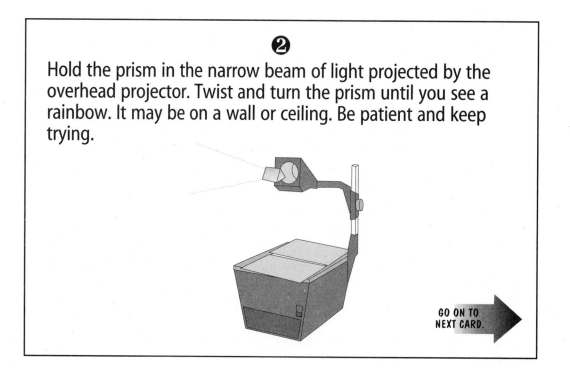

GO ON TO
NEXT CARD.

---

❸
Rainbows from Water

Place the mirror in a bowl of water as shown.

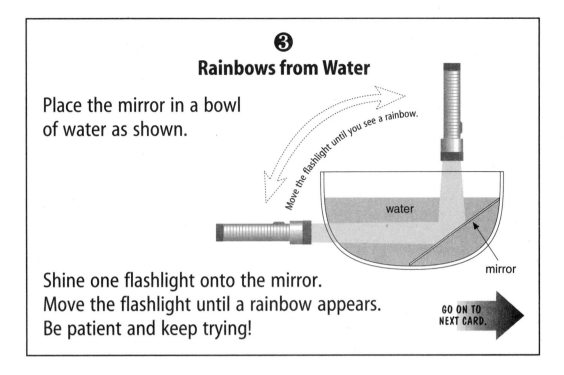

Move the flashlight until you see a rainbow.

water

mirror

Shine one flashlight onto the mirror.
Move the flashlight until a rainbow appears.
Be patient and keep trying!

GO ON TO NEXT CARD.

❹
Water Prisms

Place a glass of water on a sunny windowsill. Look for a rainbow somewhere in front of the glass.

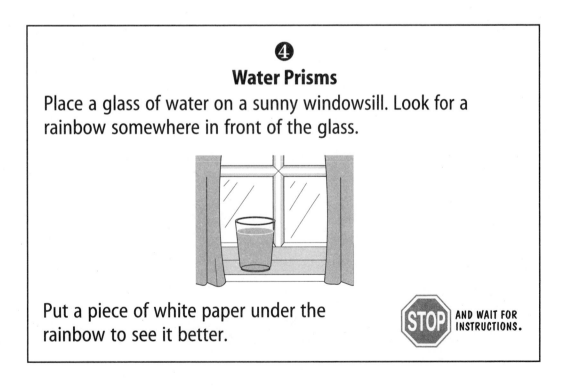

Put a piece of white paper under the rainbow to see it better.

STOP AND WAIT FOR INSTRUCTIONS.

Whirling Colors

SCIENCE CATEGORY: Light, Heat, Electricity, and Magnetism
TOPICS: Light, Properties of Colors, Persistence of Vision
OBJECTIVE: Students learn that the colors of objects depend on the colors of light that are reflected and that colors and patterns can mix visually on spinning objects. They also learn that all the colors of light mixed together form white.

In this lesson, students experiment with color-mixing spinners and conduct an experiment similar to one done by physicist James Clerk Maxwell. Ideally, this activity would follow "Colors of the Rainbow," which explores the related idea that white light can be separated into the colors of the spectrum.

- Prior to beginning the lesson, students have an opportunity to play with a variety of colorful spinning toys. They observe the objects' appearance before, during, and after spinning.

- Through a class discussion, students summarize their observations and propose explanations for why objects look different while spinning but look the same after spinning as before spinning.

- Students hear the story *Carousel* and watch what happens to the colors when the carousel turns. Does the spinning carousel look similar to the spinning toys?

- Students discuss the idea that colors of light reflect off objects and that when objects are spinning, our brains see a mixture of colors. They make spinning disks and observe what happens to the colors as the disks spin. Students also observe a commercial color-mixing disk designed to produce white light.

- To conclude the lesson, students make a "Not Spinning/Spinning" book.

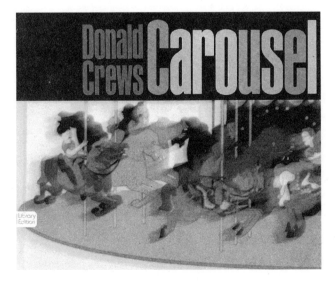

Featured Fiction Book: *Carousel*
Author and Illustrator: Donald Crews
Publisher: Greenwillow Books
ISBN: 0-688-00908-5
Summary: The brief text and illustrations recreate a ride on a carousel.

Part 1: Building Bridges

Building Student Knowledge and Motivation

Set up a center that contains a variety of colorful spinning toys. Possibilities include tops, gyroscopes, decorated disk-shaped throwing toys (such as Frisbees), and colorful yo-yos. Prior to beginning the lesson, have students spend time observing the toys in the center. Instruct them to observe the objects' appearance before, during, and after spinning and record their observations for sharing later. (Masters for several types of science journal pages are provided in the Using Science Journals section at the beginning of this book.)

Getting Ready to Read

Turn to a clean page on your science chart and label it as shown in Figure 1. Through a class discussion, have students share their observations of the toys in the center. Compile and record these observations on the chart. Help students generalize from their observations. Bring out the idea that the colors and shapes on the toys blend while the toy is spinning, but stop blending when the toy stops. Ask students for their ideas about why this happens.

Show students the cover of the book *Carousel.* Ask the students what a carousel is. Ask, "What is another name for it?" *Merry-go-round.* Ask students what they think the book has to do with the spinning toys they have been looking at. Have students carefully watch the pictures of the carousel in the story as you read aloud.

Spinning Objects			
object	before	during	after
yo-yo			
top			

Figure 1: Label your science chart.

Bridging to the Science Activity

Ask students what they observed about the pictures of the carousel and add these observations to the science chart. Ask, "What does the carousel look like before it starts? What does it look like while it's spinning? What does it look like after it stops?" Flip through the book again and look at the pictures. The students should respond that the carousel looks the same before it starts and after it stops, but it looks different while it is spinning, just like the spinning toys in the center. Ask, "If the carousel looks the same before it starts and after it stops, why does it look different while it's spinning?" Have students suggest possible reasons. Ask, "Do the spinning toys or the carousel themselves change in any way while they are spinning?" *No.* Explain that students will explore this phenomenon further by making colorful spinning objects and observing what happens to the colors as the objects spin.

Part 2: Science Activity

Materials

For the Procedure, Part A
Per class
• piece of red paper

For the Procedure, Part B
Per student
• scissors
• 1 or more of the following sets of materials to make the colored part of the spinner:
  ○ Method 1: red, orange, yellow, green, blue, and purple crayons
  ○ Method 2: several different bright colors of construction paper
  ○ Method 3: several patterns of brightly colored wrapping paper

For the Procedure, Part C
Per class
• nail or sharp pencil to poke holes in the cardboard
• animation flip book

 A set of three animation flip books (# 80-060-0808) is available from Delta Education, P.O. Box 3000, Nashua, NH 03061-3000; 800/442-5444.

• (optional) 1 or more commercial color-mixing tops, such as the following:
  ○ Color Top
  ○ Toptical
  ○ white plastic top and dry-erase marker

Color Top can be purchased from Oliphant Research International, 772 West 1700 South, Salt Lake City, Utah 84104; 801/972-1448. Toptical (#F17616) can be purchased from Frey Scientific, 905 Hickory Lane, P.O. Box 8101, Mansfield, OH 44901-8101; 800/225-FREY. Delta Education sells a white plastic top (#80-201-0128) and dry-erase markers (#80-130-8691) that can be used to color the top. Patterns drawn with the markers can be easily wiped off the top.

Per student
• scissors
• corrugated cardboard circle 6 inches in diameter

Corrugated 6-inch cake circles are available from many restaurant, food service, or grocery supply stores. If these stores do not stock this size, they can probably order them. You may need to order by the case, but if you split the order with another teacher, the cake circles can be quite inexpensive. Alternatively, you may wish to cut your own circles out of cardboard.

• glue stick
• pen with a slightly rounded bottom and a pen cap
• 2 small rubber bands

For the Science Extension
Per class
• (optional) record turntable
• commercial disk designed to produce white light, such as the Newton Color Disc

The Newton Color Disc can be purchased from Science Kit & Boreal Laboratories (#65601), 777 East Park Drive, Tonawanda, NY 14150-6782; 800/828-7777; or from Frey Scientific (#F990868), 905 Hickory Lane, P.O. Box 8101, Mansfield, OH 44901-8101; 800/225-FREY.

Getting Ready

For Part C of the Procedure, use a nail or large pin to poke a small hole in the center of the cardboard circle to help students guide the pen through the cardboard. For best spinning results, the hole should be as close to the center of the circle as possible. As a guide, lay the Unit Circle template over each cardboard circle and punch through the "x."

Procedure

Part A: Light and Color

1. Review the concept that white light is made up of a spectrum of colors. Remind students that a prism can be used to separate white light into the visible spectrum (as in "Colors of the Rainbow"). Introduce the idea that when white light hits an object, some colors of light are absorbed and some are reflected. Explain that our eyes perceive a color when an object reflects light of that color.

   While an oversimplification of what actually occurs, this statement is easier for younger children to understand than the more detailed explanation. You are probably aware that objects reflect rays of many colors. The apparent colors of some objects cannot be matched with individual colors of the spectrum. For example, brown light rays do not exist. Brown objects reflect a mixture of colors that we perceive as brown.

2. Hold up a piece of red paper and ask students to look at it. Ask, "What color of light is reflected by this paper?" *Red.* "What colors of light are being absorbed?" *Orange, green, blue, indigo, and violet.*

3. Hold up a toy from the science center, and ask students to look at it and point out some of the colors of light reflected by the toy. Explain that when we look at an object that is not moving, light reflected from different parts of the object hits different parts of our eyes. Our brain figures out where all the light is coming from and creates a mental picture.

4. Spin the object you showed in Step 3. Explain that when the object is spinning, colors of light reflected from different parts of the object hit the same part of our eyes one after the other, so fast that our brain cannot keep up with the constant changes. Therefore the colors and patterns seem blended when we look at them.

5. Through a facilitated discussion, explain that when an object spins rapidly, different colors of light bounce off almost simultaneously and travel to our eyes almost at the same time. Through a facilitated discussion, lead students to realize that the paints or dyes on spinning objects such as the toys or the carousel do not actually mix. (We conclude this because the colors are not mixed when the spinning stops.) The colors only look mixed up to our eyes as the objects spin. The artist illustrates this color mixing in *Carousel* to show us that the carousel is spinning.

Part B: Making Color Disks

Choose one or more of the following methods for making the colored disks to put on the spinners you will make in Part C. Each student will need one copy of the Rainbow Circle (template provided). Model the steps for students, then have them make their color disks using flip cards 1–3 (provided) as a reference.

Teaching Physical Science through Children's Literature

Method 1: Rainbow Circle

1. Color the sections of the Rainbow Circle with the color of crayon specified. (R = red, O = orange, Y = yellow, G = green, B = blue, and P = purple; purple replaces indigo and violet.)

2. Cut out the circle and the inside hole.

Method 2: Sliding Color Circle

This method is based on a design used by James Clerk Maxwell, an English physicist, in the mid-19th century. Maxwell was one of the first scientists to formulate the laws of color mixing and to produce results that could be easily duplicated by others. (See the Science Explanation.)

1. Trace the Rainbow Circle (including the inside hole but not the spokes) on several sheets of different-colored construction paper. Cut out the circles and the inside holes.

2. Cut a slit in each circle from the outside edge to the center hole.

3. Hold two colored circles side by side with the slits lined up. Angle the circles slightly and push the slits together. (See Figure 2.) To change the amount of each color visible, gently rotate the layers. To use more than two colored circles, stack the circles in two piles with the slits in each pile lining up. Then fit the two stacks together as before.

4. Align the paper circles so the center holes are even.

Figure 2:
Sliding color circle

Method 3: Patterned Circle

1. Trace the Rainbow Circle (including the inside hole but not the spokes) on one or more pieces of patterned wrapping paper.

2. Cut out the circle and the inside hole.

Part C: Making and Spinning the Spinner

1. Have students cut out and glue a Unit Circle (template provided) to the cardboard circle.

Students should not color the Unit Circle.

2. Tell students to push the pen up through the hole in the center of the cardboard circle and the "x" in the Unit Circle. Call this assembly (pen, cardboard, and paper circle) the spinner. The Unit Circle/cardboard will serve as the platform on which the color disks will be placed.

3. Have students select one of the color disks they made in Part B to put on the spinner.

4. Demonstrate the following (See flip card pictures for reference):

   a. Push the pen point of the spinner through the hole in the color disk and push the color disk down to the platform.

   b. Position the platform and the color disk on the pen in one of two ways: 1) If you will spin the spinner like a top, push the platform and the color disk onto the pen until they are about 1 inch from the bottom (nonwriting end) of the pen; or 2) If you will spin the spinner by rolling it between your hands, push the platform and the color disk towards the top (writing end) of the pen.

c. Put the cap on the pen, and wrap small rubber bands around the pen above and below the circles.

d. If using the Sliding Color Circle, rotate individual layers of the colored circles so that both edges of each color wedge line up with marks on the Unit Circle. You can pick any mixture and ratio of colors you want. The colors and the number of units covered by each can be recorded on the science chart.

5. Spin the spinner like a top, with the bottom (nonwriting end) down, or roll the pen back and forth between the palms of your hands. Observe the colored circles as they spin and record what colors and patterns appear.

6. Give students time to make and observe their spinners using flip cards 4–6 (provided) as a reference. Ask students to share their observations and record these on the science chart. As a class, compare and contrast observations of the spinners with observations of the spinning toys and the pictures in *Carousel*. Add these observations to the science chart.

7. Hold up a simple animation flip book. Explain, "This flip book confuses our brains just like the spinning tops." Flip through the book, displaying the animation to the class. Explain that in a flip book, one picture rapidly follows another, each reflecting light to the same part of our eyes. Thus our brain creates a mental picture that blends the individual pictures into one continuous picture that seems to move. If desired, introduce the term "persistence of vision" to describe this "eye-fooling" effect in both the tops and the flip book. Tell students that animated cartoons are made this way.

8. Put one or two commercial color-mixing tops (such as Color Top, Toptical, or Delta's white plastic top and dry-erase markers) and materials to make more colored disks for cardboard spinners in the center with the spinning toys. Add an animation flip book and a selection of nonfiction books about color and light. Give students opportunities to visit the center over the next week or so, and encourage them to add any new observations to the science chart.

Science Extension

Bring out the idea that when an object such as one of the toys or a carousel is spinning, the colors appear lighter, closer to white. Explain that with most spinning objects, we usually don't actually see white. However, if the spinning object has just the right colors on it for all of the colors of the rainbow to reflect back, we will see white light when it spins.

Show students a commercial disk designed to produce white light when spinning. One example, the Newton Color Disc, is about 8 inches in diameter and has a center hole to fit standard rotor spindles. In order to work, it must be spun very fast. One way to spin this disk is to put it on a record turntable. Students can take turns watching it spin.

 For best results viewing white, spin the disk in daylight or under a plant grow light, which simulates daylight, and spin the disk at a constant rate. Colors are skewed towards blue under most fluorescent lights and skewed towards yellow under most incandescent light.

Science Explanation

The following explanation is intended for the teacher's information. Modify the explanation for students as required.

Most of us are very familiar with combining different colors of pigment (paint, crayon, marker) to produce a variety of colors. When mixing pigments we often speak of the primary colors of pigment (cyan, magenta, and yellow) combining to form black. In contrast, mixing colors of light is a much less familiar process. The primary colors of light are different (red, green, and blue), and they mix to form white—not black!

One common way to mix colors of light is to project lights of different colors so that they shine on the same spot. But this lesson focuses on a different method of mixing colors of light—optical mixing. Optical mixing is a result of separate areas of color appearing to "fuse in the eye" because the colored object is spinning (or flipping) rapidly. This phenomenon was studied by an important Scottish physicist and mathematician of the mid 1800s, James Clerk Maxwell, and in this lesson you and your students conducted an investigation similar to a portion of Maxwell's research. Maxwell's fame rests primarily on his formulation of electromagnetic theory, but he considered his papers on color to be his most important scientific contribution.

Before we continue to discuss optical mixing, we must first review some basic ideas about color and light: In 1666, Sir Isaac Newton discovered that white light (such as the light from the sun) is actually a mixture of all the visible colors of the spectrum. (See "Colors of the Rainbow" for a more detailed discussion of Newton's work with light and prisms.) When white light (which contains many colors) shines on objects, they absorb some colors of light and reflect others. Plant cells containing chlorophyll absorb most colors and reflect the green part of the light that falls on them. The petals of a red rose absorb most colors of light and reflect primarily red light with a lesser amount of blue. Most yellow flowers reflect some red and green as well as yellow. The reflected colors of most objects are mixtures of colors. When the reflected light hits the eye, the information is processed in the brain and the perception of a particular color results.

Now we are ready to return to optical mixing: When an object is spinning, different colors of light reflecting from each color on the object fall on the same area of the retina in rapid succession. The eye cannot process information instantly, so if the object is spinning fast enough (above about 30 revolutions per second), it appears to be the average color of the various colors of light coming from it. If the proportions of the different colors on the object are just right (such as equal proportions of red, green, and blue), the spinning object will appear white. Since the colors appear to be mixed because of the processing of information in the eye, this phenomenon is called optical mixing.

In Maxwell's experiments with optical mixing, he used a top made from a tin disk divided into 100 units around the rim (rather than 16, as in our version). He placed colored paper disks on the top, slitted so that any portion of each color could be exposed. Maxwell tried different color combinations to determine what color was perceived when he spun the disk. He then recorded the "formula" for that color, such as 78% green, 14% yellow, and 8% blue. By the late 19th century, Maxwell's ideas had reached a wide public, including many artists. Optical mixture was used to explain the impressionist painting technique in which spots of different colors were to blend in the eye of the viewer. In pointillism, the spots were even smaller and more regularly applied, in the belief that optical mixture would result in more vivid colors.

Part 3: Lesson Extensions

Writing Extension

Have each student make a "Not Spinning/Spinning" book about any spinning object seen or read about during the lesson or imagined: Fold an 8½-inch x 11-inch piece of paper in half and in half again. Unfold and cut along the fold as shown in Figure 3a. Draw a picture of the object at rest on the left-hand side and a picture of the object spinning on the right-hand side (Figure 3b). Write about the object under the pictures (Figure 3c). The column on the left should describe the object at rest, and the column on the right should describe the object as it spins. Fold into a book and decorate the cover (Figure 3d).

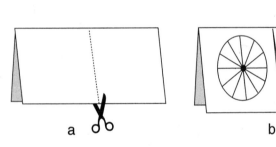

Figure 3: Make a "Not Spinning/Spinning" book.

Part 4: For Further Study

Additional Books

Nonfiction

Title: *The Science Book of Color*
Author: Neil Ardley
Publisher: Harcourt Brace Jovanovich   ISBN: 0-15-200576-5
Summary: Explains the principles of color and gives instructions for a variety of simple experiments.

References

Sarquis, M., Kibbey, B., Smyth, E. "Disappearing Colors;" *Science Activities for Elementary Classrooms;* Flinn Scientific: Batavia, IL, 1989; pp 69–71.

Sloane, P. *Color;* Design: New York, 1991; pp 58–60.

Color Wheel Templates

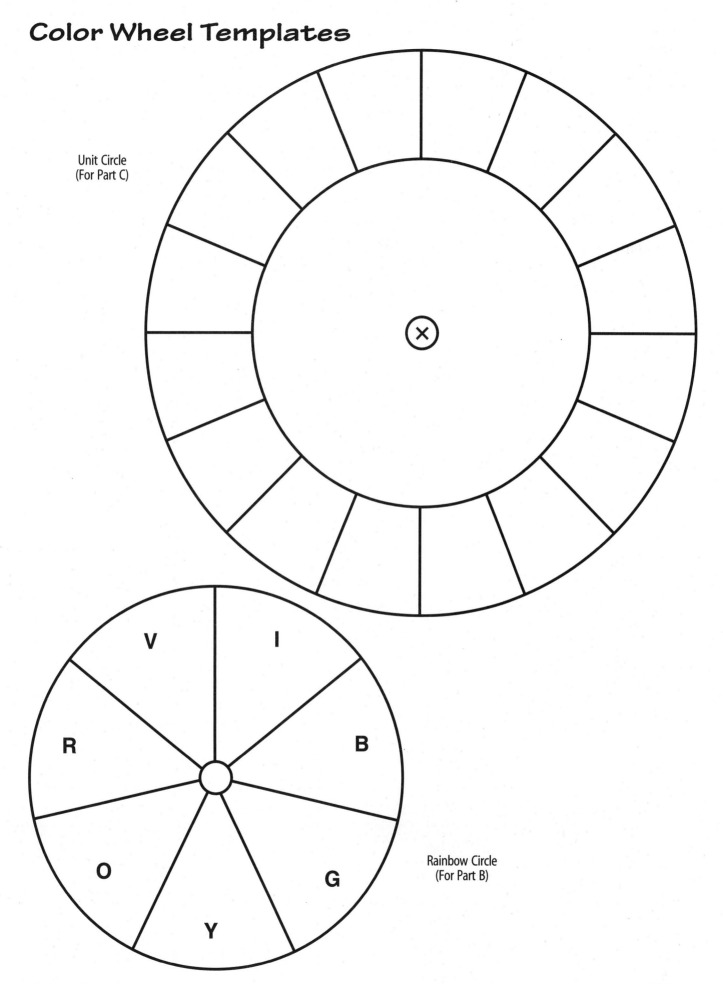

Unit Circle
(For Part C)

Rainbow Circle
(For Part B)

V   I

R   B

O   G

Y

Flip Cards

❶

Make Color Disks

Look at Cards 1–3 for three different ways to make colored disks for your spinner, and choose one or more to try.

Rainbow Circle: Color the sections of the Rainbow Circle with crayons and cut out the circle and the inside hole.

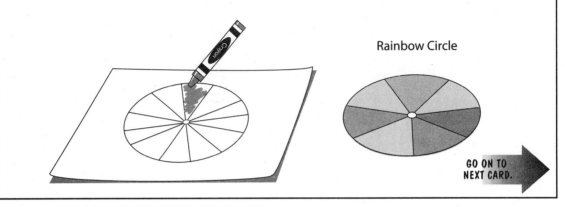

Rainbow Circle

GO ON TO NEXT CARD.

❷

Sliding Color Circle: Use the Rainbow Circle as a pattern to cut out circles of colored paper. (Also cut out the inside holes.)

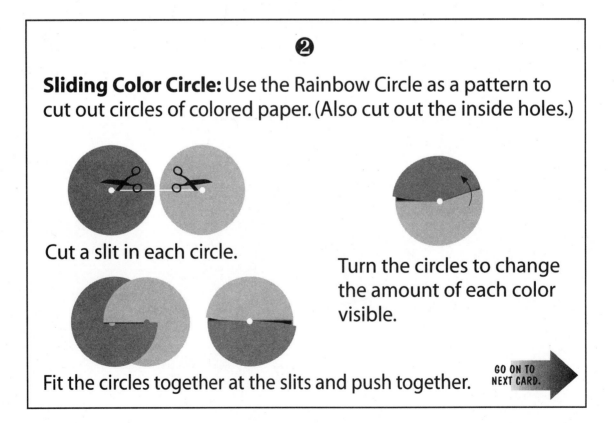

Cut a slit in each circle.

Turn the circles to change the amount of each color visible.

Fit the circles together at the slits and push together.

GO ON TO NEXT CARD.

❸

Patterned Circle: Use the Rainbow Circle as a pattern to cut out a circle of patterned wrapping paper. (Also cut out the inside hole.)

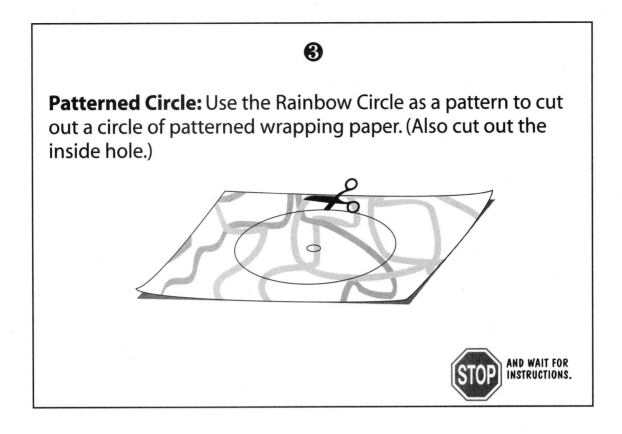

STOP AND WAIT FOR INSTRUCTIONS.

❹

Make and Spin the Spinner

Cut out the Unit Circle template and glue it onto the cardboard circle. Push a pen through the center of the spinner.

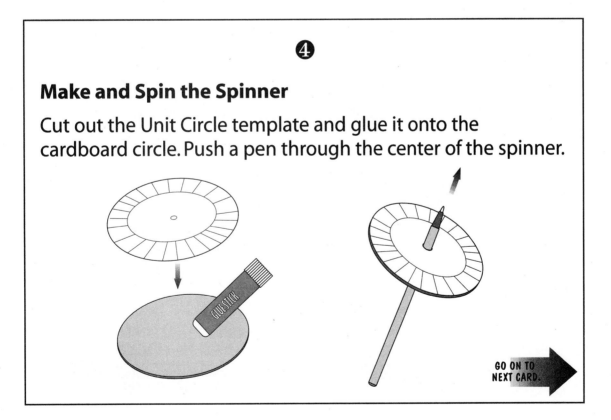

GO ON TO NEXT CARD.

❺

Put one of the the colored disks on the spinner and then put the cap on the pen.

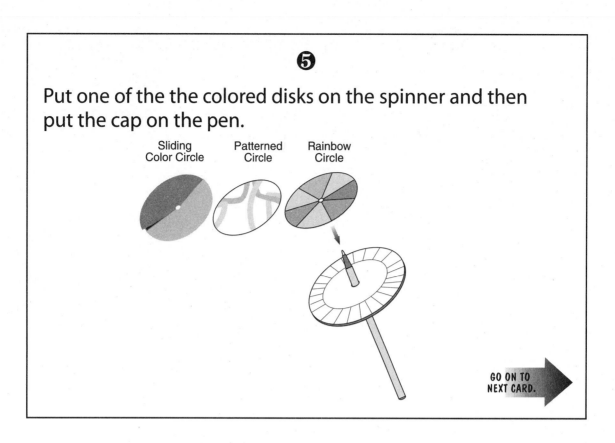

Sliding Color Circle Patterned Circle Rainbow Circle

GO ON TO NEXT CARD.

❻

Wrap rubber bands above and below the cardboard circle. Spin the spinner like a top or between your hands.

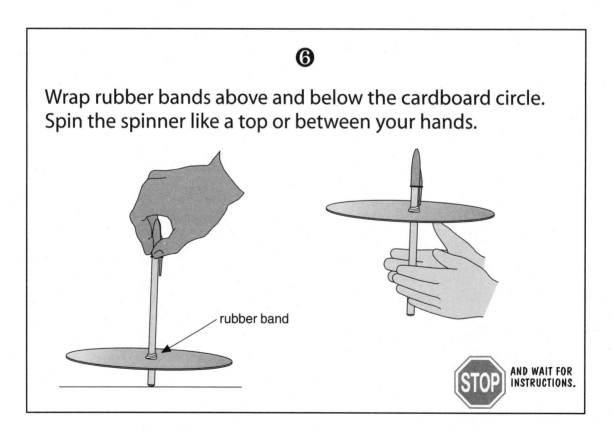

rubber band

STOP AND WAIT FOR INSTRUCTIONS.

Chemiluminescence

SCIENCE CATEGORY: Light, Heat, Electricity, and Magnetism
TOPICS: Production of Light, Effect of Temperature on Rate of Chemical Reaction, Fireflies
OBJECTIVE: Students become familiar with common sources of light. They learn that a chemical reaction produces light in both lightning bugs and lightsticks.

In this lesson, students observe the intensity of light produced by lightsticks under different temperature conditions.

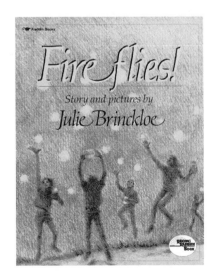

- To introduce the lesson, students examine pictures of objects that produce light. They make a list of the different items along with brief descriptions.

- As a class, students discuss the pictures and make a list of sources of light on a science chart.

- Students hear the story *Fireflies!* by Julie Brinckloe, and think about how fireflies make their light. They then hear and discuss the nonfiction book *Fireflies*, by Caroline Arnold.

- Students observe the intensity of light produced by lightsticks under different temperature conditions.

- To conclude the lesson, each group of students builds a lightstick firefly, views its light under different temperature conditions, and writes a story from a firefly's point of view.

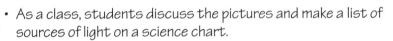

Featured Fiction Book: *Fireflies!*
Author and Illustrator: Julie Brinckloe
Publisher: Aladdin
ISBN: 0689-71055-0
Summary: A young boy is proud of having caught a jar full of fireflies, which seems to him like owning a piece of moonlight, but as the light begins to dim, he realizes he must set the insects free or they will die.

Part 1: Building Bridges

Building Student Knowledge and Motivation

Prior to beginning the lesson, set up a classroom science center with pictures of objects that produce light. Be sure to include items that produce light in different ways: the sun and other stars; filament-type light bulbs; gas-type lights, such as car headlights, street lights, and neon lights; flames, such as those from candles, bonfires, and oil lamps; and chemical sources of light such as fireflies and some deep sea creatures. Have students write lists of the different items along with brief descriptions.

Getting Ready to Read

Title a new science chart "Sources of Light." Through class discussion, add names and descriptions of light-producing items to the list. Students may suggest some items, such as the moon, that reflect light rather than produce it. Point out the difference. Without going into too much detail, also point out that light is produced in a variety of ways, such as when some materials get very hot and when electricity passes through some materials. Also mention that most sources of light are also hot.

Show students the cover of *Fireflies!* Ask students what they think the book has to do with sources of light. Ask students how many of them have ever spent a summer evening catching fireflies (or "lightning bugs"). Allow a few minutes for them to share their experiences. Tell students to think about fireflies and how they make their light as you read the story.

Bridging to the Science Activity

Have students discuss what they heard about fireflies in the story. Ask why they think the fireflies' lights became dimmer or faded while in the jar. Ask, "Where do you think fireflies' light comes from?" After hearing students' ideas, point out that fireflies do not have little light bulbs inside them, nor are they burning with fire (despite the name). Students who have held fireflies may remember that fireflies are not hot at all. Add new ideas to the "Sources of Light" chart as desired.

Read and discuss the nonfiction book *Fireflies,* by Caroline Arnold. (See Additional Books.) Tell students that the light made by a firefly is a result of a chemical reaction that produces light energy. Explain that other chemical reactions can make light and that they will be observing one popular example—a lightstick.

Part 2: Science Activity

Materials

For Getting Ready
- knife or scissors

For the Procedure, Part A

Per class

- 3 lightsticks of the same color

➤ *Inexpensive lightsticks can be purchased from the Oriental Trading Company, Inc., P.O. Box 3407, Omaha, NE 68103-0407; 800/228-2269. Make sure the lightsticks are not too old; as they age, lightsticks lose their ability to produce light.*

- flashlight
- ice
- water
- 2 clear containers such as glasses, jars, or beakers to hold about 500 mL (2 cups) each
- (optional) alcohol or metal cooking thermometer
- (optional) tongs
- access to a room that can be effectively darkened

➤ *It is easier to judge differences in light intensity if the room is darkened, but the room does not have to be completely dark.*

For the Procedure, Part B

Per class

- "cool box" made from a cooler half-filled with ice
- "warm box" made from a hair dryer and a cardboard box (See Getting Ready.)
- "room-temperature box" made from a box with a lid
- (optional) 3 alcohol thermometers

➤ *V-back metal alcohol thermometers (#80-200-1340) are easy to read and are available from Delta Education, P.O. Box 3000, Nashua, NH 03061-9913; 800/442-5444.*

Per group

- 2 plastic cups of the same size, 1 opaque and 1 clear

➤ *Make sure the clear plastic cups are not too rigid to cut as instructed in Getting Ready.*

- cap from a soft-drink bottle
- lightstick
- 4 pipe cleaners
- glue
- tape
- assorted materials for making the wings and decorating the firefly, such as construction paper, permanent markers, felt scraps, and plastic wiggle eyes

Safety and Disposal

Read and follow the precautions on the lightstick package. If the lightstick is placed in water that is too hot (more than 70°C or 158°F), the plastic might melt and the contents run into the water. (Melting doesn't cause a serious problem; the material inside the lightstick is not water-soluble, so it remains as a glowing glob in the water. However, care should be taken, as thin pieces of glass will exist in the mixture.) When finished, the lightstick can be disposed of in a solid waste container away from children. The plastic tube will contain pieces of broken glass.

Getting Ready

For Part B, pour hot tap water no hotter than 70°C (158°F), about the temperature of a hot cup of coffee, into a clear container. (Above 70°C the plastic lightstick might melt.) Make an ice-water bath by placing ice in the water in the second container.

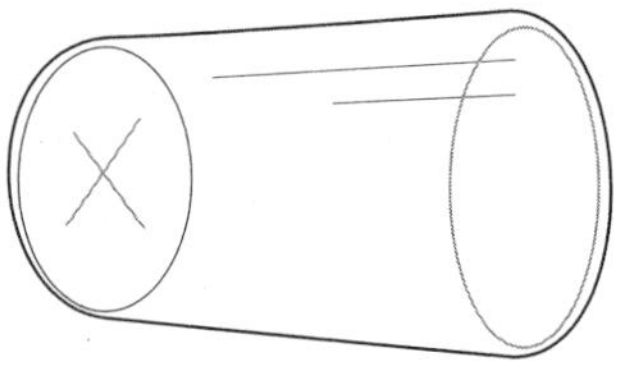

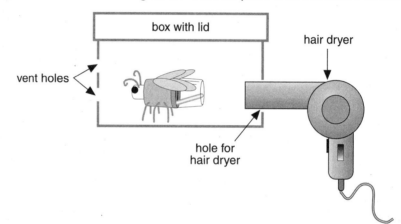

Figure 1

For Part C, use scissors or a knife to cut an X on the bottoms of the clear plastic cups. (See Figure 1.) Fill the cooler about halfway with ice. If desired, place a thermometer inside. Close the lid. For the "room-temperature box," place a thermometer inside, if desired, and close the lid. To make the "warm box" you need a hair dryer and a cardboard box with a lid. The box needs to be large enough to fit a "lightstick firefly" comfortably inside without getting too close to the hair dryer nozzle. Cut a hole in the side of a cardboard box (near the bottom) that is just large enough to insert the nozzle of the hair dryer. Also cut several ventilation holes in the side opposite the hair dryer nozzle. (See Figure 2.) Turn the hair dryer on a low heat setting and, if desired, place a thermometer inside.

Figure 2: Make a "warm box" to heat the lightstick firefly.

Procedure

Part A: Warm Light, Cool Light

1. Turn on the flashlight and set it aside so it can warm up.

2. Ask students to record observations about the lightstick *before it is activated.* Pass it around so each student has a close-up view.

3. Activate one lightstick by bending it (to break the inner glass vial; see the directions on the package) and ask students to observe.

4. Pass the *activated* lightstick and the flashlight around the class and have students make observations. Ask, "How are they similar? Different?"

Make sure students notice that the lightstick produces light without noticeable heat; the flashlight is warm.

5. Tell students that many light sources actually release most of their energy as heat and only a small amount as light. However, lightsticks give off their energy as light, not as heat.

Teaching Physical Science through Children's Literature

Part B: Bright Light, Dim Light

1. Activate the other two lightsticks. Compare the intensities of the three lightsticks. (They should be about the same intensity.)

2. Place one of the lightsticks in very hot tap water (less than 70°C). Place a second lightstick in the ice-water bath. Keep the third lightstick at room temperature as a control.

3. Allow the lightsticks to sit in the containers for the same period of time. Within a few minutes, students should observe a difference in the intensity of light from the lightsticks in the two containers.

4. Pull the glowing lightsticks out of the containers and, with the room darkened, compare their intensities with that of the room-temperature lightstick.

5. Reverse the lightsticks so that the one that was in hot water is now in the ice water and the one originally in ice water is in the hot water. Have the students observe. Ask, "How long does it take for the intensity of the glow to change?"

6. Direct students' attention to the "Sources of Light" chart. Ask, "Is there anything you want to add now?" Discuss and add to the chart as desired.

7. Remind students that the light produced by lightsticks is a result of a chemical reaction. Explain that the reaction is faster when the lightstick is in a warm place, and so more light is produced. When the lightstick is cooler, the reaction is slower. Ask, "What do you think would happen if we put one of the lightsticks in the freezer?"

Part C: Lightstick Firefly

1. Review the ideas that lightsticks produce light without heat as a result of a chemical reaction and that the intensity of the light is affected by temperature. Tell students that the light of a lightstick and the light of a firefly are similar in several ways. Explain that fireflies also produce light as a result of a chemical reaction that takes place in a part of their body called a lantern, that very little heat is produced by the firefly's lantern, and that the intensity of the firefly's light is affected by temperature.

2. Tell students that to help them think about fireflies and their lights, they will be working in groups to make model fireflies that they will call "lightstick fireflies." Distribute all materials listed for Part B, per group, except the lightsticks.

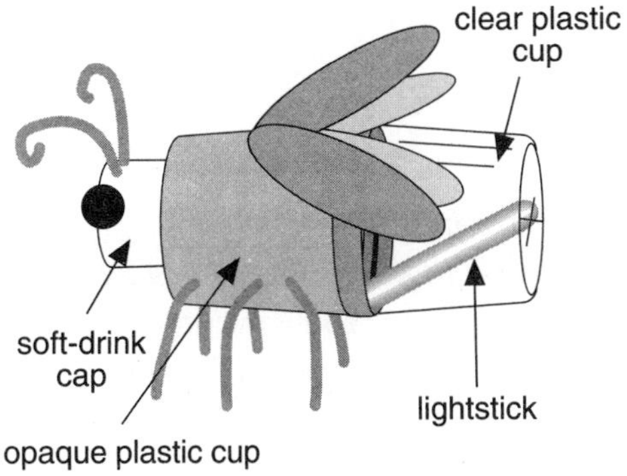

3. Review the basic parts of a firefly—head (includes eyes, mouth, antennae), thorax (has six legs and two sets of wings), abdomen (contains the light organ, or lantern).

4. Explain that they can use the provided materials any way they wish, as long as they follow these rules:

   a. The firefly must have a head made from the soft-drink cap, a thorax made from the opaque cup, and an abdomen made from the clear cup. (See Figure 3.)

   b. The eyes, mouth, and antennae must go on the head.

   c. The wings and legs must go on the thorax.

clear plastic cup

soft-drink cap

opaque plastic cup

lightstick

Figure 3

5. Give students an opportunity to work on their fireflies. After fireflies are complete, let any glue, paint, or marker used dry overnight.

6. Assign the stations for the groups to visit as follows:

   Groups 1, 4: cooler filled with ice
   Groups 2, 5: "warm box"
   Groups 3, 6: room-temperature box

7. Tell students to record the results carefully to use in a story they will be writing later.

8. Activate and pass out a lightstick to each group, and darken the room. Have each group insert their lightstick into the abdomen (clear cup) of the firefly through the "X" cut in Getting Ready.

9. Have all groups place their fireflies in the assigned stations and leave for 5 minutes. Tell students to remove their fireflies and, as a class, observe and compare the six fireflies.

10. After students have completed their observations, discuss and add to the "Sources of Light" list as desired. Then pose this question: "What do you think happens to a real firefly's light when the firefly gets warmer or cooler? As a scientist, how could you find out?"

Science Extension

Introduce the term "bioluminescence": the chemiluminescence found in living things. Explain that certain organisms (fireflies, certain types of bacteria, and some deep-sea creatures) use valuable energy to produce this chemical light, and that organisms do not use up energy without gaining some benefit. Through class discussion, have students brainstorm the possible benefit bioluminescence could have for organisms that produce it. Students can then do follow-up research to find out more about bioluminescence.

Science Explanation

The following explanation is intended for the teacher's information. Modify the explanation for students as required.

Sources for light include fusion (such as in the sun and other stars), heating something until it glows (such as the filament in a lightbulb), and passing electricity through certain gases (such as in a halogen light bulb). The energy given off by these light sources includes a significant amount of heat as well as light. For example, in an electric arc light, only 10 percent of the energy is light, and the other 90 percent of the energy produced is given off as heat.

Chemical reactions can also produce light. Combustion reactions, for example, often produce light energy as well as heat energy. A small number of chemical reactions produce light without heat at room temperature. The light produced by such nonthermal reactions is called chemiluminescence. When such light is produced within biological systems, it is called bioluminescence.

In this activity, you observe an example of chemiluminescence when you mix the two components of a lightstick. A lightstick consists of a sealed plastic tube that contains two solutions. One solution contains a fluorescent dye and a chemical called phenyl oxalate ester. The other solution, dilute hydrogen peroxide, is in a thin glass vial within the plastic tube. The lightstick is activated by bending the plastic tube, which causes the glass vial to break so the two solutions can interact. When mixed, the two solutions react and give off energy in the form of visible light.

In general, the rate of a chemical reaction increases as the temperature increases. Thus, at a higher temperature, the lightstick's glow is brighter. Likewise, at a lower temperature, the lower light intensity indicates that the reaction rate is less. Since each lightstick contains a fixed amount of material, the lower the temperature, the longer the lightstick will glow (but with less intensity). If an activated lightstick is stored in a freezer, the rate of reaction becomes so slow that there is no perceptible glow; however, when removed from the freezer and warmed, the lightstick will give off light, even after being stored for several months.

Fireflies (or lightning bugs) are not actually flies; they are beetles (order, Coleoptera; family, Lampyridae). Many members of this well-known group possess a "tail light"—segments near the end of the abdomen with which the insects are able to produce light. These luminous segments can be recognized, even when they are not glowing, by their yellowish-green color. The flickering light is produced by an organ called a lantern on the underside of the firefly's abdomen. To produce the light, a chemical reaction takes place in the lantern in which two compounds—luciferin and the enzyme luciferase—react with oxygen. Nearly 100 percent of the energy given off by this chemical reaction appears as light. The firefly controls the blinking by controlling the air supply to the lantern organ. A distinct blinking pattern is characteristic of each species of firefly, and is used to attract a mate of its own species. The females of many firefly species cannot fly and are called glowworms.

Part 2: Lesson Extensions

Writing Extension

Using the notes from Part C of the Procedure, have students write stories about their lightstick fireflies and their adventures. Instruct students to be sure to use their observations as part of the stories.

Math Extension

Have students record and make bar graphs of the length of time a lightstick will glow under the three temperature conditions used in the experiment.

Cross-Cultural Integration

This section is intended for teacher background. You may wish to use the information in this section to develop age-appropriate activities for your classroom.

Fireflies, with their seemingly magical lights, have fascinated people around the world for thousands of years. Many customs and legends have sprung up in different lands about these little beetles. In Japan, firefly festivals are celebrated every summer. People come together to catch fireflies, put them in cages, and row out to the middle of a lake or river. The people open their cages at the same time, sending clouds of flickering fireflies into the night sky. In Central and South America, Japan, and the West Indies, people make firefly lamps by catching fireflies and putting them in cages or net bags. Sometimes people wrap fireflies in pieces of net and wear them; in South America, women wear them on clothing or in the hair as glowing "jewelry." In the West Indies, people who hunt or fish at night wear netted fireflies on their wrists and ankles to keep track of each other in the dark.

Fireflies are mentioned in ancient literature from many countries, including India, China, and Greece. The *Shih Ching,* written in China about 3,000 years ago, describes the beetle's intermittent glow. Another Chinese legend tells of a poor but resourceful student who lived almost 2,000 years ago. Unable to afford lamp oil, Ch'e Yin collected fireflies and used their light to study at night. Fireflies also appear in Japanese folklore; according to one legend, fireflies are the ghosts of brave warriors who died fighting for their country.

Part 4: For Further Study

Nonfiction

Title: *Fireflies*
Author: Caroline Arnold   Illustrator: Pamela Johnson
Publisher: Scholastic   ISBN: 0-590-46944-4
Summary: Discover how fireflies grow and why they light up. Find out how people in other parts of the world use fireflies to decorate their clothes and even have special festivals for these tiny beetles.

Title: *Nature's Living Lights: Fireflies and Other Bioluminescent Creatures*
Authors: Alvin and Virginia Silverstein   Illustrator: Pamela Carroll
Publisher: Little, Brown   ISBN: 0-316-79119-9
Summary: Describes bioluminescent insects, plants, and sea animals and the uses these creatures make of their self-generated lights.

Title: *Animals That Glow*
Author: Judith Janda Presnall
Publisher: Franklin Watts   ISBN: 0-531-20071-X
Summary: A study of insects and other animals that are bioluminescent, including fireflies, glowworms, and squids.

References

Borror, D.; Delong, D. *An Introduction to the Study of Insects;* Holt, Rinehart, and Winston: New York, 1971; pp 285–287.

Kohn, B. *Fireflies;* Prentice-Hall: Englewood Cliffs, NJ, 1968; pp 43–51.

Matthews, R.W.; Matthews, J.R. *Insect Behavior;* John Wiley & Sons: New York, 1978; p 236.

Perkins, R., Greenwich High School (Connecticut) and Assistant Director of Institute for Chemical Education, University of Wisconsin, Madison, WI 53706, personal communication.

Sarquis, M.; Sarquis, J.L.; Williams, J.P. "Investigating the Effect of Temperature on Lightsticks;" *Teaching Chemistry with TOYS: Activities for Grades K–9;* McGraw-Hill: New York, 1995; pp 269–273.

Shakhashiri, B. Z. *Chemical Demonstrations;* University of Wisconsin: Madison, WI, 1983; Vol. 1, pp 125, 146–152, 158.

Are Mittens Warm?

SCIENCE CATEGORY: Light, Heat, Electricity, and Magnetism
TOPICS: Heat, Insulation, Temperature
OBJECTIVE: Students learn that mittens and other clothing are not actually warm but can trap our body heat to help us stay warm.

In this lesson, students gather data to investigate the role of mittens in keeping our hands warm. Students discover that mittens do not produce heat on their own, but keep our hands warm by holding in the heat from our hands.

- Prior to beginning the lesson, students dress cut-out figures in clothes appropriate for summer and winter weather. They will discuss parts of the world that are summer-like most of the year and parts of the world that are winter-like most of the year.

- Through a class discussion, students decide where in the world their cut-out people would be comfortable living based on how they are dressed.

- Students hear the story *Mama, Do You Love Me?* and look for examples of warm clothing worn by the Inuit characters in the story.

- To answer the question "Are mittens warm?" students measure the temperature of their hands with and without mittens as well as the temperature of the mittens themselves.

- To conclude the lesson, students hear the book *Eskimo Boy* by Russ Kendall. This book investigates the lifestyle and clothing of a seven-year-old Eskimo boy and his family. Students then make a cut-out figure of an Eskimo (Inuit) character, dress him or her, draw an appropriate setting for the character, and write about him or her.

Featured Fiction Book: *Mama, Do You Love Me?*
Author: Barbara Joosse
Illustrator: Barbara Lavallee
Publisher: Chronicle Books
ISBN: 0-87701-759-X
Summary: A child living in the Arctic learns that a mother's love is unconditional.

Part 1: Building Bridges

Building Student Knowledge and Motivation

Enter the room dressed half for winter and half for summer. For example, you might wear shorts and sandals with a winter coat, scarf, and hat. Tell the students that you need help dressing appropriately for the weather. Discuss what kinds of clothing are appropriate for warm weather and for cold weather and have the students help you choose an appropriate outfit.

After the discussion, provide each student with two cut-out figures and clothing. (Master provided. If necessary, enlarge the pictures to make them easier for students to handle.) Tell students to dress one cut-out figure in clothes appropriate for summer and the other figure in clothes appropriate for winter.

Getting Ready to Read

Turn to a clean page in your science chart and divide it into two columns. Label one "Summer" and the other "Winter." Through a class brainstorming session, list in each column the types of clothing that would be appropriate for that season.

Show students a map of North and South America. Discuss what areas on the map are winter-like most of the time and what areas are summer-like most of the time. Give several students a chance to stick their cut-out figures on the map in areas the figures are appropriately dressed to live in.

Hold up a copy of *Mama, Do you Love Me?* Ask, "Do you think the people in the story live in a cold place or a warm one?" *Cold.* "What do you see that makes you think that?" Ask students to look for different kinds of warm clothes worn by the characters as you read the story.

Bridging to the Science Activity

Ask students what the story is about. Ask, "What did you see in the story that tells you how the Inuits keep warm?" Discuss the traditional clothing shown in the book, including parkas, mukluks, and mittens. Ask students if they ever wear clothes like these. Do they feel warmer in these clothes? Pass some mittens around the room and ask students to describe how they feel. Ask, "Are they warm or cold to the touch?"

Put a clean medicinal thermometer under your tongue to take your temperature and read the result aloud. Talk about body temperature and what it measures. Ask, "Are all parts of the body at this temperature?" Using body temperature as a frame of reference, discuss air temperature and how it affects us. What feels warm to us? What feels cold? What feels comfortable? Use responses to lead into a discussion of warm and cold climates. Talk about average or high temperatures in warm climates and average or low temperatures in cold climates. Ask, "How do you think people in these places feel when the temperature is so high/low?" Talk about the kinds of clothing people in these places wear.

As a class, brainstorm possible explanations for why we feel warmer when wearing mittens and other winter clothing. Accept all ideas without further discussion. Tell students they will be making some observations and gathering some data to help them answer this question.

Part 2: Science Activity

Materials

For the Procedure
Per class
- clock with minutes marked

Per group
- mitten
- large stuffed animal with a leg or paw that a mitten will fit onto
- dial thermometer or V-back alcohol thermometer with calibrations between 15–40°C (about 60–100°F)

Dial thermometers under the name "pocket test thermometer" (#80-070-4923) and V-back metal thermometers (#80-200-1340) are easy to read and are available from Delta Education, P.O. Box 3000, Nashua, NH 03061-9913; 800/442-5444. (Dial thermometers are easier to read than V-back thermometers but are also more expensive.)

For the Science Extensions
All materials listed for the Procedure plus the following:
❷ Per class
- glove made of the same material as the mitten

❹ Per class
- mittens of different materials, such as knit mittens, fur-lined mittens, and down-filled mittens

❺ Per class
- several thin mittens and one thick mitten

Safety and Disposal

No special safety or disposal procedures are required.

Procedure

	Temperatures			
item	group 1	group 2	group 3	group 4
room — predicted				
room — actual				
palm — predicted				
palm — actual				
fist — predicted				
fist — actual				
empty mitten — predicted				
empty mitten — actual				
palm with mitten — predicted				
palm with mitten — actual				
paw with mitten — predicted				

Figure 1

1. Make a science chart as shown in Figure 1.

2. As a class, consider whether the room feels cool or warm. Have students volunteer predictions for the temperature of the air in the room. Emphasize that predictions are not wild guesses, but are based on related previous experiences. In this case, if the students know the temperature of a given object, then they could conclude an object that feels cooler must have a lower temperature. For example, if students are told that the average human body temperature is 98.6°F, they could conclude that an object that feels warm to them must have a temperature higher than 98.6°F, and an object that feels cooler must have a temperature below 98.6°F.

DATA SHEET

3. Have students work in cooperative groups. Tell each group to decide on a prediction for room temperature, record it on their Data Sheet (master provided), and then read the thermometer's actual temperature. Have a volunteer from each group write the group's prediction and actual temperature on the class science chart.

➤ *If your students do not already know, instruct them in the proper use, handling, and reading of the thermometers they will use.*

4. Have each group complete the following steps for items 2–6 on the Data Sheet:

   a. Considering previous data, predict the temperature for each item and record the prediction on the Data Sheet.

➤ *Instruct students not to put the mitten on until they need to measure temperatures with it on. If the mitten has been recently worn, it will affect the temperature reading. (See the Science Explanation.)*

   b. Position the thermometer as indicated for each item.

   c. Wait 2 minutes. While waiting, have a member of the group record the group's prediction on the class chart.

   d. Read the thermometer without moving it.

   e. Record the temperature on the Data Sheet.

   f. Have a member of the group record the actual temperature on the class chart.

5. The following questions can be used to discuss the lesson.

   a. What was the room temperature? How does that compare to body temperature?

   b. What was the temperature when the thermometer was in the palm of your open hand? What was the temperature when your hand was closed into a fist? How do these temperatures compare to normal body temperature?

   c. What temperature was recorded with the mitten on? How does it compare to the temperature recorded in your open hand with no mitten? How does it compare with the temperature of the stuffed animal paw with the mitten on?

   d. Why do you think wearing a mitten made your hand feel warmer? Are mittens warm?

   e. Discuss predictions versus experimentation—why we want to predict and why it's okay for predictions to be "wrong."

   f. Did each group get exactly the same temperatures? Name some reasons why they might not have.

Science Extensions

1. To determine the effect of the air temperature on the activity, try the activity outside on a cold day and compare the temperatures recorded.

2. Try repeating the Procedure with gloves made from the same type of cloth as the mittens and compare the results.

3. Test the insulating properties of a wet mitten.

Teaching Physical Science through Children's Literature

4. Test mittens of different materials, such as knit mittens, fur-lined mittens, and down-filled mittens.

5. Compare the insulating properties of several layers of thin mittens to one thick mitten.

Science Explanation

> *The following explanation is intended for the teacher's information. Modify the explanation for students as required.*

The goal of this activity is for students to discover that mittens are "warm" because they help to hold in heat from the body and minimize its loss into the air. In other words, mittens act as insulators. Humans are warm-blooded animals. We typically maintain a body temperature of 37°C (98.6°F). Except on very hot days, we usually lose some of our body heat to the air and our surroundings. This is because heat flows from materials with higher temperatures to materials with lower temperatures. One of the purposes of clothing is to hold in our body heat and minimize this heat loss. This is the reason we change the amount and kind of clothes we wear as the weather changes.

In this activity students are asked the question, "Are mittens warm?" Students typically know that mittens are worn in cold weather to keep their hands warm. Depending on their age and maturity, some students may believe that the warmth comes from the mitten itself. With further questioning and collecting of temperatures under various conditions, however, students discover the insulating ability of mittens and the role mittens play in keeping their hands warm.

The first several temperatures are taken to allow students to discover that, except in very warm places, (a) air temperature is usually less than body temperature, and (b) the temperature of a hand (either open or close fisted) is typically below "normal" body temperature because heat is lost to the cooler surrounding air.

The final steps of the activity are done to show the insulating ability of the mitten. By itself, the not-recently-worn mitten should have the same temperature as the air temperature. With your hand in the mitten, the temperature is higher because your hand is providing heat to warm the thermometer. This temperature is also greater than the previously recorded temperature of the palm without the mitten. The mitten prevents the cold air from the outside from making contact with your hand; the mitten insulates your hand from the cold surroundings. Thus, our hands are warmer when we have mittens on.

Part 3: Lesson Extensions

Writing Extensions

1. Read aloud the book *Eskimo Boy,* by Russ Kendall. This book describes the lifestyle and clothing of a seven-year-old Eskimo boy and his family. Have students make a cut-out figure of an Inuit character, dress him or her, and draw an appropriate setting for the character. Ask each student to explain in writing

why his or her character is dressed the way he or she is. Also have each student describe the kind of person he or she is, where he or she lives, and what he or she does for fun.

2. Explain that our language is enriched by borrowing words from other languages and incorporating them into our own and that American English has developed from the languages of many ethnic groups. Have students pick Inuit words from *Mama, Do You Love Me?* and *Eskimo Boy* that they think have been incorporated into the English language. Then have students use a dictionary to check for these words and write definitions for the words they find. Have students use classroom references to find a picture of each.

Cross-Cultural Integration

 This section is intended for teacher background. You may wish to use the information in this section to develop age-appropriate activities for your classroom.

Description of Inuit People

The name "Eskimo" comes from a native American word meaning "eaters of raw meat." However, most native Arctic people call themselves "Inuit," which means "the people." One Inuit person is called an Inuk. There are many different Inuit nations, and each has its own language and traditions. Most Inuit live in the Arctic—the area around the North Pole. It is one of the coldest regions on earth. During the winter, there are months when the sun doesn't shine; in summer, there are months when the sun never sets. Greenland, northern Canada, and parts of Russia are all part of the Arctic region. This description of Inuit people focuses on traditional Inuit lifestyles. Although many Inuit people no longer live this way, these traditions are still carried on.

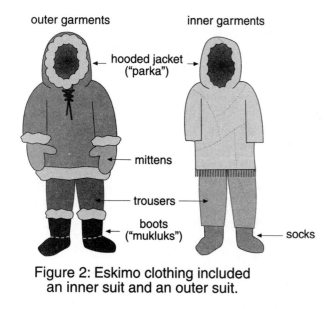

Figure 2: Eskimo clothing included an inner suit and an outer suit.

The Inuit people have survived in their harsh environment for thousands of years by following a special way of life. Most Inuits lived near the sea, which provided them with most of their food. They hunted mostly seals and caribou, but they also hunted musk oxen, walruses, polar bears, whales, and birds. They made clothes from caribou skins and the skins of other animals, and they trimmed these clothes with fur such as fox and wolverine. Inuit clothing consisted of an inner suit of hooded jacket, trousers, and socks, and an outer suit of another hooded jacket, trousers, boots, and mittens. These layers of clothing helped keep them warm in the winter, but usually the Inuits wore only the inner suit or a suit of sealskin during warmer weather. Men, women, and children wore the same type of clothing. (See Figure 2.)

In the Arctic, no forests can grow—only small, scattered trees. Therefore, while many Inuit sleds and boats were made of wood, it was not relied on as a fuel. Instead, the Inuits usually burned oil made from the blubber of seals and other sea mammals to produce heat and light. These lamps cooked food very slowly, so the Inuits usually ate their meat raw. They sometimes ate berries and other parts of certain plants, but in most areas these foods were available only during the warmest months, and only in small amounts.

Unlike many other Native American groups, the Inuit people had no tribes and no chiefs. They usually lived in family groups which included parents, unmarried children, and married sons and their wives and children. These families often moved regularly, following game. Most families had a summer home and a winter home. During the summer, most Inuits lived in tents made of sealskin or caribou skin. During the winter, most Inuits lived in sod houses. Some Inuits also made dome-shaped houses of snow. These snowhouses were usually used as temporary shelters when traveling, but some Inuits used them as permanent winter homes. These snow houses were only slightly warmer than the outdoors, but they felt much warmer because they shut out the wind. (See Figure 3.)

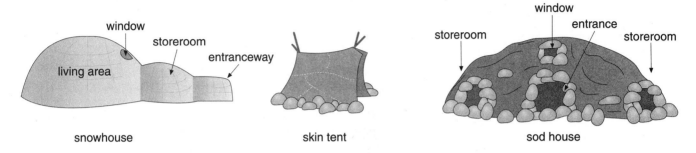

Figure 3: Types of Eskimo dwellings included the snowhouse, skin tent, and sod house.

The Inuits used boats (kayaks and umiaks) to travel and hunt on rivers, lakes, and the sea. They used dogsleds to travel on snow and ice. To travel over land in the summer they walked. To pass the time during the cold, dark, winter months, the Inuits played many games. The men especially liked tests of strength and skill, such as wrestling, tug of war, and even trapeze acts (on strings of skin strung across the inside of a house). The Inuits also liked singing, telling stories, and dancing to the beat of drums. The Inuits decorated their clothes with furs and with carved ivory buttons and buckles. They also drew and carved on tools, weapons, and other items, such as children's toys.

Inuits in different regions mostly spoke languages very similar to each other. Many Inuit words consist of one-syllable words strung together, sometimes in chains of five or more syllables. Inuits did not have a system of writing.

The ancestors of Inuits came from northeastern Asia. They may have moved to Alaska across a land bridge that connected Asia and northern North America until about 10,000 years ago. From Alaska, the Inuits later spread eastward across the North American Arctic in two major waves. Inuits of the second wave met Vikings on Greenland in about 1100 A.D. In the 1500s, European explorers began to meet Inuits. Russians and other European explorers first met Alaskan Inuits in the 1700s. In the 1800s, European whalers and fur traders entered Inuit territory. Many Inuits began to work for and trade with the Europeans. Unfortunately, the Europeans also brought diseases new to the Inuits, such as measles and smallpox, and many Inuits died.

During the 1900s, the Inuits' way of life underwent many changes. Inuits in many countries hunted and trapped for trade. But when populations of game animals began to decline, many Inuits were forced to adopt different lifestyles and find jobs in other industries, such as construction and fishing.

Part 4: For Further Study

Additional Books

Fiction

Title: *The Mitten*
Author and Illustrator: Jan Brett
Publisher: Scholastic   ISBN: 0-399-21920-X
Summary: This story is a retelling of a Ukrainian folktale about animals who find shelter inside a small boy's mitten.

Title: *50 Below Zero*
Author: Robert Munsch   Illustrator: Michael Martchenko
Publisher: Annick Press Ltd.   ISBN: 0-920236-91-X
Summary: A boy's father sleepwalks outside on a cold winter night while wearing only pajamas. The father freezes solid and the boy thaws him out.

Title: *The Jacket I Wear in the Snow*
Author: Shirley Neitzel   Illustrator: Nancy Winslow Parker
Publisher: Greenwillow Books   ISBN: 0-590-43945-6
Summary: A young girl names all the clothes that she must wear to play in the snow.

Nonfiction

Title: *Keeping Warm, Keeping Cool*
Author and Illustrator: Joan Elma Rahn
Publisher: Atheneum   ISBN: 0-689-30995-3
Summary: Describes how living things, especially animals and human beings, adapt to environmental temperature changes in order to conserve heat in cold weather and lose heat in hot weather.

Title: *Eskimo Boy*
Author: Russ Kendall
Publisher: Scholastic   ISBN: 0-590-43696-1
Summary: Describes the life of a seven-year-old Eskimo boy living in a small Alaskan village.

Name _____   Date _____

Data Sheet

Are Mittens Warm?

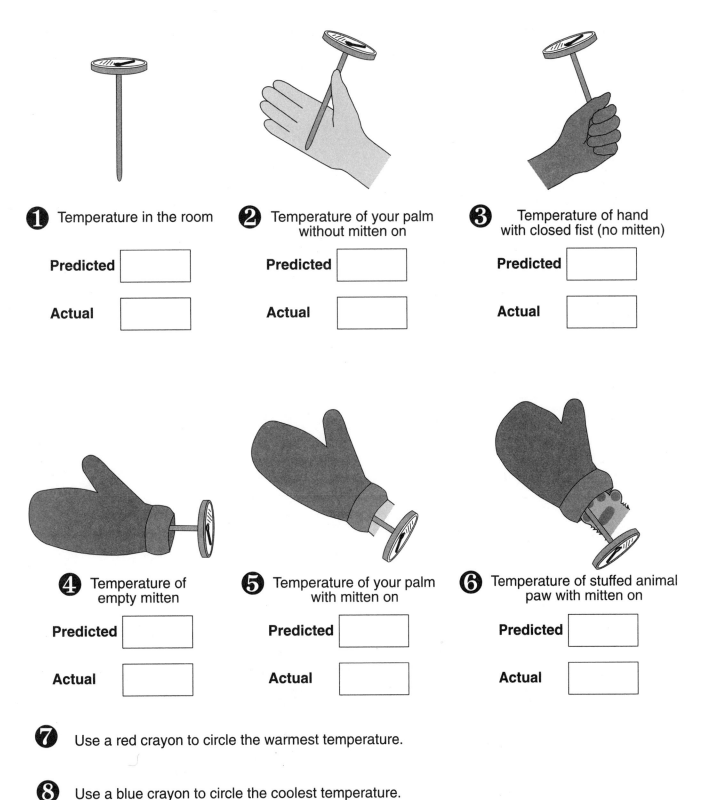

① Temperature in the room

Predicted [   ]

Actual [   ]

② Temperature of your palm without mitten on

Predicted [   ]

Actual [   ]

③ Temperature of hand with closed fist (no mitten)

Predicted [   ]

Actual [   ]

④ Temperature of empty mitten

Predicted [   ]

Actual [   ]

⑤ Temperature of your palm with mitten on

Predicted [   ]

Actual [   ]

⑥ Temperature of stuffed animal paw with mitten on

Predicted [   ]

Actual [   ]

⑦ Use a red crayon to circle the warmest temperature.

⑧ Use a blue crayon to circle the coolest temperature.

Are Mittens Warm?

1. Cut out the two figures and their clothes.
2. Dress one figure for winter weather and one for summer.

Is It Really Magic?

SCIENCE CATEGORY: Light, Heat, Electricity, and Magnetism
TOPIC: Static Electricity
OBJECTIVE: Students observe some effects of static electricity and learn a scientific explanation for a seemingly magical event.

In this lesson, students observe that static electricity can cause some objects to be attracted to each other in a way that seems magical. Students learn that scientists must discount the idea of magic when trying to explain events. It is helpful if students have some familiarity with the effects of static electricity.

• Prior to beginning the lesson, students practice a variety of commercial magic tricks and try to determine how they work.

• As a class, students discuss their ideas about magic and list their proposed explanations for the magic tricks on a science chart.

• Students hear the story *The Wartville Wizard* and listen for examples of magic. Through a class discussion, students brainstorm other possible explanations besides magic for the way things stuck together in the story.

• Students use balloons and a variety of other items to observe that static electricity can make objects stick together.

• To conclude the lesson, groups of students present science-based magic tricks from books in the *Science Magic with…* series to the class and explain the science behind them.

Featured Fiction Book: *The Wartville Wizard*
Author and Illustrator: Don Madden
Publisher: Macmillan
ISBN: 0-689-71667-2
Summary: Wartville is being buried in trash. One man realizes he has the power to get rid of all the trash forever. The people of Wartville must make some positive changes.

Part 1: Building Bridges

Building Student Knowledge and Motivation

Demonstrate several simple commercial magic tricks for the class. Turn to a clean sheet on your science chart and label three columns: "Magic Trick," "Is It Really Magic?" and "How We Think It Works." Ask students, "Were these tricks really magic? Why or why not?" Brainstorm as a class, recording all ideas in the "Is It Really Magic?" column but not commenting at this time. Place the magic tricks in a center along with their instructions and several books about magic or famous magicians. Over several days, give groups of students time to practice the magic tricks and try to determine how they work.

Simple magic tricks such as "magic nail box," "penny change to dime," "magic ball," and "magic coloring books" are available in kits at toy stores or individually from magic stores or a magic supply company such as Metro Magic, 1855 South University Dr., Davie, FL 33324; 954/473-2385.

Getting Ready to Read

Hold up each magic trick from the center in turn and ask students for their proposed explanations. Record all ideas in the "How We Think It Works" column. (For younger students, discuss one magic trick each day for several days until all the magic tricks have been discussed.)

Show the cover of *The Wartville Wizard* and ask students what they think the book has to do with magic. Tell students to listen for examples of magic as you read the story.

Bridging to the Science Activity

For lower grades, we do not recommend that you discuss positive and negative charges. However, these concepts are appropriate for older students; thus, we have provided two separate Bridging to the Science Activity ideas.

For lower grades

Tell the class you are going to perform a magic trick. Show the class an inflated balloon, and then hold it against the wall and let go. (The balloon falls.) Tell the class you will make the balloon stick to the wall. Hide the balloon in a "magic" box or behind a "magic" screen and secretly charge the balloon by rubbing it with a wool cloth. As you are charging the balloon, use magical gestures and words (such as "abracadabra"). Bring out the balloon and demonstrate with a flourish that it sticks to the wall. Ask, "Is this trick magic? Why or why not?" List this trick on the science chart and record ideas in the "Is It Really Magic?" column.

Tell the class, "I performed this trick as a magician. A magician doesn't tell how a trick works. Now let's look at this trick from a scientist's point of view. A scientist looks for explanations." Have the class brainstorm possible reasons the balloon stuck to the wall the second time. Students may say that the box was magic, that your gestures or words were magical, or that you have secretly placed tape on the wall or balloon. List all responses in the "How We Think It Works" column, but do not comment on responses at this time. Based on this list, repeat your trick several more times, testing each factor listed but not charging the balloon. When you have tested all of the suggested factors, and if none of those factors involved rubbing the balloon, tell students, "Maybe the balloon stuck because I charged it by rubbing it with this cloth." Charge the balloon in view of the class and show them that it sticks to the wall. Tell students, "The balloon sticks to the wall because of static electricity. Now we will do a science activity in which we will use static electricity to make things stick to each other, like the trash stuck to the people in *The Wartville Wizard*."

For upper grades

Develop a class definition of "magic." Through a class discussion, have students brainstorm possible explanations besides magic for the way things stick together in the story. Tell students that magic is a fun explanation for events in a story, but that a scientist trying to explain an event must look for an explanation based on scientific methods and ideas. Tell students they will be making balloons and a variety of other items stick together in a way that seems magical and that they will be learning that we have a scientific explanation for these events.

Ask, "Have you ever seen a balloon stick to someone's head? How do you make it stick?" *Rub it on someone's hair.* Demonstrate by rubbing a balloon on your hair. This will put a negative charge on the balloon. Explain that when some objects rub together, negative charges move from one to the other. Bring the charged balloon near your hair; your hair and the balloon will attract. Explain that when the negative charges left your hair, your hair became positively charged. Since negative and positive charges attract, the balloon and your hair stuck together. Now, charge two balloons by rubbing on your hair. Ask, "Are these balloons negative or positive charged?" *They are negatively charged.* Ask, "What will happen when they come near each other?" *They will push each other away.* Demonstrate for the students.

Part 2: Science Activity

Materials

For the Procedure
Per pair of students
- 2 different-colored balloons
- single-ply sheet of facial tissue
- small paper cup containing about 3 ounces puffed rice
- small paper plate
- (optional) wool cloth

 Some hair textures do not generate a charge very well. In this case, use a wool cloth.

Safety and Disposal

For health reasons, be sure that two students do not rub their hair on the same balloon. Caution students not to eat the salt and pepper or get either in their eyes. No special disposal procedures are required.

Getting Ready

Inflate the balloons and tie them closed.

Procedure

Part A: Testing the First Set of Items

1. Have one student in each pair tear tissue into little pieces and put them on the plate while the other gently rubs the balloon on his or her hair.

   A piece of wool cloth may be used as an alternative to hair. Be sure that each student in each pair has a different-colored balloon (so they can tell them apart) and that only one student rubs his or her hair on any one balloon.

2. Explain to the students that they have now charged their balloons.

3. Have students in each pair take turns holding the charged balloon over the plate. Ask, "What happens?" *The tissue sticks to the balloon.* Explain that they have seen static electricity in action. Have students dispose of the tissue pieces.

4. Have one student in each pair pour the puffed rice on the plate. Have the other student rub the balloon on his or her hair and wave the charged balloon over the puffed rice. Ask, "What happens?" *The charged balloon picks up the pieces of rice.* Have students dispose of the puffed rice and save the cups for Part B.

5. Ask, "What other examples of static electricity have you experienced?" *Static cling on clothes coming out of the dryer, hair standing up after being combed, being shocked when taking off a sweater, or walking across a carpeted room and being shocked when reaching for a metal doorknob or another person.*

6. Discuss how static electricity could be mistaken for magic. Ask, "How could you show someone who doesn't know about static electricity that the balloon in this activity is not really magic?" Discuss various methods.

7. Tell students that tomorrow they will be testing items from home to see if they can be picked up by a charged balloon. Tell them to bring five items from home (such as small seeds, spices, and small pieces of paper or tissue) to test. If desired, send a letter home to parents explaining the project.

Part B: Testing Items from Home

1. Have students work in pairs to see if they can pick up their objects from home with a charged balloon.

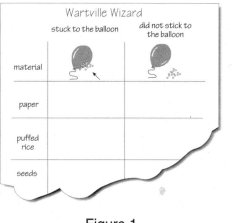

Figure 1

2. If an object sticks to the balloon, have the students save it in a cup. If an object does not stick, tell them to put it in a pile.

3. Make a large chart with two columns labeled "Stuck to the Balloon" and "Did Not Stick to the Balloon." (See Figure 1.) For younger students, you may want to add a picture cue to each label, such as a picture of a balloon with (or without) things stuck to it.

4. Have each pair of students glue small samples of the items they tested to the appropriate areas of the chart. (They should save some of each item for use in the first Writing Extension.)

5. Post the chart for use during the first Writing Extension.

6. Place all leftover items from home in the science center. Encourage students to bring in new items for the center. Tell students to bring their own balloons

when they visit the science center. Give them the opportunity to visit the science center, test items with their balloons, and add new items to the science chart.

Science Extensions

1. Experiment with different sizes of paper to find out the maximum size that the balloon can lift.

2. Divide the class into small groups. Privately assign each group a science "magic trick." One source for such tricks is a series of books entitled *Science Magic with…*, by Chris Oxlade (Barron's). Topics in the series include machines, shapes and materials, magnets, forces, sound, light, water, and air. Another book is *The Klutz Book of Magnetic Magic*, by Paul Doherty (Klutz, ISBN 1-878-25786-2). This book includes 10 round magnets and a Brazilian 50 centavo piece. Tell each group to practice their "trick" and prepare to present their trick and explain the science behind it to the class. Have each group present their tricks and discuss. You may wish to have students demonstrate and explain their magic tricks as a take-home activity.

Science Explanation

The following explanation is intended for the teacher's information. Modify the explanation for students as required.

Atoms are the building blocks of matter. Atoms are made of smaller particles that have electric charges—protons are positively charged and electrons are negatively charged—as well as neutrons, which have no charge. Electrons can sometimes move from one atom to another. For example, when you rub a balloon against your hair, the friction causes some of the electrons from your hair to be transferred to the balloon. After this exchange, the balloon becomes negatively charged with an excess of electrons, and the hair is positively charged with a shortage of electrons. Some materials are affected this way more than others, and scientists do not yet completely understand why particular objects become charged the way they do.

Objects with the same net charge repel each other; for example, two negatively charged objects repel, as do two positively charged objects. After you rub your hair with a balloon, this repulsion causes the positively-charged strands of hair to repel each other and therefore stand on end. Objects with opposite charges attract each other. If the students have studied magnets, explain that electric charges have the same rules of attraction as magnetic poles. (Like poles repel, and opposite poles attract.) As in magnets, the closer the charges are to one another, the bigger the force.

Objects can attract each other when one is negatively charged (such as the balloon) and the other is not charged (such as the tissue paper and rice used in this activity). For example, when a negatively charged balloon is brought near neutral tissue paper, the negative charge on the balloon causes some of the electrons on the surface of the tissue paper to shift slightly, creating a small region of positive charge on the tissue. This positive region is then attracted to the balloon, and the tissue jumps to the balloon's surface.

Part 3: Lesson Extensions

Writing Extensions

Figure 2

- Put two containers in a central location in the room. Label these like the chart used in Part B of the Procedure. After students glue samples of their items on the chart, have them place the leftover materials in the appropriate container. Remind students about Jimmy VanSlammer in *The Wartville Wizard*—he was so covered with trash that only his legs showed. Have students draw a picture of what they think Jimmy looked like under all that trash. Depending on students' grade level, have students write appropriately about static electricity and the objects that they will glue to Jimmy. Next, have students glue onto their picture of Jimmy samples of some of the items that stuck to the balloon. (See Figure 2.)

- Have students write stories about events or objects that at first seem magical but turn out, under closer inspection, not to be magical at all. Have them include in their stories descriptions of how they (or the main character) find a scientific explanation.

Part 4: For Further Study

Additional Books

Nonfiction

Title: *The Klutz Book of Magnetic Magic*
Author: Paul Doherty   Illustrator: Buc Rogers
Publisher: Klutz Press   ISBN: 1-878257-86-2
Summary: A collection of science/magic activities that explores the science of magnetism and the tricky things you can do with magnets.

Title: *Science Magic* series
Author: Chris Oxlade
Publisher: Barron's
Summary: This series contains books on science magic with magnets, forces, machines, shapes and materials, sound, light, air, and water.

References

Barhydt, F. *Science Discovery Activities Kit;* The Center for Applied Research in Education: West Nyack, NY, 1982.

Hewitt, P. *Conceptual Physics;* Little, Brown: Boston, 1985; pp 322–335.

Paulu, N. *Helping Your Child Learn Science;* U.S. Department of Education: Washington, D.C., June 1991.

Sarquis, M.; Kibbey, B; Smyth, E. "Electric Wand;" *Science Activities for Elementary Classrooms;* Flinn Scientific: Batavia, IL, 1989; pp 14–15.

Taylor, B.A.P.; Poth, J.E.; Portman, D.J. "Magic Balloon;" *Teaching Physics with TOYS: Activities for Grades K–9;* McGraw-Hill: New York, 1995; pp 79–83.

Tolman, M.; Morton, J. *Physical Science Activities for Grades 2–8;* Parker: West Nyack, NY, 1986.

Section 3:
Position and Motion of Objects

Keep Your Balance

SCIENCE CATEGORY: Position and Motion of Objects
TOPICS: Balance, Gravity, Center of Gravity, Engineering
OBJECTIVE: Students will learn that objects balance more easily when the center of gravity is below the support point.

In this lesson, students build balance toys from a given set of objects. They then apply their knowledge of balance to design a new toy from assorted everyday objects.

- Prior to beginning the lesson, students play with and observe a variety of homemade and commercial balance toys.

- As a class, students describe and discuss the toys, offering ideas about how they balance. Students then take turns walking on a make-believe high wire and offer ideas about how they kept their balance. These ideas are recorded on a science chart.

- Students hear the story *Mirette on the High Wire* and look for examples of balance in the story. Through class discussion, they add to the chart.

- Students use craft sticks, wire, and weights to construct balance toys.

- Students use assorted everyday objects to make balance toys of their own invention.

- To conclude the lesson, each student writes a set of instructions for making a balancing toy like the one he or she invented.

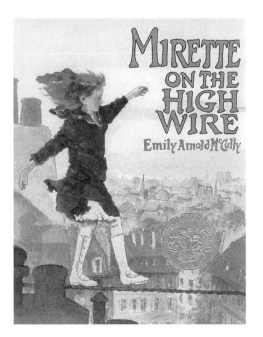

Featured Fiction Book: *Mirette on the High Wire*
Author and Illustrator: Emily Arnold McCully
Publisher: G.P. Putnam Sons
ISBN: 0-399-22130-1
Summary: Mirette sees the Great Bellini walking on a clothesline outside the boarding house where she lives. She wants to learn how to be a wire-walker. The Great Bellini teaches her, and Mirette travels with the Great Bellini as a wire-walker in the circus.

Part 1: Building Bridges

Building Student Knowledge and Motivation

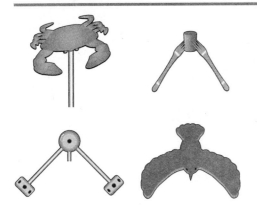

Figure 1

Set up a classroom science center with assorted commercial and homemade balance toys. (Some examples are shown in Figure 1.) Commercial balance toys come in many forms, including wire figures on bases, lightweight cardboard animals (such as butterflies) with weights on the wings, and molded plastic animals (often birds with outstretched wings). Toy and novelty catalogs are good sources for these types of toys. Give students opportunities to play with the toys over several days prior to the lesson. Ask them to record a name and description for each toy, tell whether they found it hard or easy to balance, and write some ideas about how they think it balances. (Masters for several types of science journal pages are provided in the Using Science Journals section.)

Getting Ready to Read

Divide a science chart into two columns: "What or Who Is Balancing" and "Why It Balances." As a class, have students discuss the toys from the science center, sharing their ideas about how they balance. Record their ideas on the chart.

Place a 6-foot-long piece of masking tape in a straight line on the floor. Tell the students to pretend that it is a tightrope or high wire, like ones they may have seen at the circus. Remind them that if they step on the floor and not on the tape, they have fallen off! Have each student walk quickly across the tape with their arms firmly at their sides. Ask the students if they have any ideas that would make it easier to walk across their make-believe high wire. Have each student try his or her idea. Give everyone a chance to walk across again. Instruct students to watch each person carefully for clues about how people keep their balance. After everyone has taken a turn, add observations to the science chart.

Bring out the book *Mirette on the High Wire*. Ask, "What is the girl on the cover doing? How is this similar to what you just did on the tape? How is it different? What do you think the book has to do with balance?" After sharing ideas, tell students to look for examples of balance in the story.

Bridging to the Science Activity

Bring out the science chart. Ask students what characters from the story should be added to the chart under "What or Who is Balancing." *Mirette and the Great Bellini.* Flip through the book again, pausing at pages that show Mirette or Bellini balancing on the wire. Add observations to the "Why It Balances" column.

Ask, "Can everyone balance on a high wire? Why or why not? Which is harder, balancing on a high wire or balancing one of the balance toys on your finger?" After discussing ideas, tell students that there is an important difference between walking on a high wire, a line of tape, or a balance beam and balancing any of the toys from the center. Tell students that they will be making some toys of their own to learn why some things are easy to balance and why keeping your balance on a high wire is very difficult.

Part 2: Science Activity

Materials

For the Procedure, Part A
Per class
- several commercial and/or homemade balance toys

Per student
- Popsicle™ or craft stick
- 24-inch length of 20- or 22-gauge soft wire

➤ *A good source for this wire is discarded telephone cable. Call the Public Relations Department of your local telephone company or the telephone company account manager for your school.*

- 1 or more of the following to use as weights:
  - 2 paper clips
  - 2 hex nuts
  - 2 ⅜-inch flat washers
- (optional) additional weights

For the Procedure, Part B
Per class
- assorted materials for each student to make a balance toy, such as straws, clay, Styrofoam™ balls, wire, forks, cardboard, washers, pennies, corks, marshmallows, pencils

Safety and Disposal

Caution students to work in their own space when bending wire, keeping it well away from their eyes and the eyes of other students. No special disposal procedures are required.

Procedure

Part A: Making a Balancing Stick

1. Distribute a wooden Popsicle or craft stick to each student.

2. Tell students you have been trying to balance the stick upright on your fingertip and that you would like them to show you how they would do it. Let them try for a little while.

3. Attempt to balance a stick on your fingertip again. Move your hand back and forth in an exaggerated attempt to keep the stick from falling. Ask, "If I practiced long enough, could I learn to keep this stick balanced on my finger?" Discuss the idea that, like Mirette, you could learn to balance the stick with practice.

4. Balance several of the commercial and homemade toys on your fingers, one at a time. Move your hands around to demonstrate that the toy will not fall even if it tips. Tell students, "We need to find out why I can balance this so much more easily than the stick. Let's look at ways the stick and the balance toy are different. That will give us some clues." Through a facilitated class discussion, help students bring out the idea that the commercial or homemade toy has some parts that hang or extend below your fingertip. Suggest that they use the stick, wire, and weights to test the idea that something extending downward makes an object easier to balance.

5. Distribute wire and objects you are using for weights. Give students time to work in small groups to find a way to use these items to make their sticks balance.

Do not demonstrate a solution. Some teachers are initially concerned about giving students such an open-ended task and are pleasantly surprised at their students' creativity. Figure 2 shows some examples of student solutions.

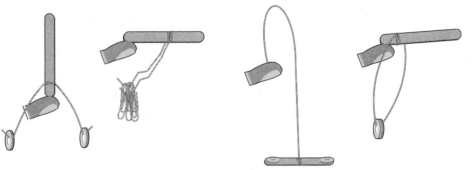

Figure 2: Many different designs are possible for the balancing stick.

6. As individuals find solutions, have them share with their neighbors. If some students are still having trouble finding a solution, have one or more students demonstrate their balancing sticks so that others can use their ideas.

7. Bring out the commercial balance toys again. Ask students to compare and contrast the commercial toys and their balancing sticks, using a Venn diagram if desired. Through a facilitated discussion, lead students to observe that in all types of balance toys, some part of the toy hangs below the support point.

8. Show students some of the pictures of Mirette and Bellini balancing. Ask, "What is the support point when they are balancing on the high wire?" *The wire itself.* "Is anything hanging below the wire when they walk?" *No.* "So how can they balance?" After discussion, bring out the idea that the characters can balance on the wire without something extending below the wire, but that it is very difficult for them—they are much less stable than the balance toys.

9. Introduce the idea that every object or person has something called a center of gravity. This center of gravity is in one particular spot on the object or person. Explain that an object balances when its center of gravity is directly above or below the point of support. When the center of gravity for an object or person is above the support point (such as the fingertip or wire), it is very difficult to balance. When the center of gravity is below the support point, it is much easier to balance.

10. Ask, "Do you think Mirette's center of gravity is above or below the wire? *Above.* "Why do you think so?" *No part of her is below the wire, and she found it hard to balance and had to practice a lot.* "Where was the craft stick's center of gravity before the wire and weights were added?" *Above the finger.* "What happened to the stick's center of gravity when the wire and weights were added in such a way that the stick balanced easily?" *It became lower than the tip of the finger.*

11. Ask students to use the terms "point of support" and "center of gravity" to describe how a tightrope walker balances. *A tightrope walker balances when her or his center of gravity is directly over the point of support (the rope).* Ask students to use the same terms to describe how a tightrope walker falls. *A tightrope walker falls when his or her center of gravity is not directly over the point of support.* Ask, "What pulls the falling tightrope walker down?" *Gravity.*

Part B: Inventing New Toys

1. Have each student choose one item from the variety of objects available and demonstrate that this object will not easily balance in some position. (For example, a pencil will not easily balance vertically on a fingertip, or a Styrofoam ball will not easily balance on the head of a pin.)

2. Next, have each student select and use additional materials to turn his/her object into a stable balance toy. Remind students to apply what they have learned about balance and center of gravity as they build their toys.

3. Have students complete the Balance Invention Data Sheet (provided).

The Balance Invention Data Sheet works well as an assessment of student understanding of balance and center of gravity.

4. Leave the commercial balance toys and materials for inventing and building balance toys in the science center for further exploration. Also include assorted nonfiction books on balance and a copy of *Mirette on the High Wire* for rereading.

Science Explanation

The following explanation is intended for the teacher's information. Modify the explanation for students as required.

The center of gravity of an object or connected group of objects is the point at which the weight of the object behaves as if concentrated. The center of gravity may be located where no actual material exists. An object balances when its center of gravity is directly above or below the point of support. Any object with its center of gravity below its point of support is stable because when it is tipped, gravity pulls it back into position. An object can balance with its center of gravity above the point of support, but the object is unstable. If the object is tipped even a little, gravity pulls it away from the balanced position. Tightrope walkers are unstable because their center of gravity is above their point of support (the rope). They need to be very skilled at keeping their center of gravity directly over the rope. This task is difficult because their center of gravity is relatively high above the rope; if they tip even a small bit, gravity pulls them away from their balanced position, and they fall (unless they can move their center of gravity back over the rope very quickly).

In Part A of the Procedure, students try to balance the stick on end with no other mass added. Under these conditions, the stick's center of gravity is well above the point of support (the fingertip), and the stick falls. The stick balances when wire and additional mass are used to move the center of gravity to a point below the support point.

Changing the position of the added mass changes the behavior of the balancing stick. For example, if all of the additional mass is concentrated directly below the stick in a small area, the toy balances but becomes less stable. If part of the additional mass is moved upward and outward, the center of gravity of the whole system is redistributed and moves upward and outward. In response, the whole system tilts or rotates to move the center of gravity back down. (Try this maneuver to see how it works.) If the center of gravity moves up to a point above the point of support, the whole system may rotate off its support point.

Changing the amount of mass also changes the behavior of the balancing stick. Adding more mass below the support point lowers the center of gravity and makes the toy more stable. Removing mass from below the support point raises the center of gravity, making the toy more difficult or impossible to balance.

Part 3: Lesson Extensions

Writing Extensions

Balance carefully.
Always walk on the wire slowly.
Look where you are walking.
A net under you is important.
Never balance alone.
Center of gravity is the key.
Exciting adventure!

1. Have each student write a set of instructions for making a balancing toy like the one he or she invented in Part B of the Procedure. Tell students the instructions must include the following: drawing of the toy, name for the toy, list of materials used, step-by-step instructions for making the toy, and an explanation of how the toy works. Students can then take turns reading their instructions to the class and demonstrating their toys.

2. Have groups of students make acrostic poems from such words as "balance" or "high wire." A sample is provided at left.

Cross-Cultural Integration

➤ *This section is intended for teacher background. You may wish to use the information in this section to develop age-appropriate activities for your classroom.*

History of the Circus

Tightrope walking like Mirette learned to do is a form of acrobatics, a main component of the modern circus. Acrobatics developed in China about 4,000 years ago. There is evidence in Egyptian wall paintings that acrobats, musicians, and dancers entertained villagers. In the third century B.C., a menagerie parade in Egypt lasted from sunrise to sunset and included numerous wild beasts.

The Olympic games held in ancient Greece featured chariot races and men standing on the bare backs of two horses that raced around a track. In Rome, an elephant is said to have walked a tightrope.

The tradition of roving entertainers continued through the Middle Ages and Renaissance in fairs, plays, and marketplaces. During the Middle Ages, individuals performed circus-type acts on street corners. They walked on tightropes, juggled, and performed balancing acts. Many of these acts included a trained bear, horse, or monkey. At the end of the show, the performers would pass among the spectators and ask for money.

The modern circus was developed in England during the 1700s by Philip Astley and soon spread to America. The early circuses were small shows with riding acts, jugglers, and clowns. The first real American circus was Rickett's circus in Philadelphia in 1792. Many of the early circuses were mobile, performing under tents in the open air. For many years, circuses traveled from town to town in colorful wagons pulled by horses. In each town, youngsters earned tickets to the circus by watering the elephants or doing other chores.

With bad roads and no street lights, travel was very hazardous for the early circuses. When a uniform rail gauge and a device for loading the wagons onto cars were invented, circuses could travel much farther by train, spurring rapid circus growth. As circus empires grew, so did personal fortunes. The trip from the railroad station into town became an elaborate circus parade, complete with beautifully carved wagons drawn by up to 40 horses. Bringing up the rear was the calliope, tooting its melody. For many rural communities, the traveling circus was the only form of entertainment for families to enjoy outside of church-sponsored outings.

With the Great Depression, many circuses failed. Later, with the coming of television, fewer people ventured out to see live performances, and the circus continued to struggle. Although it was once thought that television and video games would lead to the end of the circus' popularity, circuses are as well attended today as they have been in the past 75 years. Approximately 100 circuses travel throughout the United States every year, and an estimated 20 million people in the United States attended a circus in 1995. The Ringling Bros. and Barnum & Bailey circus, the largest and most well-known circus in the country, has been performing for over 125 years.

Part 4: For Further Study

Additional Books

Fiction

Title: *The Balancing Girl*
Author: Berniece Rabe   Illustrator: Lillian Hoban
Publisher: Trumpet Club   ISBN: 0-440-84277-8
Summary: A physically challenged child amazes her classmates with her balancing tricks. Her most amazing feat is a domino city.

Title: *The Twelve Circus Rings*
Author and Illustrator: Seymour Chwast
Publisher: Harcourt Brace Jovanovich   ISBN: 0-15-200627-3
Summary: This is a counting book in which the story centers around a boy and his sister arriving for a day at the circus. They begin at the first ring with one daredevil on a high wire.

Title: *Circus*
Author and Illustrator: Lois Ehlert
Publisher: HarperCollins   ISBN: 0-06-020252-1
Summary: Leaping lizards, marching snakes, a bear on the high wire, and others perform in a somewhat unusual circus.

References

Machotka, H. *The Magic Ring: A Year with the Big Apple Circus;* Morrow: New York, 1988.
Matsumoto, J. "Big Top's Appeal Timeless," *Variety.* 1995, 359(12), 44–45.
Taylor, B.A.P.; Poth, J.E.; Portman, D.J. "Balancing Stick;" *Teaching Physics with TOYS: Activities for Grades K–9;* McGraw-Hill: New York, 1994; pp 45–52.

Keep Your Balance

Balance Invention—Data Sheet

Draw a picture of the object you will balance.	Draw a picture of your balance invention.

Describe your balance invention and explain how it works.

Ramps and Cars

SCIENCE CATEGORY: Position and Motion of Objects
TOPICs: Inclined Planes, Motion, Gravity
OBJECTIVE: Students learn that energy is needed to push a car up a ramp and that the height of the ramp affects the distance traveled and how quickly the car moves down the ramp.

In this lesson, students use a toy racetrack and car to explore the effects of ramp height on the movement of a toy car. Students will observe, compare, measure, and communicate their findings through charts, graphs, and discussion.

- Prior to beginning the lesson, students have an opportunity to play with ramps and toy cars in a classroom activity center and look for ramps in their environment.

- Through a class discussion, students talk about various kinds of ramps they have seen and the ways they are used.

- Students hear the story *The Lazy Bear* and look for something similar to a ramp in the story.

- Students discuss the hills in the story and how far and fast Lazy Bear's ride was on each hill. They also discuss the difference in effort between going up a hill or ramp and going down.

- Students conduct an experiment to determine the effect of ramp height on the movement of a toy car.

- To conclude the lesson, students write a story about Lazy Bear riding down the different ramp heights tested by the class. They discuss which ride he likes best and why.

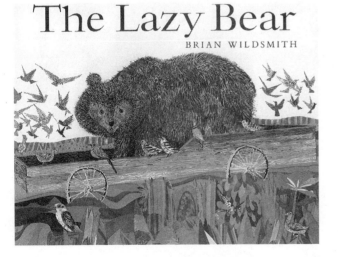

Featured Fiction Book: *The Lazy Bear*
Author and Illustrator: Brian Wildsmith
Publisher: Oxford University Press
ISBN: 0-19-272158-5
Summary: A bear discovers a wagon and sits inside it. To his surprise, he rolls down the hill. He enjoys the ride so much that he does it again and again. He lets his animal friends ride down the hill, but they must push the "lazy bear" up the hill. What should they do?

Part 1: Building Bridges

Building Student Knowledge and Motivation

Three or four days before beginning the lesson, set up a center in the classroom with a simple ramp and assorted cars for students to play with. Ask students to look for examples of ramps they see every day and be prepared to describe them to the class.

Getting Ready to Read

As a class, discuss different kinds of ramps (for example, wheelchair ramps, slides, loading ramps, and ramps in parking garages). Ask, "What are ramps used for?" Also ask, "Is it as easy to walk up a ramp as down?" Tell students, "We've talked about ramps in our environment. Now we're going to read about a bear who used something like a ramp."

Show students the cover of *The Lazy Bear.* Tell them to listen to the story and look for something similar to a ramp.

Bridging to the Science Activity

After you finish reading, briefly discuss the "ramps" in the story, referring back to the pictures as necessary. Make the point that the sides of the hills are like ramps. Ask students, "Which was easier in the story: riding down the hill or pushing the wagon up the hill?" Draw students' attention to the picture of the hill when the animals push the Lazy Bear over the other side. Ask, "Are both sides equally steep? Which side is steeper? How is this ride different from the other ones? Which ride did the Lazy Bear and his friends like best?" Tell students that they will be testing toy cars and ramps to decide which ride the Lazy Bear and his friends would like best. Students must be told that while science activities are fun, this is not a play activity. They must follow directions and move the cars only when instructed to do so.

Part 2: Science Activity

Materials

For the Procedure
Per class
- 3 same-sized blocks or books
- Hot Wheels®- or Matchbox®-type race car

Be sure to use the same car for the entire experiment.

- 5–6 feet of straight plastic race car track

Darda®, Hot Wheels, and Majorette® make racetrack sets suitable for this activity, but since only the straight pieces are needed for the activity, buying complex sets is not cost-effective. Darda and Hot Wheels sell accessory sets with just straight track pieces, but not all toy stores carry them. Students may have track at home that they can bring in. (See Getting Ready.)

- 4-foot-long board to use as a ramp
- any or all of the following items to measure and record distances:
  - meterstick, ruler, measuring wheel, or tape measure
  - premarked measuring strip taped to the floor and crayons or markers
  - 4 each of 3 different-colored stickers
  - about 300 feet of adding machine tape
- digital stopwatch
- (optional) wall chart made in 1 of the following ways (See Getting Ready):
  - paper or posterboard mounted on the wall or bulletin board
  - drawn on the chalkboard

Safety and Disposal

No special safety or disposal procedures are required.

Getting Ready

This activity requires three basic components: a track on a board that can be elevated on one end, a means of measuring the distance traveled by the car, and a means of recording and displaying the results of the experiments. These components (described below) can be set up in a variety of ways to suit your classroom. Make sure you have enough floor space to allow cars to come to rest on their own (10–20 feet beyond the end of the ramp). Usually a classroom or hall has adequate space.

1. Prop a board up at one end to form a ramp. Lay the plastic racetrack on the surface of the board. (See Figure 1.) Tape the plastic track to the upper end of the ramp. Make sure the track extends beyond the board (as shown) to provide a smoother transition from the track to the floor.

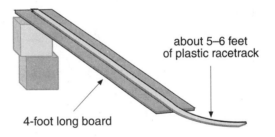

about 5–6 feet of plastic racetrack

4-foot long board

Figure 1: Set up the racetrack with a board underneath.

2. Choose a method for marking and measuring the distances the car travels for the three different elevations of the track. Below are some ideas:

   - After each trial for one elevation, have students mark the car's position on the floor with the same color of sticker. Repeat, using a different-colored sticker for each elevation of the ramp. Then students can measure the distances using a meterstick, ruler, measuring wheel, or tape measure. Students who cannot yet measure distance in these ways can measure distance by counting the numbers of floor tiles traveled by the car.

   - Tape a long strip of paper to the floor along the path the cars will run. Measure and mark distance intervals, such as half-meters, along the paper. After each trial, students can use the paper strip to measure the distance the car traveled to the nearest half-meter (or whatever unit you used). If desired, students can mark the distances on the paper strip using crayons, markers, or colored stickers.

- After each trial, roll a piece of adding machine tape from the end of the ramp to the position of the car. Tape the paper strips in the appropriate position on a chart as shown in Figure 2. If desired, you can have students measure the lengths of the strips. But even without measuring, the relative distances are clearly visible.

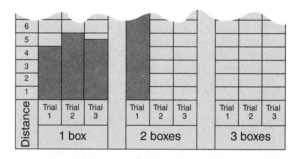

1 Box	
Trial 1	← If using paper strips, attach the end of the first strip here.
Trial 2	
Trial 3	
2 Boxes	
Trial 1	
T l 3	

Figure 2: The paper strips in this type of chart will be the actual distances the cars traveled.

3. Use a bar graph to record distances traveled, measured in either half-meters or floor tiles. (See Figure 3.)

Figure 3: A bar graph can represent the distances traveled.

Procedure

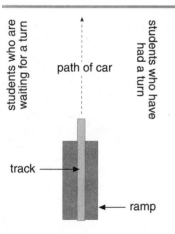

students who are waiting for a turn

path of car

students who have had a turn

track

ramp

Figure 4

Do the following procedure as a whole-class activity. Students can participate as releasers, markers, measurers, timers, watchers, or recorders. With three trials of each of three ramp heights (a total of nine trials), and six jobs per trial, every student should have a chance to participate. The following classroom management strategy has been effective with this activity: Set up the ramp and track. Have all students stand on one side of the track. Call the first group of six students to the ramp. After they have completed their jobs, have them stand to the other side of the track. (See Figure 4.) Call the second group to the ramp. Repeat until everyone is standing on the other side of the ramp. Give students second turns as needed to complete all trials.

1. Review and, if desired, have students practice the tasks that will be performed by the person in each role:

   - Releaser—releases the car
   - Timer—times the ride
   - Watcher—calls out when the car stops
   - Marker—marks where the car stops
   - Measurer—measures the distance the car travels
   - Recorder—records distance and time data

2. Show students the three blocks. Demonstrate how high the ramp will be with one, two, and three blocks under it.

3. Place one block under one end of the board. The track will extend beyond the edge of the board to lie on the floor.

4. Have a Releaser push the car up the ramp to the top of the track and hold it there. Ask, "What did he/she use to push the car?" Students may answer "hand." Through discussion, make the point that he/she used energy to push the car. (A person's hand requires energy to move.)

5. Make sure the Timer has a stopwatch ready. Instruct the timer to start the stopwatch when you say "Go" and stop the stopwatch when the Watcher says "Stop."

6. Make sure the Releaser is ready. Instruct the releaser to let go as soon as you say "Go." Make sure the student does not push the car.

7. Make sure the Watcher is ready. Instruct the watcher to say, "Stop" as soon as the car reaches the bottom of the ramp.

8. Say, "Go," causing the Releaser to let go of the car and the Timer to start the stopwatch.

9. After the car comes to rest, have Markers, Measurers, and Recorders do their jobs.

10. Do two more trials at this ramp height to see if the car stops at about the same place.

11. Add one more block under the ramp for a total of two blocks, and do three trials at this ramp height.

12. Ask students to consider the distances the car travelled with one block and with two. Then, based on the data gathered so far, have them predict the distance the car will travel with three blocks.

   Prediction is introduced at this stage of the activity because prior to this, students may not have enough knowledge of the behavior of cars and ramps to make a meaningful prediction. Explain to students that "prediction" without knowledge is not science; it is only a random guess.

13. Add one more block under the ramp for a total of three blocks, and do three trials at this ramp height.

14. Create a class display of results.

Class Discussion

1. Ask students to look at the display of results from the experiment. Ask, "Were the results exactly the same for all three trials at a height of one block?" *No.* Explain that scientists do the same experiment over and over to make sure of their results. Introduce the ideas of variability and experimental error. Sometimes, something can happen during one trial of an experiment to make the results of that trial very different from all the others. Ask, "What kinds of things happened (or could have happened) with some of our trials to cause varying results?" *Someone could push the car instead of just letting go, a wheel could get stuck, or something on the floor could stop the car.*

2. As a class, look at the display of results and discuss the following questions. Older students can calculate average values and answer these questions based on their calculations.

   a. With which ramp height did the car travel the farthest? Why?

   b. With which ramp height did the car travel down the ramp fastest? Why?

   c. When did the car stop closest to the ramp?

   d. Why is it harder to go up a ramp than down? Why was it hard for Lazy Bear's friends to push him up the hill?

3. Reread the part of the story where the bear's friends make a plan to teach the bear a lesson. Ask, "In the story, down which side of the hill did the bear go faster? How can you tell?" Point out and discuss the word "hurtling" and the phrase "faster and faster sped the wagon." Ask students to examine the illustration and compare the two sides of the hill to the ramps in the experiment. Ask, "How did the bear's experiences on the hill compare to our results in the experiment?"

Science Explanation

The following explanation is intended for the teacher's information. Modify the explanation for students as required.

In this activity, you observe that the toy car rolls farther as the incline of the track becomes steeper. The car rolls farther with a steeper incline because it is moving faster when it reaches the bottom of the ramp. The faster the car is moving when it leaves the ramp, the more distance it can cover before friction slows and stops it.

So why is the car moving faster when it reaches the bottom of a steeper incline? To understand why, we need to think about how the force of gravity acts on objects. If you hold a toy car in the air and drop it, it falls to the ground. When you place the same toy car at the top of an inclined ramp and let go, the car rolls down the ramp. In both cases the car moves because the force of gravity acts on it. This force of gravity is the weight of the car. But the car falls to the ground much faster than it rolls down the ramp. Why? In addition to a small effect from friction, there is another important factor.

When you hold the car in the air and drop it, the entire force of gravity (or weight) acts straight down with no opposing force, causing the car to accelerate and reach

Teaching Physical Science through Children's Literature

the ground quickly. (See Example 1 in Figure 5.) When the car is sitting on a level track, the force of gravity pulling down is equal and opposite to the track force pushing up, and the car does not move. Notice that the track force is perpendicular to the track. When we angle the track upward, the track force remains perpendicular to the track and no longer cancels out the force of gravity: the car rolls down the ramp. As we angle the track higher, the track force decreases more and the car rolls faster. When the track is completely vertical, the track force disappears, just as if the car had been dropped.

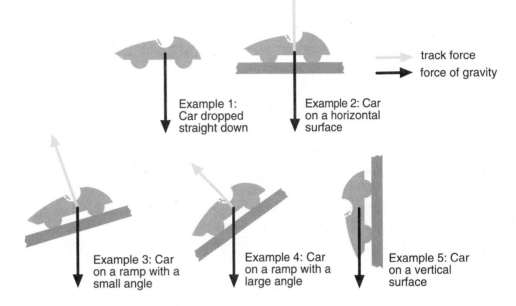

Figure 5: As the angle of the track changes, the track force changes.

You can illustrate this phenomenon in a simple demonstration. Begin by attaching a rubber band to the back of a car. Place this toy on the incline and while holding the rubber band in one hand raise the incline with the other. Notice that the rubber band stretches more and more as you raise the board. (See Figure 6.) This indicates that as the angle of the incline increases, more of the weight of the car points down the incline.

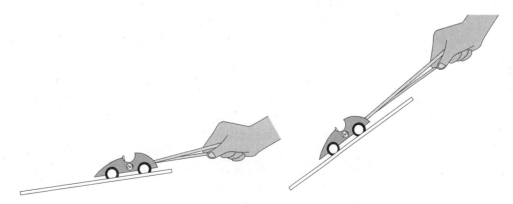

Figure 6: As the slope increases, so does the pull on the rubber band.

Part 3: Lesson Extensions

Writing Extension

Have students write stories in which the Lazy Bear rides in the car on the ramps the class tested. Have students respond to the following questions in their stories: Which ride went farthest? Which ride was shortest? Which ride was fastest? Which ride does the Lazy Bear like best and why? What if the Lazy Bear told you he wanted to go even farther? What kind of ramp would you build? To help students test their hypotheses, put a car in the classroom science center with materials to make ramps of different heights and lengths, a copy of *The Lazy Bear,* and a selection of nonfiction books on motion and vehicles.

Math Extension

Have students average the distance data from the three trials for one of the ramps tested. Have them round the average to the nearest whole number. Point out the use of averaging to compare the performances of athletes in baseball, bowling, and basketball.

Part 4: For Further Study

Additional Books

Nonfiction

Title: *The Way Things Work*
Author: David Macaulay
Publisher: Houghton Mifflin   ISBN: 0-395-42857-2
Summary: Text and numerous detailed illustrations introduce and explain the scientific principles and workings of hundreds of machines, including a lawn sprinkler, pneumatic drill, electric guitar, and a smoke detector.

Title: *Force & Motion*
Author: Peter Lafferty
Publisher: Dorling Kindersley   ISBN: 1-879431-85-8
Summary: Explores the principles of force and motion, describing how they have been applied in modern times.

Title: *Wheels*
Author: Byron Barton
Publisher: Crowell   ISBN: 0-690-03951-4
Summary: Highlights the invention of the wheel and its importance and uses.

Title: *Transport on Land, Road, & Rail*
Author: Eryl Davies
Publisher: Franklin Watts   ISBN: 0-531-15741-5
Summary: Surveys the development of land transportation in relation to the needs, skills, and technologies of people living at different periods in history.

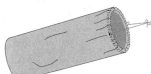

Catch the Wind

SCIENCE CATEGORY: Position and Motion of Objects

TOPICS: Using Wind to Do Work, Forces, Engineering

OBJECTIVE: Students learn that wind—moving air—can be used to do work and that, even though we can't see wind, we can see its effects.

In this lesson, students make sailboats and observe how the boats move. Students communicate observations about the wind through discussion and in writing.

- Prior to beginning the lesson, students observe wind socks outside the classroom and learn that even though wind is invisible, its effects are visible.

- As a class, students brainstorm a list of things that catch the wind.

- Students hear the story *Mirandy and Brother Wind* and discuss how Mirandy uses the wind to help her. Then students brainstorm a list of ways we use the wind to help us.

- Students design sails and test their designs by measuring the distance their boats travel.

- Students use their observations of the individual sail designs to design and test improved sail designs.

- To conclude the lesson, students apply what they've learned about wind in one or more writing exercises.

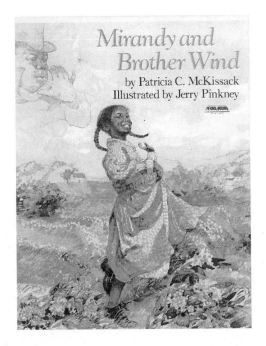

Featured Fiction Book: *Mirandy and Brother Wind*

Author: Patricia McKissack

Illustrator: Jerry Pinkney

Publisher: Alfred A. Knopf, Inc.

ISBN: 0-394-88765-4

Summary: Tomorrow night is Mirandy's first cakewalk, and somehow, some way, she's going to be kicking up her heels with Brother Wind! But how do you catch the Wind? With neighbors up and down Ridgetop suggesting all manner of strategies, and friend Ezel laughing at each foiled one, Mirandy grows ever more determined: she'll get hold of that Brother Wind yet!

Part 1: Building Bridges

Building Student Knowledge and Motivation

Several days before beginning the lesson, put some wind socks outside the classroom window and set out some magazines and books on sailing and the force of air. Allow students to observe the wind socks and discuss their observations. Emphasize that wind cannot be seen—only its effects are visible.

Getting Ready to Read

Have students sit in a circle with a fan blowing on them, or if possible, take the children outside if there is a breeze. Ask students, "What do you feel? Can you catch the wind?" Label a science chart with two columns: "Things that Catch the Wind" and "How We Make Wind Work for Us." Brainstorm and record on the chart a list of things that catch the wind. Explain that in the story you're about to read, Mirandy wants to catch the wind. Ask, "Do you think she can? Why do you think she would want to catch the wind?"

Students may be confused by the way the author treats Brother Wind as a real person in the story. Show students a few pictures of Brother Wind. Ask how the illustrator shows that Brother Wind is not actually a person, like the other characters in the story. *He is blue-tinted and we can see through him, unlike the other characters.* Why might the author and illustrator want to portray the wind the way they do? Remind them of what they learned from observing the wind socks—wind is invisible, but its effects are visible. Talk about using imagination to "see" something that is invisible and to describe an invisible thing to someone else.

Bridging to the Science Activity

After reading *Mirandy and Brother Wind,* engage students in a discussion. Ask, "How did Mirandy get the wind to work for her in the story?" Have students use a quilt or blanket to imitate Mirandy's first attempt to catch Brother Wind. "Does it work? Why or why not?" Act out the other two ways Mirandy tried to catch Brother Wind (with the cider bottle and in the barn). Ask students, "How did she finally catch him? Can we catch the wind and make it work for us?" Brainstorm ways we use the wind to help us, and record the ideas on the science chart in the "How We Make Wind Work for Us" column. *Sailing, flying kites, etc.* Tell students that they are going to make sails for milk carton sailboats that will move by "catching the wind."

Part 2: Science Activity

Materials

For the Procedure
Per class
- hot-melt glue gun and glue
- several large disposable plastic wallpaper troughs (each about 2½ feet long)

Inexpensive disposable plastic wallpaper troughs are available at many discount and home-decorating stores.

- water
- several inexpensive plastic tape measures

You will need at least one tape measure per trough, and you may choose to have two per trough. (See Getting Ready, Step 3.)

Per student
- 6-inch straw
- paper

The paper will be used for sails. The purpose of this activity is to determine what makes a good sail for the milk-carton boats; therefore, provide students with a variety of papers.

- scissors
- (optional) crayons

Per 2 students
- ½-pint milk carton

The tall kind works better than the shorter, square kind.

For the Science Extensions
❶ Per student
- tag board
- scissors

❷ Per wind sock
- rectangle of taffeta or ripstop nylon about 21 inches x 24 inches
- colorful scraps of lightweight fabric or permanent markers
- plastic lid from a 5-pound coffee can
- scissors
- 3-yard length of yarn
- (optional) white glue

Per class
- hot-melt glue gun or stapler

Safety and Disposal

The teacher or an adult assistant should be the only one to hand the hot-melt glue gun. Use extreme caution as hot glue can cause serious burns. No special disposal procedures are required.

Getting Ready

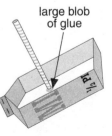

large blob of glue

Figure 1

1. Cut the milk cartons in half lengthwise and, if necessary, staple the opened end closed. (One milk carton will make two boats.)

Use caution when working with hot-melt glue.

2. Hot-glue a straw to the bottom of each boat. (See Figure 1.)

3. Hot-glue the tape measure to one side of each wallpaper trough as shown in Figure 2. Be sure not to stretch the tape. If desired, glue one tape measure with the inches side up and a second tape measure on the other side of the trough with the centimeters side up.

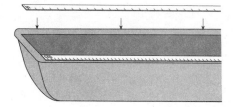

Figure 2: Hot-glue one or two tape measures to the sides of the trough.

Procedure

Part A: Making Initial Observations

1. Show the students one of the milk carton boats and tell them they will be creating and testing paper sails for the boats. Ask students to consider the list they made of things that catch the wind. Discuss some of the features these items have in common. Ask, "Based on what you know about things that catch the wind, how could you make a sail that would catch the most wind and move the boat furthest? What shape would it be? What material would you make it from?"

2. Give students time to select their paper and make their sails. Students may cut the paper into shapes, fold the paper, etc. If time allows, students can decorate their sails with crayons.

3. After the students cut out their sails, have them make two small slits to put the straw through. Remind students to start with small cuts and make them bigger only after trying to push the straw through the two cuts. (The sail will slip down the straw if the cuts are too big to hold the straw snugly.)

4. Explain that in an experiment, we want to keep everything the same except the one thing we are testing. Ask, "What are we testing in this experiment?" *The sail.* Through facilitated discussion, have the class come up with a list of things they need to try to keep the same in the experiment. *The boat, the mast, the container and water the boat sails in, the amount of air in the sail.*

5. Explain that the class has already kept everything on the list the same except the amount of air in the sail. To fairly compare the sails, students need to try to blow close to the same amount of air into the sail each time. Tell students to take a normal breath and blow once when testing sails.

6. Using the wallpaper troughs of water, have students take turns blowing into the sail to move the boat across the water; then have them measure and record the distances their boats traveled. Tell students to carefully observe how well their sails worked and to think about how they could redesign their sails to make the boats travel even farther. (In Part B they will have a chance to design a new sail as part of a team.)

Part B: Using Observations to Develop Sail Designs

1. Label four columns on a science chart as shown in Figure 3.

Teaching Physical Science through Children's Literature

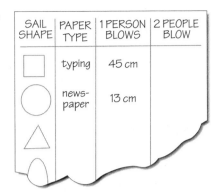

SAIL SHAPE	PAPER TYPE	1 PERSON BLOWS	2 PEOPLE BLOW
▢	typing	45 cm	
◯	news-paper	13 cm	
△			
⬭			

Figure 3: Make a science chart.

2. Divide students into teams to design and test new sails. Tell the teams to use the results they observed in Part A as a basis for developing a new sail design. Have students discuss the success of their first sail with their teammates so the team can come up with one new design based on all of the members' observations. (How well did the material seem to work? Was the shape effective or did it not work well? Was the sail too big or too small?) Give each team time to design a new sail, trace it on the chart in the "sail shape" column, indicate what kind of paper they used in the "paper type" column, and attach the sail to their boat.

3. Have each team sail their boat, with one team member giving one strong blow on the sail and the others noting and recording the spot where the boat stops. Have them write the distance traveled in the "1 person blows" column.

 Emphasize that students should blow only once.

4. Have each team increase the force of blows by having two people give one strong blow on the sail at the same time. Have them record the distance traveled in the "2 people blow" column.

5. If time allows, have each team design and test other sails, recording the distances traveled when blown by one person and by two people.

6. As a class, discuss any general conclusions students can draw from data on the chart. For example, do certain sail shapes help the boats to travel farther? Do boats with larger sails travel farther than those with smaller ones? Do two people blowing at once make the boat go further? Are there variables other than the size, shape, and material of the sail that would affect how far it went? (Examples: how close the sail was to the base of the boat, how hard the student was able to blow, other sources of wind during the experiment.)

7. Return to the science chart from Getting Ready to Read. Ask students what the items in the Things that Catch the Wind column have in common with each other and with the sails tested in Parts A and B. Let students suggest reasons for what they have observed in the activity.

Part C: Testing New Ideas About Sailboats

1. Review the idea that in an experiment we want to keep everything the same except the one thing we are testing. Explain that in the first part of the experiment we changed only the sail, but we changed more than one thing about the sail (for example, the paper type, the shape, and the size). Tell students that to make the experiment better, you want them to test their sails

Catch the Wind

again but change only one thing about the sail at a time. For example, they could make sails of the same shape out of the same paper and vary only the size of the sail.

2. Leave the water troughs, sail-making materials, and sailing magazines in a classroom science center.

3. Challenge students to test some of the ideas discussed in Part B, Step 6. For example, if bigger sails seem to help the boats travel further, what if the sail is even bigger? Can a sail be too big? What if three people blow on the sail? What if two people blow from opposite sides?

4. Leave the science chart out for students to record new sail shapes and measurements.

Science Extensions

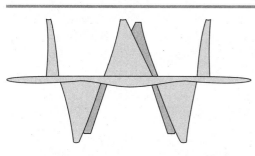

Figure 4: Sections of an air wheel folded up and down alternately

1. The same concept of using wind to help move objects can be demonstrated using an air wheel (a "wind roller"). Copy the Air Wheel Template (provided) onto tag board. Cut around the outside of the circle. Punch a small hole in the center and cut on the dotted lines. Fold the sections up and then down, alternately, until all sections are folded. When you are finished, four sections will point out from one side of the wheel, and four sections will point out from the opposite side. (See Figure 4.) Take the wheel outside on a windy day. Ask students to try to make the wheel move. If students hold the wheel on its edge on the ground, let the wind catch it, and release it, the wheel will move along nicely. The distance traveled can be measured and graphed.

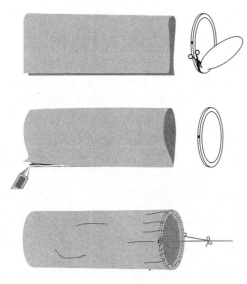

Figure 5: Make a wind sock with fabric and a coffee can lid.

2. As a class project, make one or more wind socks to catch the wind. For each wind sock, use a rectangle of taffeta or ripstop nylon about 21 inches x 24 inches. Leave the fabric out where students can take turns gluing lightweight scraps onto the fabric or drawing on it with permanent markers. Cut out the center of the plastic lid from a 5-pound coffee can so only the edge remains, forming a ring. Fold the material roughly in half lengthwise and lay it flat in front of you, so that the edge on the bottom extends slightly beyond the edge on top. (See Figure 5.) Working a few inches at a time, hot-glue the two long edges together to make a tube. (Work quickly so that the glue doesn't dry before the seam is made.) Wrap the plastic ring with the material, stapling it on or hot-gluing it to the ring with a glue gun. Punch two holes on opposite sides of the covered ring. Thread the yarn or heavy string through the two holes in the plastic ring and material and knot it. Take the wind sock outside to catch the wind.

Science Explanation

 The following explanation is intended for the teacher's information. Modify the explanation for students as required.

All matter is made up of very small particles. In gases these particles are in constant motion. By blowing, the students exhale gas particles from their lungs. While an individual gas particle has little effect on an object it hits, if an extremely large number of gas particles hit an object, they can have a very noticeable effect. In this activity, students force air (or wind) into the sail, which causes enough gas particles to collide with the sail to push the boat a short distance.

Part 3: Lesson Extensions

Writing Extensions

1. Ask students to write about the experiment, responding to the following questions: "What did we do? How did we do it? Did our sails work well? Which sail made the boat sail the farthest? least far?" Have the students compare their sail designs.

2. Take students outside on a day when the wind is blowing. Have them sit down in a circle in the grass to experience the wind using their five senses. Ask the following questions:

   - How does the wind feel?
   - How does the wind look?
   - How does the wind taste?
   - How does the wind smell?
   - How does the wind sound?

   Return to the classroom. Give each student a sheet of paper and ask them to draw one thing about the wind that they experienced through their senses. When the drawings are complete, take dictation or allow students to write about their pictures. Examples: The wind felt _____. The wind looked _____. Put the drawings together in a class book for everyone to read.

3. Wind words: Ask students to share all of the "wind words" they can think of—words that would tell about the wind. As students brainstorm, write the words on chart paper. As a further extension, students can categorize the words into naming words (nouns) or action words (verbs).

4. Wind idioms: List several idioms that use wind in the phrase (for example, "run like the wind," "knocked the wind out of my sails," "the wind beneath my wings"). Ask students to pick an idiom, copy it onto a piece of drawing paper, and illustrate its meaning. These pictures could also be collected in a class book.

Math Extension

Using data collected in Part B, rank students' boats from "traveled least distance" to "traveled most distance." Draw the vertical and horizontal axes of a graph on the chalkboard. Label the horizontal axis with units of distance and the vertical axis with names of students in the order determined above. Have students tape their sails under their names. Each student should make a bar on the graph to indicate how far his or her boat traveled. As a class, look at the graph. Can any conclusions be drawn about the most effective shape and size of a sail?

Cross-Cultural Integration

➤ *This section is intended for teacher background. You may wish to use the information in this section to develop age-appropriate activities for your classroom.*

A cakewalk, like the one Mirandy and Ezel perform in the story, is a dance of African-American 19th-century origin made popular and diffused through imitations of it in blackface minstrel shows (especially the "walk-around finales") and later, vaudeville and burlesque. The cakewalk is thought to have originated with American slaves parodying their white owners' high manners and fancy dances; the name is supposedly derived from the prize (presumably a cake) given to the best dancers among a group of slaves. No specific dance steps were associated with the cakewalk, but it featured couples prancing, strutting, parading arm in arm, with bows back and forward, salutes to spectators, and high kicks with arched backs and pointed toes. The couples moved around in a large square, keeping time with fiddle and banjo music. As the dancers paraded by doing flamboyant kicks and complicated swirls and turns, the elders judged them on appearance, grace, precision, and originality of moves. In the 1890s, "cakewalk contests" were organized as public entertainments in northern American cities and featured in all-black musicals of the late 1890s (notably Will Marion Cook's *Clorindy, or The Origin of the Cakewalk,* 1898). The cakewalk became an international hit in the social dancing of the period from 1898–1903. During this time, while the cakewalk was popular, a multithematic instrumental march with syncopated melodic rhythms developed, the simplest of which became a trademark in 2/4 time. Cakewalks formed a subgenre of ragtime and American marching band repertoires.

Part 4: For Further Study

Additional Books

Fiction

Title: *Gilberto and the Wind*
Author and Illustrator: Marie Hall Ets
Publisher: Puffin Books   ISBN: 0-14-050276-9
Summary: Gilberto describes his playmate, the wind, and the games they play together.

Title: *Iva Dunnit and the Big Wind*
Author: Carol Purcy   Illustrator: Steven Kellogg
Publisher: Deal Books   ISBN: 0-14-054651-0
Summary: A pioneer woman with six children uses her wits and strength to save her prairie home during a fearsome windstorm.

Nonfiction

Title: *Air*
Author: Kitty Benedict   Illustrator: Etienne Delessert
Publisher: Creative Education   ISBN: 0-88682-547-4
Summary: Discusses the physical properties and importance of air.

Title: *Air Is All Around You*
Author: Franklyn M. Branley   Illustrator: Holly Keller
Publisher: Harper & Row   ISBN: 0-06-445048-1
Summary: This book contains easy activities and explanations to help young
         children understand the concept of air.

Air Wheel Template

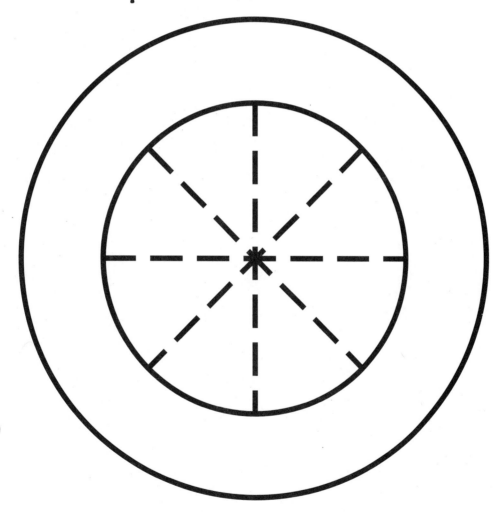

Folded Paper Kites

SCIENCE CATEGORY: *Position and Motion of Objects*
TOPICS: *Wind and Kites, Aerodynamic Forces, Engineering*
OBJECTIVE: *Students learn that the force of the wind makes a kite move and that many different styles of kites can move in the wind.*

In this lesson, students build three styles of simple paper kites and compare the kites' ability to move in the wind. Ideally, this lesson should follow "Catch the Wind."

- Prior to beginning the lesson, students have a chance to look at sample kites as well as pictures of many different kinds of kites and write descriptions of each.

- As a class, students discuss the kites, sort them into different categories, and consider why people make so many different types of kites.

- Students hear the story *The Emperor and the Kite* and listen for the special way the kite in the story is used.

- Students use paper and string to make simple kites. They fly the kites and compare the performance of the different kites. Students are challenged to raise up a basket of food, as Djeow Seow did with her kite in *The Emperor and the Kite*.

- To conclude the lesson, students write about their kites, describing their kite-flying experiences.

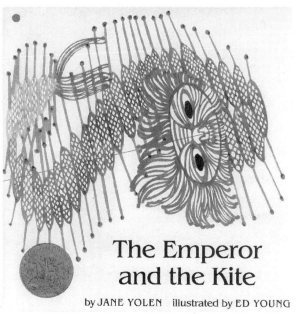

The Emperor and the Kite
by JANE YOLEN illustrated by ED YOUNG

Featured Fiction Book: *The Emperor and the Kite*
Author: Jane Yolen
Illustrator: Ed Young
Publisher: Philomel Books
ISBN: 0-399-21499-2
Summary: When the emperor is imprisoned in a high tower, his smallest daughter, whom he has always ignored, uses her kite to save him.

Part 1: Building Bridges

Building Student Knowledge and Motivation

Set up a classroom science center with a diverse collection of kites and pictures of kites. Make sure the kites or pictures represent the widest possible variety of kite styles and shapes. (The nonfiction book list in Part 4: For Further Study provides many sources.) Over a period of several days prior to the lesson, give groups of students an opportunity to visit the science center. Have each group of students look at all the kites carefully and write a brief description of each.

Getting Ready to Read

Title a new science chart "Types of Kites." Through class discussion, decide on categories to organize descriptions of the kites. Many categories are possible, including shape, size, color, cultural origin, use, and construction materials. Label the chart with the chosen categories, and through class discussion fill in a description of each kite. Pose the question, "Why do people make so many different kinds of kites?" Give students time to propose ideas, but don't comment further.

Show students the cover of *The Emperor and the Kite*. Ask, "Does the kite on the cover of this book look like any of the kites we just discussed? Let's add it to our list." Tell students, "The kite in this story was used for something very unusual. As I read, listen for how the kite was used."

Bridging to the Science Activity

Ask students, "How was the kite used in the story?" *The youngest daughter uses her kite to keep her father alive in prison and finally to rescue him.* "Why did she need a kite to do this? Why didn't she just throw the food up to the window?" *The window was too high. She was not strong enough.* "Why was the kite able to go so high?" *The wind's force makes the kite fly and even carry other objects.* Direct students' attention to the science chart. Ask, "Do you have anything to add to this kite's description after hearing the story?" Add student responses to the chart. Ask, "No matter what its shape, size, or color, what does a kite have to be good at?" *Flying, catching the force of the wind.* Tell students, "We have seen many kinds of kites. Now you will make some kites of your own and see how well the wind can push them."

Part 2: Science Activity

Materials

➤ **For the Procedure, Part A**
The materials listed here are for each student to make all three kites. An alternative would be to assign each student to make one particular kite.

Per student
*   3 sheets of paper, two 8½-inch x 11-inch and one 8½-inch x 14-inch
➤ *Any lightweight paper will do, such as paper used for photocopying.*

*   2 straws
*   6-inch length of thread

- 2 15-inch lengths of thread
- (optional) hole reinforcements
- 2 10-foot strips of 1-inch-wide crepe paper

Per group
- scissors
- hole punch
- tape
- stapler and staples

For the Procedure, Part B
Per student
- string reel made from a 6-inch x 3-inch piece of corrugated or other stiff cardboard (See Getting Ready.)
- 30-foot length of thread for kite line

Possibilities include quilting thread, buttonhole twist, or invisible thread similar to fishing line (but not strong enough to cut students' hands). Have several spools of thread available so that students can take turns measuring and cutting the thread as part of the Procedure. (See Part B.)

For the Procedure, Part D
Per group
- tiny wicker basket (such as a doll-sized basket from a craft store)
- 6-inch length of string
- lightweight food small enough to fit in basket
- 5- to 6-foot dowel rod or other pole

Safety and Disposal

Follow kite flying safety rules: never fly a kite with metallic or wire line, in wet or stormy weather, near electric power lines or antennas, near an airport, above streets or highways, in or above crowds of people, or without gloves in windy weather. If a kite becomes entangled in a power line or antenna, cut the string and call the power company. Teachers should state the kite-flying boundaries. No special disposal procedures are required.

Getting Ready

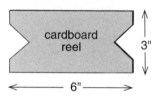

Figure 1

1. Make a copy of the Scientific Sled design (provided) on white or colored paper for each student.

2. To save time, you may wish to cut bridle strings, cut the crepe paper in half for the tails, or make the string reels in advance. To make the string reels, notch the ends of each 6-inch x 3-inch piece of cardboard as shown in Figure 1.

Procedure

Part A: Making the Kites

1. Have students make the three types of kites (Scientific Sled, Flying Cloak, and Swooper) using the instructions on the flip cards (provided).

2. If desired, demonstrate the cuts and folds needed for each type of kite.

Part B: Preparing Reels

1. If you have not already done so, have students cut their cardboard string reels as described in Getting Ready.

2. Have each student take a turn making a kite reel as follows: Tape the end of the thread on the spool to one notched end of the reel. Turn the reel about 45 complete turns to wind about 30 feet of thread onto it. This reel of thread is the kite line.

➤ *Group members can count out loud together to help keep track of the number of turns.*

Part C: Checking the Wind

1. Explain that flying a kite successfully requires observing the wind—both its direction and speed. Introduce students to the Beaufort wind scale for estimating wind speed. (See Table 1.)

			Table 1: Beaufort Scale
Beaufort Number	Type of Wind	Wind Speed (miles per hour)	Description
0	calm	less than 1	Calm; smoke rises vertically.
1	light air	1–3	Direction of wind shown by smoke but not by wind vanes.
2	light breeze	4–7	Wind felt on face; leaves rustle; ordinary vane moved by wind.
3	gentle breeze	8–12	Leaves and small twigs in constant motion; wind extends light flag.
4	moderate breeze	13–18	Raises dust and loose paper; small branches are moved.
5	fresh breeze	19–24	Small trees in leaf begin to sway; crested wavelets form on inland water.
6	strong breeze	25–31	Large branches in motion; telegraph wires whistle; umbrellas used with difficulty.

2. Explain to students that the folded paper kites will fly best in a steady wind of 8–10 mph (a "3" on the Beaufort Scale). In higher winds they will need extra tails for stability. In gusty wind they may turn inside out.

3. Have students estimate the wind speed using the Beaufort scale descriptions. Have them repeat their estimations several times to determine of the wind is steady. If conditions are good, it's time to fly the kites.

Part D: Flying the Kites

1. Remind students that kite flying is a process of trial and error: every kite is different, every kite flyer is different. Encourage students to use problem-solving techniques if their kites do not fly well at first.

2. With a student volunteer, demonstrate the kite launching procedure illustrated on the Kite Flying Instruction Sheet (master provided). Once the kite is flying, demonstrate how to take up kite line with the reel if the kite begins to fall, and to let line out if the kite pulls on the line.

3. Instruct students to launch and fly their kites.

4. Fill several tiny wicker baskets (such as a doll-sized basket from a craft store) with a lightweight food. Tie strings to the baskets. Use a 5- to 6-foot dowel rod

Teaching Physical Science through Children's Literature

or other pole to serve as a target height that represents the Emperor in the tower. Give each student a chance to tie a basket to a kite and see if he or she can fly it up to the "tower."

Part E: Discussion

1. Bring out the science chart and compare the kites described on the chart with the kites the students made. Lead students to make observations about their own kites and add these observations to the science chart.

2. Pick up one of the kites used in class and drop it to the ground. Ask, "Why does it fall?" *Gravity.* Ask, "Why did the kites fly in the wind?" *The wind pushed them.* Remind students that kites depend on the force of the wind pushing on them to fly. Ask, "Do you think it was windy or still during the days that Djeow Seow's father was imprisoned? Why do you think so?" Discuss students' ideas. Then reread and discuss parts of *The Emperor and the Kite* that refer to the wind. For example, "Her toy was like a flower in the sky. And it was like a prayer in the wind," and "The wind was raging above, holding the kite in its steely grip."

Science Explanation

The following explanation is intended for the teacher's information. Modify the explanation for students as required.

For any flying object to remain in the air (including kites, gliders, and powered aircraft), an upward force must be present that can overcome the downward force of gravity (weight) plus any other downward forces exerted on the object. In aerodynamics, the upward force is called lift. In addition to the up and down forces, flying objects also have another pair of forces acting on them called thrust and drag. Thrust propels the object forward, and drag holds it back. A kite will hover in the same place in the sky when each pair of forces (lift and downward forces and thrust and drag forces) are equal and opposite. (See Figure 2.)

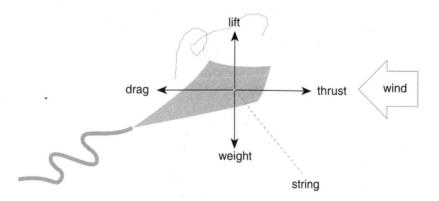

Figure 2: Various forces act on a flying kite.

In kites, lift is provided primarily from the wind's angle of attack. The kite is usually tipped so that the leading edge points upward. At this angle the kite deflects the air downward. According to Newton's third law, if the kite has exerted a downward force on the air, the air must exert an upward force (lift) on the kite. The wind also provides a component of the drag force. The tail of the kite increases drag but also increases stability. The tension on the kite string provides components of two different forces: downward force and thrust force.

Part 3: Lesson Extension

Writing Extension

Have each student write about his or her kites and kite-flying experiences from Part D of the activity. Each student should write as if he or she were the daughter in the story, trying to send food to the emperor. The story should describe the kite and the student's attempts to fly the basket up to the "tower."

Cross-Cultural Integration

 This section is intended for teacher background. You may wish to use the information in this section to develop age-appropriate activities for your classroom.

Though today's kites are primarily a recreational pastime, the history of kite usage is quite rich. The "kite" (a word of English origin, referring to a bird of prey), Spanish "cometa" (comet), and Chinese "feng-cheng" (wind harp) all refer to the brightly colored, high-flying devices that have been around for more than 2,000 years. Each country and culture has used kites over the years for many purposes, ranging from military to meteorological.

Ancient Egyptian hieroglyphics refer to kites. Early Egyptians used banana leaves, cloth, bamboo, lightweight wood, silk, and plant vines to construct their kites. Chinese documents dating back to the third century B.C. describe wooden kites that may have developed from peasants tying strings to their straw hats or from hunters shooting arrows with rope attached for easy retrieval. One interesting early use of kites occurred in 196 B.C. during the Han Dynasty. Soldiers wanted to dig a tunnel under the enemy's fort but did not know how far to dig. Kites were flown directly over the enemy's fortification; the line was brought back in and measured to estimate the distance to dig. The soldiers dug a tunnel and surprised the enemy, emerging victorious. Also, kites carrying bamboo instruments that moaned and wailed in the wind were sent up over enemy troops on dark, moonless nights as a scare tactic. Kites and wind sock pennants were also used to identify military units, signal troops for miles around, or carry fireworks.

After the 105 A.D. invention of paper in China, paper kites could be constructed and shared through trading among various cultures, where the kite underwent changes in form and function. The high cost of paper initially limited paper kiting to the wealthy. As paper became more affordable, kites were incorporated into religious, social, and political festivals. Messages of goodwill, family crest prayers of health and happiness, warnings to enemies or evil spirits, and even advertising slogans were cast into the skies for all to see.

Kites eventually began to be used in scientific experiments and for meteorological observations. In 1749, the Scottish team of Alexander Wilson and Thomas Melville attached protected thermometers to six or more kites in tandem. This experiment, the first documented kite experiment in Europe, took place 30 years before the first balloon flight and about 150 years before the invention of the airplane. By releasing the bundled thermometers with timed fuses, these kite scientists proved their hypothesis that colder temperatures existed in the upper atmosphere. During a thunderstorm in the summer of 1752, a few years after Wilson and Melville's experiments, Benjamin Franklin conducted his famous key-on-a-kite experiment. This experiment led to the invention of the lightning rod and to further studies of electricity.

Innovative minds also employed the kite to move or lift objects. In 1825 Englishman George Pocock invented the charvolant, or kite carriage, which pulled a carriage of passengers across the countryside at a speed of 25 miles per hour. Kites could also tow sleds across the ice or boats over water.

In the 1890s, Australian Lawrence Hargrave created the box kite, a revolutionary kite design. He chose not to patent the design, because as a scientist he believed his designs and accomplishments belonged to all people and should be available to anyone who could put them to good use.

Hargrave's studies in aerodynamics and the uses of a three-dimensional kite led to the invention of the airplane; Wilbur and Orville Wright used the Hargrave kite design for their studies of wind dynamics. After experimenting with the box kite design and aerodynamics, the Wright brothers made three gliders between 1900 and 1903. The brothers also built their own engine and propellers to create the first man-carrying airplane, which first flew in December 1903 in the strong winds of the North Carolina coast.

In the 1940s, NASA scientist Francis Rogallo designed the parawing, a flexible cloth square. He believed a kite should conform to the wind—not the other way around. His design was used for the space program's capsule landings. This twist on the kite concept developed into popular activities like parasailing, wind surfing, and hang gliding.

Kites are still used for festivals and sporting events. In Japan, the Boys' Festival, dating back to 1550, features kites decorated with paintings of heroes or messages of health and happiness. Carp kites are used to represent an adolescent boy's struggle to manhood, like the mature carp's struggle upstream to reach spawning grounds. In Korea, a family kite-flying festival begins the new year. The children and parents release kites high in the sky, hoping that the wind god will then blow the kites far away to distant lands, carrying away any evil spirits that may affect the future prosperity of the children. In India, kite fighting with glass-coated kite line is a popular sport. The friction from tangled lines cuts the loser loose.

The popularity of kites as fascinating toys and subjects of aerodynamic research continues. The Massachusetts Institute of Technology has created a Kite Experimentation Laboratory. Millions of kites continue to be sold yearly.

Part 4: For Further Study

Additional Books

Fiction

Title: *Kite Flier*
Author: Dennis Haseley
Illustrator: David Wiesner
Publisher: Macmillan
ISBN: 0-689-71668-0
Summary: As his son grows, Kite Flier makes spectacular kites for special occasions, and his hair flies as each one soars overhead. When the boy becomes an adult, father and son make a magnificent memory kite from the pieces of all the old kites.

Title: *The Kite*
Author: Alma F. Ada
Illustrator: Vivi Escriva
Publisher: Santillana
ISBN: 1-56014-228-6
Summary: A resourceful mother helps her children make and fly a kite. Contains a surprise ending.

Title: *Mike's Kite*
Author: Elizabeth MacDonald
Illustrator: Robert Kendall
Publisher: Orchard Books
ISBN: 0-153-003200
Summary: On a windy day, Mike's kite blows away, pulling him and all the many people who try to help him.

Nonfiction

Title: *Catch the Wind!: All About Kites*
Author: Gail Gibbons
Publisher: Little, Brown, and Company
ISBN: 0-316-30955-9
Summary: Two children visit Ike's Kite Shop and learn about kites and how to fly them. Includes instructions for building a kite.

Title: *One-Hour Kites*
Author: Jim Rowlands
Publisher: St. Martin's Press
ISBN: 0-312-03218-8
Summary: This book contains patterns for 25 kites.

Title: *The Ultimate Kite Book*
Authors: Paul and Helene Morgan
Publisher: Simon and Schuster
ISBN: 0-671-74443-7
Summary: A catalog of the world's classic kites. Gives information on the long tradition kiting has enjoyed in the Far East, where kites still play a central role in folklore and legends.

References

The American Heritage History of Flight; Josephey, A., Ed.; American Heritage: New York, 1962; pp 85–87.

Newman, L.S. *Kite Craft: The History and Processes of Kitemaking Throughout the World;* Crown: New York, 1974; p 29.

Teaching Physical Science through Children's Literature

Flip Cards

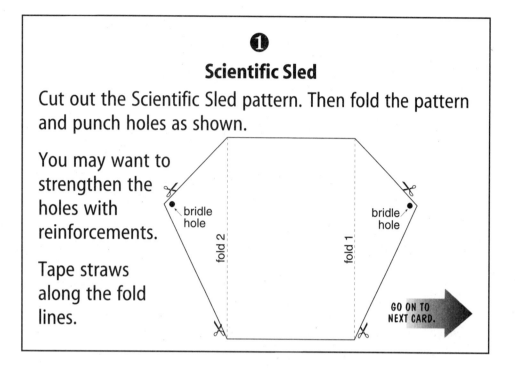

①

Scientific Sled

Cut out the Scientific Sled pattern. Then fold the pattern and punch holes as shown.

You may want to strengthen the holes with reinforcements.

Tape straws along the fold lines.

bridle hole

bridle hole

fold 2

fold 1

GO ON TO NEXT CARD.

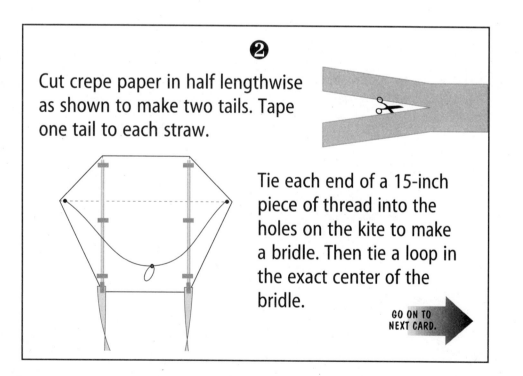

②

Cut crepe paper in half lengthwise as shown to make two tails. Tape one tail to each straw.

Tie each end of a 15-inch piece of thread into the holes on the kite to make a bridle. Then tie a loop in the exact center of the bridle.

GO ON TO NEXT CARD.

Flying Cloak

Fold an 8½-inch by 14-inch piece of paper in half. Then pull one side of the sheet around in a curve.

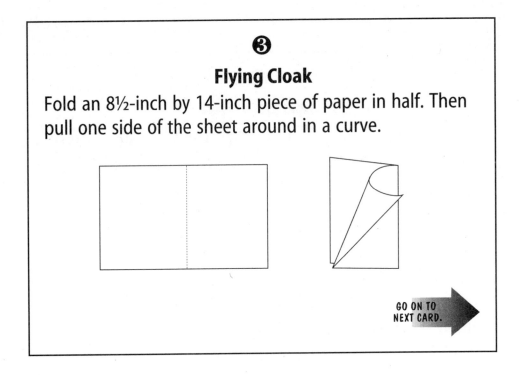

GO ON TO NEXT CARD.

❹

Staple the curve against the center fold 1½ inches from the tip. Let the point of the curve overlap on the center fold. Repeat on the other side.

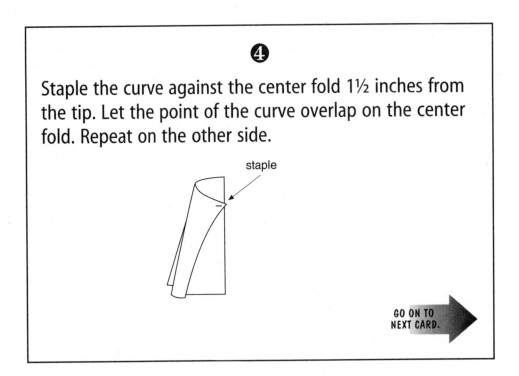

staple

GO ON TO NEXT CARD.

Punch a hole in the center fold 3½ inches from the top of the kite. You may want to strengthen the hole with reinforcements. Attach your kite line through the hole.

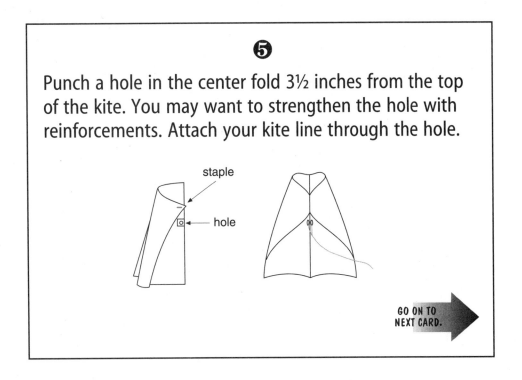

GO ON TO
NEXT CARD.

❻

Swooper

Fold an 8½-inch by 11-inch piece of paper in half. Then fold each end to the middle, accordion style, so the paper is divided in fourths.

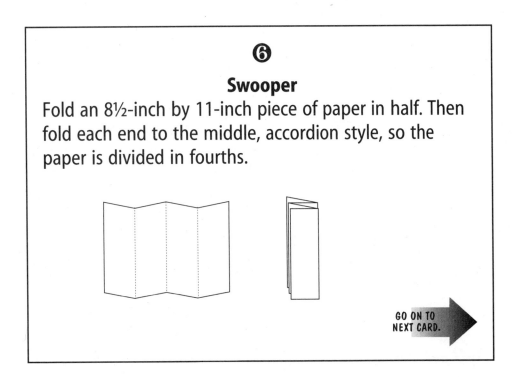

GO ON TO
NEXT CARD.

❼

Punch a hole for the tail at the base of the long side on the middle crease.

Punch holes for the bridle on the short sides of the kite 2 inches from the top. You may want to strengthen the holes with reinforcements.

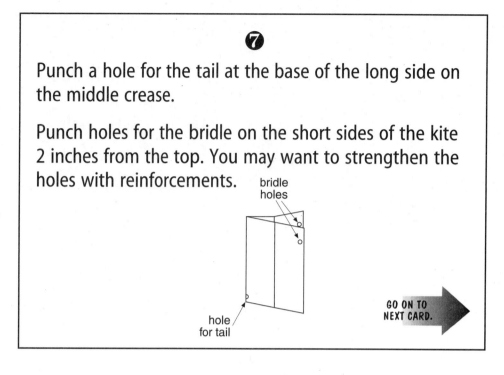

bridle holes

hole for tail

GO ON TO NEXT CARD.

❽

Punch a hole in the tail near one end. Loop a 6-inch piece of thread through the hole at the base of the kite and the hole in the tail. Tie the ends of the thread.

Tie the ends of a 15-inch piece of thread in the two holes on the short sides of the kite to make a bridle. Then tie a loop in the exact center of the bridle.

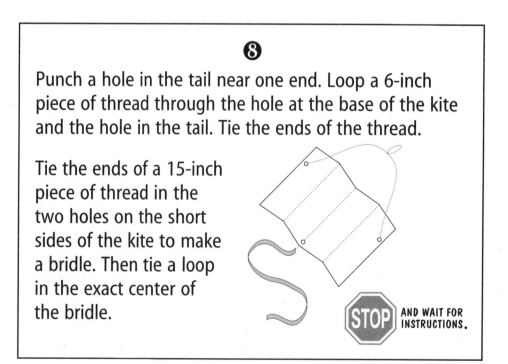

STOP AND WAIT FOR INSTRUCTIONS.

Folded Paper Kites

1. Never run with the kite.

2. Use two people to launch the kite.

3. Have one person hold the kite by the bottom, facing the other person who is holding the line.

4. On a given signal, the person holding the kite releases it, without throwing it, and the person holding the line pulls in the line as fast as he or she can.

5. The farther apart the two people are, the faster the kite will climb.

Folded Paper Kites

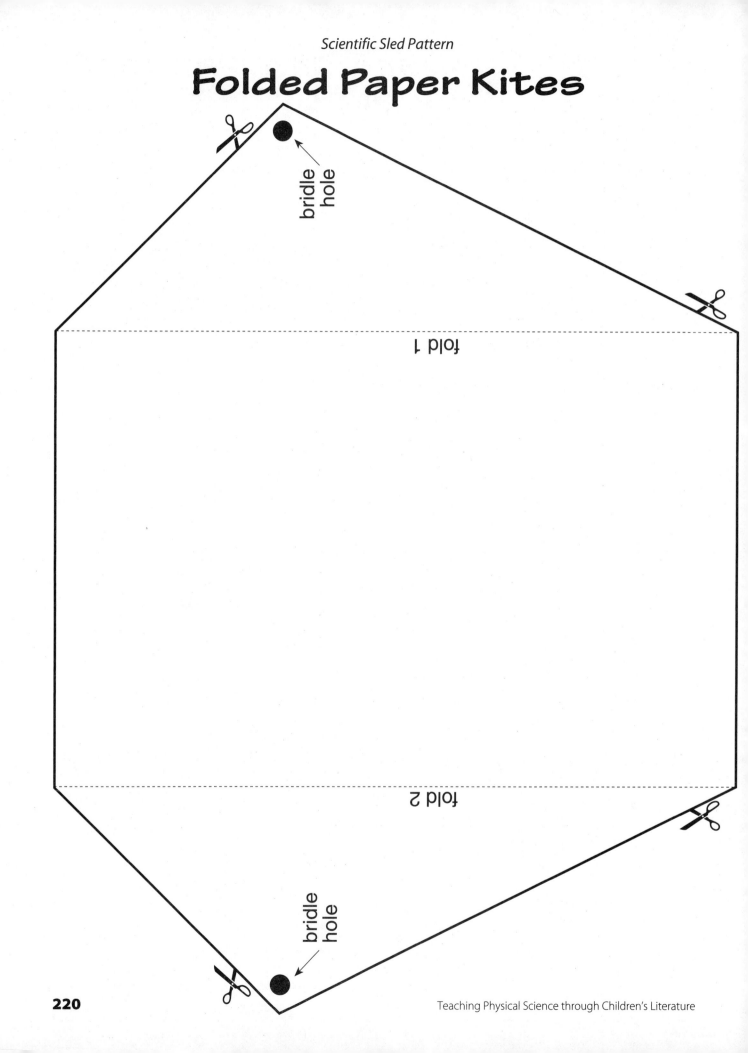

bridle
hole

fold 1

fold 2

bridle
hole

Rubber Band Banza

SCIENCE CATEGORY: Position and Motion of Objects

TOPICS: Sound, Design of Musical Instruments

OBJECTIVE: Students review ideas about sound and vibration and apply these ideas to learn how a stringed instrument makes music.

In this lesson, students make a banza to explore sound and how stringed musical instruments work. Students should already be familiar with the idea that sound is produced by vibrating objects.

- Prior to beginning the lesson, students spend time in a center where they can make sounds with a variety of objects. They also have access to a variety of written materials and pictures relating to sound.

- Through a class discussion, students categorize the ways they made sounds in the center (such as banging, blowing, and plucking) and create a sound web chart.

- Students hear the story *The Banza* and decide how Cabree makes sounds with her banza (banjo).

- Students make banza-like instruments of their own using pans or boxes and rubber bands. They review the idea that vibrations cause sound and experiment with ways to change the pitch and loudness of the sounds their instruments make.

- To conclude the lesson, students use what they have learned about the banza and about sound to add details and explanations to a laminated picture of a banza.

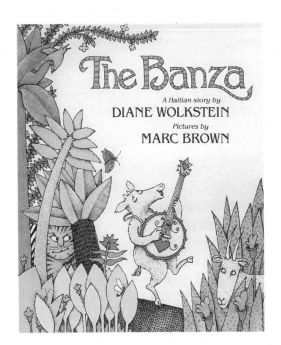

Featured Fiction Book: *The Banza*

Author: Diane Wolkstein

Illustrator: Marc Brown

Publisher: Dial Books for Young Readers

ISBN: 0-14-054605-7

Summary: Seeking refuge from a storm, a tiger and a goat meet in a cave and decide to be friends. Teegra the Tiger leaves Cabree the Goat a special gift—a banza (banjo)—for Cabree's protection. Later, alone, Cabree finds herself face-to-face with 10 hungry tigers. Using her banza, she plays a ferocious song that sends the tigers slinking off in fear.

Part 1: Building Bridges

Building Student Knowledge and Motivation

Prior to beginning the lesson, set up a sound exploration center where students can use a variety of objects to make sounds in the following ways: banging, plucking, strumming, and shaking. (We are not suggesting making sounds by blowing because of the difficulty of keeping such objects sanitary.) Also include pictures of objects that produce sound (including musical instruments) and nonficton books about sound, such as *The Science Book of Sound,* by Neil Ardley. (See Additional Books.) Divide students into pairs, and give each pair time in the center to explore all the sounds. While in the center, each pair should name or draw each object and describe how they made sounds with that object. Encourage students to bring other sound-making items from home.

Getting Ready to Read

Turn to a clean sheet on your science chart. Involve the students in creating a sound web chart. Write "making sounds" in the middle of the chart. Have students name the different ways they made sounds in the sound center (such as shaking, plucking, and banging) and web these categories out from "making sounds." (See Figure 1.) Have students name the objects they used to make each type of sound and add these to the web as appropriate. (Save the web chart to use later.) Ask, "What is the name for all the kinds of sounds made with things like flutes, guitars, and drums?" *Music.* Read the title *The Banza.* Explain that this story is about a goat named Cabree who made music with a instrument called a banza. Tell students, "As you listen to the story, I want you to decide how Cabree made this music." Point to the categories on the sound web. "Did she bang? Shake? Strum?"

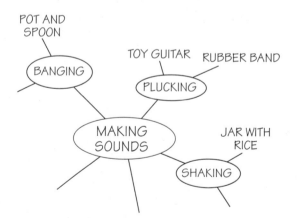

Figure 1: An example of a sound web chart

Figure 2

Divide the students into groups and give each group an object from the sound exploration center. Bring out a Cabree face mounted on a stick to use as a cue. (See Figure 2.) Tell the students that you will read a story that requires their participation. When you hold up the picture of Cabree's face, they should quietly "play" their instruments in time with a tempo you give. When you lower the picture, they should immediately stop playing and give the instrument to another person in their group. Demonstrate the tempo they should follow as they play. Students who do not have instruments can clap their hands. Have the students practice as a group playing at this tempo. Then have them practice starting and stopping on cue. When the students are able to play as a group reasonably well, read the story. When you reach the parts where Cabree sings her ferocious song, hold up the cue and have the students softly play and clap as you read the lyrics in a singsong voice.

Bridging to the Science Activity

Ask students which categories on the sound web describe how Cabree made sounds (music) with her banza. Ask, "Were the sounds always the same?" *No.* Discuss the different types of sounds Cabree's banza could make. Tell students that they will make rubber band banzas of their own to find out more about how Cabree used her banza to make different sounds.

Part 2: Science Activity

Materials

Figure 3

For the Procedure
Per class
• stringed instrument such as a guitar, banjo, violin, or cello

Per student or group
• small, rigid rectangular pan or box, no wider than 5 inches and about 8 inches long

A small, non-disposable loaf pan is ideal. An inexpensive half-pint freezer container with a hole cut in the lid also works well. (See Figure 3.) The lip of the lid acts as a ready-made bridge. (See Part B, Step 2 of the Procedure.)

• 4–5 rubber bands with different lengths and widths
• 3 pens, markers, or pencils

Safety and Disposal

Remind students that the rubber bands are to be used only as specified in the procedure and definitely not as projectiles. No special disposal procedures are required.

Procedure

Flip-cards are provided for the steps in this Procedure. They may be used for student reference as you demonstrate and/or as a reference in a follow-up science center.

Part A: How Does a Banza Make Sounds?

1. Instruct each group to look at the pan or box and rubber bands. Ask, "How can we use these objects to make something similar to Cabree's banza?" Through a facilitated discussion, lead students to suggest putting the rubber bands around the box to make "strings."

2. Have each group put the rubber bands around the box and experiment with their "banzas." Give students time to explore making different sounds.

3. Ask students why the banzas make sounds. Review the idea that vibrating objects cause the air around them to move. This air in turn transmits the energy or motion to the air which makes our eardrums vibrate, telling our brains we have heard a sound. Ask, "What part of your banza vibrates?" Students will probably answer "rubber bands." Explain that the rubber bands do vibrate, but so does the entire box. To demonstrate, have one student pluck a rubber band on the banza very hard, and have the other students gently touch the side of the banza right away. They should feel the vibrations of the box.

4. Have students describe the sounds they made. Ask, "What kind of sound did Cabree use as a warning? Which of the sounds you made with your banzas would be the best warning?"

Part B: How Can We Change the Sounds?

1. Explain, "We've talked about the different sounds you can make with your banzas. Some sounds are loud, some are soft. Some sounds are high, others are low. Why might we want to produce different sounds?" *Different kinds of sounds are needed to make music. Playing the same note at the same volume all the time would not be interesting or pleasing.* Bring out a stringed instrument such as a guitar, banjo, violin, or cello. Ask, "How is this instrument similar to your rubber band banzas?" *It has strings of different sizes strung over the opening of a hollow object.* Tell the students that their rubber band banzas are really stringed instruments and that you will show them how sounds can be produced and changed in the same ways on their banzas and your instrument.

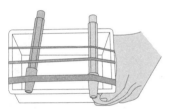

Figure 4

2. Tell students that before they start experimenting with their banzas, they need to make their banzas more like your stringed instrument in one way: they need to make "bridges" to allow the rubber bands to vibrate more freely. Show the students the bridge on your instrument. Then have them place two pens (or pencils or markers) underneath the rubber bands of their banzas, one on each side. (See Figure 4.) Now they are ready to experiment with their banzas.

3. Develop the idea of amplitude as follows:

   a. Gently pluck a string on your instrument. Ask the students to describe the sound. *Soft.* Pluck the same string more forcefully. Ask the students to describe the sound. *Louder.* Ask, "What did I do differently to produce these sounds?" *The first time, you plucked gently. The second time, you plucked more forcefully.* Discuss the idea that how forcefully the strings are plucked determines how loud the sounds are.

   b. Have students use their banzas to create loud and soft sounds the same way you did. Tell students to carefully watch the vibration of the rubber band with a soft pluck and a hard pluck. Ask, "What difference can you see?" *The hard pluck made the rubber band vibrate up and down much higher and lower.* Explain that the size of the vibration is called its amplitude.

4. Discuss the idea that tension affects the pitch (how high or low something sounds to us) as follows:

   a. Pluck one of the middle strings on your instrument continually while turning the string's tuning peg to tighten it. Ask, "What happens to the pitch as I play?" *The pitch rises.* Next, pluck the string continually while turning the peg to loosen the tension. Ask, "What happens to the pitch now?" *It becomes lower.* Ask the students "What did I do to make the sound change?" *You turned the string's tuning peg.* Explain that turning the peg pulls the string tighter or makes it looser. How tightly a string is pulled is its "tension." Tell the students that the tension of a string affects its pitch; the higher the tension is, the higher the pitch is. The lower the tension is, the lower the pitch is. A string that is less tense vibrates more slowly than a string that is more tense. An object that vibrates slowly makes a low sound; one that vibrates rapidly makes a high sound. The number of times something vibrates each second is its frequency. Scientists can measure the frequency of a sound with special equipment. When we hear a sound, we cannot tell what its frequency is, but we can tell how high or low it sounds to us. We use the word "pitch" to describe this highness or lowness.

b. Demonstrate how to change the tension of rubber bands on a banza. The rubber band banzas do not have pegs, so in order to change the pitch, you must pull the slack of each band to the top or bottom of the banza. To increase the tension, pull the rubber band toward the bottom of the banza. Friction from the sides of the pan will hold the slack in place; you don't need to hold the band as you play. To decrease the tension, pull the slack to the top. Have the students experiment with changing the tension of their banza strings.

5. Discuss the idea that the length of the vibrating string affects pitch as follows:

a. Pluck one of the strings of your instrument repeatedly, moving your finger along the neck of the instrument. Ask students to describe what they hear. *As your finger moves down the string (away from the pegs), the pitch rises. As your finger moves toward the pegs, the pitch lowers.* Discuss how pressing the string against a different spot on the neck of the instrument changes the sound by varying the length of the vibrating part of the string.

b. Show students how to use a pen, pencil, or marker to change the length of the vibrating part of the rubber band "strings" on their banzas. (See Figure 5.) Give them time to experiment with their banzas.

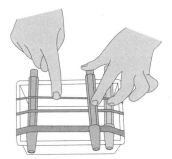

Figure 5

6. Develop the idea that the size of the string helps determine its pitch as follows:

a. Pluck the thickest string on your instrument. Then pluck the thinnest string. Ask, "What was the difference between these two sounds?" *The pitch of the first sound was low; the pitch of the second sound was high.* Ask students what the difference is between the two strings you plucked. *The low string is thicker than the high string.* Also have the students observe the material the strings are made of (e.g., wire, nylon, or "catgut"). Explain, "The thicker string vibrates more slowly than the thinner string. Because it vibrates more slowly, it has a lower frequency and thus a lower pitch."

b. Have students adjust the rubber bands on their banzas to have approximately equal tension. Then have students play their banzas to observe how the size of each rubber band affects its pitch. Remind them to keep the lengths of the rubber bands constant. In the case of the rubber band banzas, size includes length, width, and thickness. Some rubber bands that are narrower in width but longer in length will produce lower pitches than rubber bands that are thicker but shorter. The material a band is made of may also affect its pitch. Students will need to experiment to determine the relative pitches of their particular instruments' strings.

7. Add several rubber band banzas, flip cards, and (if possible) stringed musical instruments to the sound center. Provide copies of *The Banza*, *The Science Book of Sound*, and other nonfiction books. Make the center available for one or more weeks for further exploration. Encourage students to add observations to the science chart as they make discoveries in the center.

Science Extension

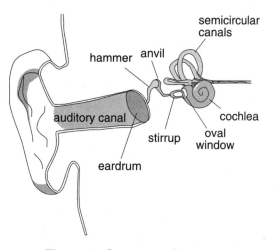

Figure 6: Components of the ear

For older students, discuss how the ear receives sound. The eardrum can be compared with an instrument—the drum. Hearing is the process of picking up and interpreting wavelike air pressure disturbances we call sound waves. These waves are produced when a physical force causes an object to vibrate, such as the plucking of a string, the beating of a drum, or air traveling over human vocal cords. These forces produce sound waves, which are funneled into the ear. Sound passes through the auditory canal to the eardrum. The eardrum vibrates much like the head of a drum when the sound waves reach it. This vibration causes three small hinged bones in the ear to vibrate too—the hammer, anvil, and stirrup. The stirrup in turn flexes the membrane of a small oval "window" in a structure called the cochlea. When the cochlea's membranes vibrate, a signal is sent to the brain that lets us hear. (See Figure 6.)

Science Explanation

➤ *The following explanation is intended for the teacher's information. Modify the explanation for students as required.*

When any object that can vibrate is disturbed, it will vibrate at its own special set of frequencies (rates of vibration), which together form its special sound. These frequencies are called the object's natural frequencies, and they depend on factors such as the material, elasticity, and shape of the object. Sound is produced when the energy from the vibrating object gets transferred to gas particles in the air that are moving freely and happen to collide with the vibrating object. These gas particles pass their energy to adjacent particles and eventually transmit the energy to the ear and cause the eardrum to vibrate, sending messages to the brain which let us know if we have heard a sound. We give the name "music" to collections of sounds that are changed in a controlled manner and are considered pleasing by the listener. Of course, what is considered pleasing varies with culture, age, and experience.

Musical instruments are built to produce pleasing sound vibrations through various methods. Stringed instruments, a large group of musical instruments that includes the violin family, guitars, banjos, harpsichords, and harps, produce sound when a string is caused to vibrate. Vibrations may be produced by drawing a bow across the strings (as with the violin family), or by plucking (as with guitars, banjos, harpsichords, and harps). Other parts of the instrument act as a sounding board to amplify the vibrations produced by the strings.

When playing a stringed instrument, different sounds (or notes) are produced by producing different rates of vibration in the strings. The rate of vibration is known as the frequency. Higher sounds are produced by faster rates of vibration, or in other words, by higher frequencies. Lower sounds are produced by slower rates of vibration, or in other words, lower frequencies. The brain interprets frequency detected by the ear primarily in terms of a subjective quality called pitch. In a stringed instrument, many factors contribute to the creation of different pitches. The strings have different masses and are under different amounts of tension. These differences contribute to different frequencies of vibration and therefore different notes. Changing the length of the string also changes the frequency of the vibration and thus the pitch.

The loudness or softness of a note can be changed by plucking or bowing the string more forcefully or more lightly. Plucking the string more forcefully makes it move a greater distance, increasing the amplitude (or height) of the vibration. When the string vibrates with greater amplitude, it passes more energy to surrounding air particles, and thus more energy reaches the ear. When the string is pulled only a small distance, it transfers less energy to the air particles and, consequently, to the ear.

The rubber band banza is a simple kind of stringed instrument; it consists of strings (rubber bands) stretched over the opening of a box that acts as a sounding board. It can produce different pitches and loudnesses in much the same way as other stringed instruments.

Part 3: Lesson Extension

Writing Extension

Divide students into small groups. Give each group a laminated "banza mat" 8½ inches x 11 inches, or larger if desired. (See Figure 7.) Also provide several strands of yarn of different widths, tape, and several colored washable markers. Tell the students to design a mat that can teach someone else how a banza *makes* sounds and how the player can *change* those sounds. Explain that students may complete their design by writing, drawing, and/or taping strings on their mats.

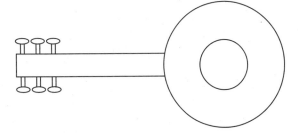

Figure 7: Sample mat design

Cross-Cultural Integration

➤ *This section is intended for teacher background. You may wish to use the information in this section to develop age-appropriate activities for your classroom.*

Haiti is a country in the West Indies. It is not an island itself, but it joins the Dominican Republic to form an island known as Hispaniola, which is situated in the Caribbean between the islands of Cuba and Puerto Rico. Most Haitians are descendants of west African slaves. However, Haiti's culture also shows European influences. It is the only Latin American country whose European culture is predominantly French. (Typically European influences in Latin America are Spanish.)

Music and Musical Instruments of Haiti

Music and musical instruments in Haiti are influenced by both European and African ancestors. Generally, the elite music is more European-inspired, while the folk music is inspired by west African traditions. The instruments used in Haitian folk music are made in villages or in huts in the mountains.

The drum is the most common instrument and is used for dancing, cult rites, work music, and assembly calls and signals. Drums range in height from 18 inches to 6 feet. Drumheads are covered with either cowhide or goatskin and are played using either some type of stick or the bare hand. The sound a drum makes depends on its size, the materials it is made with, what is used to strike the drumhead, and where the drumhead is struck.

The ganbo, a bamboo stamping tube, is another type of percussion instrument found in Haiti. It, too, originated in Africa. The stamping tube is like an inverted drum made from bamboo. One end is closed by a membrane and the other end is left open. The closed end is struck hard on the ground and the sound comes from the open end.

Horns, trumpets, rattles, ratchets, and flutes are also heard in Haitian folk music. The word "banza" originally referred to a banjo-like instrument like the one Cabree played in the book *The Banza*, but it is now used to describe a homemade fiddle used in European-influenced dances.

Part 4: For Further Study

Additional Books

Nonfiction

Title: *The Science Book of Sound*
Author: Neil Ardley
Publisher: Harcourt Brace Jovanovich   ISBN: 0-15-200579-X
Summary: Simple experiments demonstrate basic principles of sound and music.

Title: *The Magic School Bus in the Haunted Museum: A Book About Sound*
Author: Linda Beech   Illustrator: Bruce Degen
Publisher: Scholastic   ISBN: 0-590-48412-5
Summary: The class is thrilled about their upcoming concert at the Sound Museum…
    until they find that the spooky mansion is more of a thrill than they bargained for.

Title: *Sound Experiments*
Author: Ray Broekel
Publisher: Childrens Press   ISBN: 0-516-41686-3
Summary: Discusses sound, pitch, sound travel, sound waves, vibration, frequency, length, and thickness with simple experiments to demonstrate each concept.

References

Courlander, H. *The Drum and the Hoe: Life and Lore of the Haitian People;* University of California: Berkeley, 1960.

Harlan, J. *Science Experiments for the Early Childhood Years,* 4th ed.; Merrill: Columbus, OH, 1988; pp 227–228.

Hewitt, P. *Conceptual Physics,* 5th ed.; Little, Brown: Boston, 1985; pp 280–305.

Macaulay, D. *The Way Things Work;* Houghton Mifflin: Boston, 1988; pp 234–235.

Flip Cards

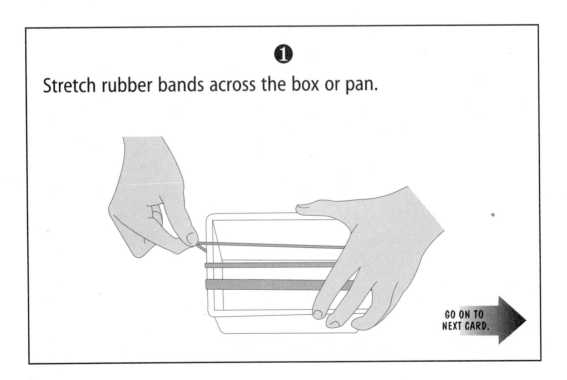

❶

Stretch rubber bands across the box or pan.

GO ON TO NEXT CARD.

❷

Pluck the rubber bands.

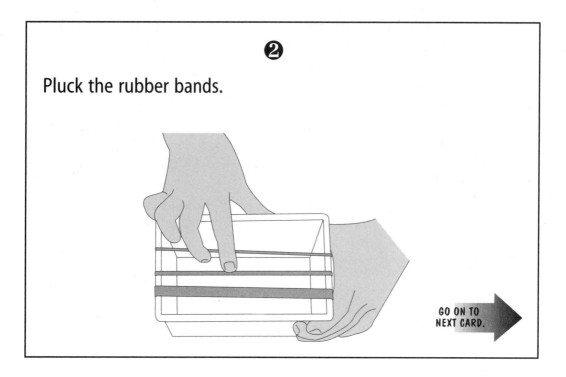

GO ON TO
NEXT CARD.

❸

Make bridges by placing two pens
(or pencils or markers) underneath
the rubber bands.

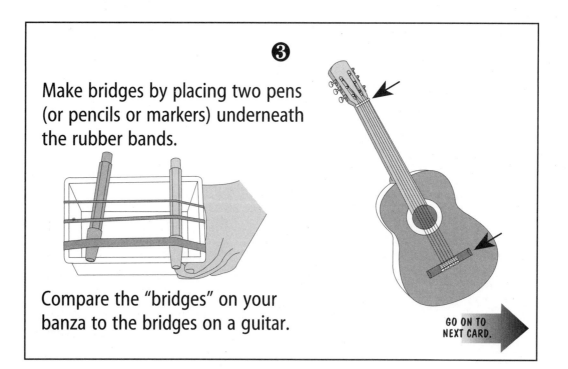

Compare the "bridges" on your
banza to the bridges on a guitar.

GO ON TO
NEXT CARD.

❹

Pluck the rubber bands gently then harder, and notice the difference in how loud the sounds are.

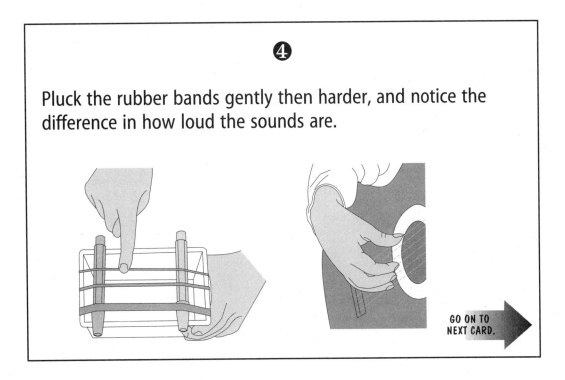

GO ON TO NEXT CARD.

❺

Change the tension in one of your bands by pulling it tighter. What happens to the pitch (how high or low the sound is) when you pluck this band? Compare this to turning the tuning peg on a guitar.

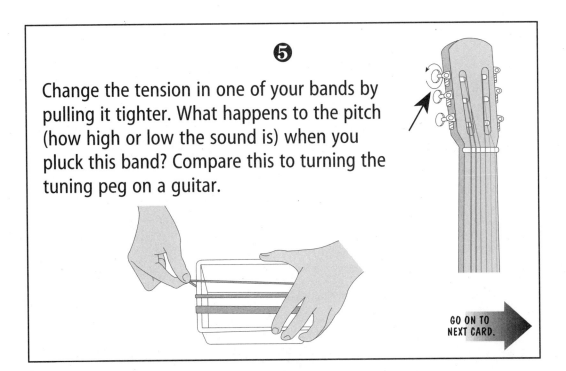

GO ON TO NEXT CARD.

❻

Change the length of the bands using a pen. What happens to the pitch? Compare this to changing the pitch on a guitar by pressing your fingers in different positions on the neck.

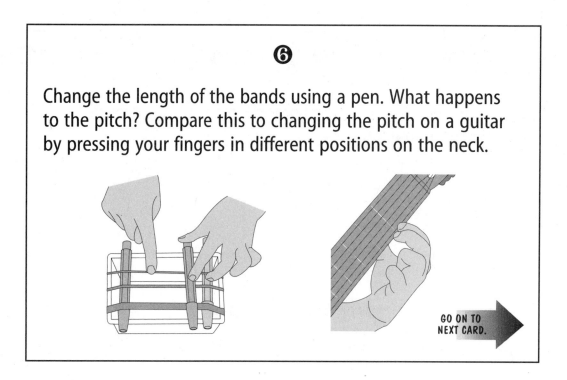

GO ON TO NEXT CARD.

❼

Pluck the thickest band on your instrument, then the thinnest. Notice the difference in how high the sound is (pitch). Look at the thicknesses of the strings on the guitar.

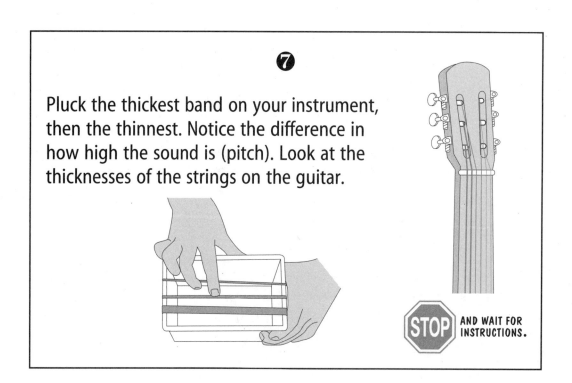

STOP AND WAIT FOR INSTRUCTIONS.

● The Center for Chemical Education

Built on a tradition of quality programming, materials development, and networking between academia and industry, Miami University's Center for Chemical Education (CCE) encompasses a multifaceted collaboration of cross-grade-level and interdisciplinary initiatives begun in the mid-1980s as Terrific Science Programs. These initiatives are linked through the centrality of chemistry to the goal of fostering quality hands-on, minds-on science education for all students. CCE activities include credit coursework and other opportunities for educators at all levels; K–12 student programs; undergraduate, graduate, and postgraduate programs in chemical education; materials development, including teacher resource materials, program handbooks, and videos; and public outreach efforts and networking to foster new and existing partnerships among classroom teachers, university-based science educators, industrial scientists, and professional societies.

Professional Development for Educators

Credit Courses
The Center for Chemical Education offers a variety of summer and academic-year workshop-style courses for K–12 and college teachers. While each workshop has a unique focus, all reflect current pedagogical approaches in science education, cutting-edge academic and industrial research topics, and classroom applications for teachers and students. Short courses provide opportunities for educators to enrich their science teaching in a limited amount of time. All courses offer graduate credit.

Noncredit Courses
Academies allow CCE graduates and other teachers to attend special one-day sessions presented by leading science educators from around the United States. Offerings include seminars, mini-workshops, and share-and-swap sessions.

Internships
Through 8- to 10-week summer internships, program graduates work as members of industrial teams to gain insight into the day-to-day workings of industrial laboratories, enabling them to bring real-world perspectives into the classroom.

Fellowships
Master teachers at primary, secondary, and college levels do research in chemical education and undertake curriculum and materials development as Teacher Fellows with the Center for Chemical Education. Fellowships are available for the summer and the academic year.

K–12 Student Programming

Summer Camps
A variety of summer camps are available to area elementary, middle, and high school students. These camps not only provide laboratory-based enrichment for students, but also enable educators in summer courses to apply their knowledge of hands-on exploration and leadership skills. Satellite camps are offered at affiliated sites throughout the country.

Science Carnivals
Carnivals challenge elementary school students with hands-on science in a nontraditional atmosphere, encouraging them to apply the scientific method to activities that demonstrate scientific principles. Sponsoring teachers and their students host these carnivals for other students in their districts.

Super Saturday Science Sessions
High school students are introduced to industrial and research applications of science and technology through special Saturday sessions that involve the students in experiment-based problem-solving. Topics have included waste management, environmental sampling, engineering technology, paper science, chemical analysis, microbiology, and many others.

Ambassador Program	Professional chemists, technicians, and engineers, practicing and recently retired, play important roles as classroom ambassadors for high school and two-year college students. Ambassadors not only serve as classroom resources, but are also available as consultants when a laboratory scenario calls for outside expertise; they mentor special projects both in and out of the classroom; and they are available for career counseling and professional advice.

Undergraduate and Graduate Student Programming

Teaching Science with TOYS Undergraduate Course	This undergraduate course replicates the Teaching Science with TOYS teacher inservice program for the preservice audience. Students participate in hands-on physics and chemistry sessions.
General Chemistry Initiative	This effort is aimed at more effectively including chemical analysis and problem-solving in the two-year college curriculum. To accomplish this goal, we are developing and testing discovery-based laboratory scenarios and take-home lecture supplements that illustrate topics in chemistry through activities beyond the classroom. In addition to demonstrating general chemistry concepts, these activities also involve students in critical-thinking and group problem-solving skills used by professional chemists in industry and academia.
Chemical Technology Curriculum Development	Curriculum and materials development efforts highlight the collaboration between college and high school faculty and industrial partners. These efforts will lead to the dissemination of a series of activity-based monographs, including detailed instructions for discovery-based investigations that challenge students to apply principles of chemical technology, chemical analysis, and Good Laboratory Practices in solving problems that confront practicing chemical technicians in the workplace.
Other Undergraduate Activities	The CCE has offered short courses/seminars for undergraduates that are similar in focus and pedagogy to CCE teacher/faculty enhancement programming. In addition, CCE staff members provide Miami University students with opportunities to interact in area schools through public outreach efforts and to undertake independent study projects in chemical education.
Degree Program	Miami's Department of Chemistry offers both a Ph.D. and M.S. in Chemical Education for graduate students who are interested in becoming teachers of chemistry in situations where a comprehensive knowledge of advanced chemical concepts is required and where acceptable scholarly activity can include the pursuit of chemical education research.

Educational Materials

	The Terrific Science Press publications have emerged from CCE's work with classroom teachers of grades K–12 and college in graduate-credit, workshop-style inservice courses. Before being released, our materials undergo extensive classroom testing by teachers working with students at the targeted grade level, peer review by experts in the field for accuracy and safety, and editing by a staff of technical writers for clear, accurate, and consistent materials lists and procedures. The following is a list of Terrific Science Press publications to date.
Science Activities for Elementary Classrooms (1986)	Science SHARE is a resource for busy K–6 teachers to enable them to use hands-on science activities in their classrooms. The activities included use common, everyday materials and complement or supplement any existing science curriculum. This book was published in collaboration with Flinn Scientific, Inc.

Polymers All Around You! *(1992)*	This monograph focuses on the uses of polymer chemistry in the classroom. It includes several multipart activities dealing with topics such as polymer recycling and polymers and polarized light. This monograph was published in collaboration with POLYED, a joint education committee of two divisions of the American Chemical Society: the Division of Polymer Chemistry and the Division of Polymeric Materials, Science and Engineering.
Fun with Chemistry *Volume 2* *(1993)*	The second volume of a set of two hands-on activity collections, this book contains classroom-tested science activities that enhance teaching, are fun to do, and help make science relevant to young students. This book was published in collaboration with the Institute for Chemical Education (ICE), University of Wisconsin-Madison.
Santa's Scientific Christmas *(1993)*	In this school play for elementary students, Santa's elves teach him the science behind his toys. The book and accompanying video provide step-by-step instructions for presenting the play. The book also contains eight fun, hands-on science activities to do in the classroom.
Teaching Chemistry with TOYS *Teaching Physics with TOYS* *(1995)*	Each volume contains more than 40 activities for grades K–9. Both were developed in collaboration with and tested by classroom teachers from around the country. These volumes were published in collaboration with McGraw-Hill, Inc.
Palette of Color *Monograph Series* *(1995)*	The three monographs in this series present the chemistry behind dye colors and show how this chemistry is applied in "real-world" settings: • The Chemistry of Vat Dyes • The Chemistry of Natural Dyes • The Chemistry of Food Dyes
Science in Our World *Teacher Resource Modules* *(1995)*	Each volume of this six-volume set presents chemistry activities based on a specific industry—everything from pharmaceuticals to metallurgy. Developed as a result of the *Partners for Terrific Science* program, this set explores the following topics and industries: • Science Fare—Chemistry at the Table (Procter & Gamble) • Strong Medicine—Chemistry at the Pharmacy (Hoechst Marion Roussel, Inc.) • Dirt Alert—The Chemistry of Cleaning (Diversey Corporation) • Fat Chance—The Chemistry of Lipids (Henkel Corporation, Emery Group) • Chain Gang—The Chemistry of Polymers (Quantum Chemical Company) • Chemistry of Metals (Armco, Inc., scheduled 1996)
Teaching Science with TOYS *Teacher Resource Modules* *(scheduled 1996)*	The modules in this series are designed as instructional units focusing on a given theme or content area in chemistry or physics. Built around a collection of grade-level-appropriate TOYS activities, each Teacher Resource Module also includes a content review and pedagogical strategies section. Topics to be released in 1996 include the following: • Mechanical Energy and Energy Conversions (intermediate) • Linear Motion (primary) • Using Your Senses to Explore Matter (elementary) • States of Matter and Changes of State (middle school)

Terrific Science Network

Affiliates	College and district affiliates to CCE programs disseminate ideas and programming throughout the United States. Program affiliates offer support for local teachers, including workshops, resource/symposium sessions, and inservices; science camps; and college courses.
Industrial Partners	We collaborate directly with over 40 industrial partners, all of whom are fully dedicated to enhancing the quality of science education for teachers and students in their communities and beyond.

Outreach   On the average, graduates of CCE professional development programs report reaching about 40 other teachers through district inservices and other outreach efforts they undertake. Additionally, graduates, especially those in facilitator programs, institute their own local student programs. CCE staff also undertake significant outreach through collaboration with local schools, service organizations, professional societies, and museums.

Newsletters   CCE newsletters provide a vehicle for network communication between program graduates, members of industry, and other individuals active in chemical and science education. Newsletters contain program information, hands-on science activities, teacher resources, and ideas on how to integrate hands-on science into the curriculum.

For more information about any of the CCE initiatives, contact us at:

Center for Chemical Education
4200 East University Blvd.
Middletown, OH 45042
(513) 727-3318
FAX (513) 727-3223
e-mail: CCE@muohio.edu
http://www.muohio.edu/~ccecwis/

Center for Chemical Education Staff

Mickey Sarquis, Director
Bruce L. Peters, Jr., Associate Director
Billie Gerzema, Administrative Assistant

Assistants to Director

Susan Gertz   Mark Sabo
Lynn Hogue

Project Coordinators and Managers

Richard French   Andrea Nolan
Betty Kibbey   Ginger Smith
Carl Morgan   Amy Stander

Research Associates and Assistants

Kersti Cox   Anne Munson
Stephen Gentle   Thomas Nackid
Susan Hershberger   Michael Parks
Amy Hudepohl   Lisa Taylor
Baird Lloyd

Program Secretaries

Victoria Burton   Ruth Willis

Graduate Assistants

Michelle Diebolt   Richard Rischling
Nancy Grim   Annette Souder
Julie Hust

Appendix B:

● Literature Index

	Featured Book	Fiction Book	Nonfiction Book

The list below is an alphabetical index of the books used or suggested for further study in each of the activities.

Title, Author, and ISBN

A

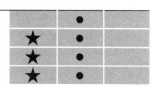

Title	Featured Book	Fiction Book	Nonfiction Book
Africa Dream, Eloise Greenfield, 0-06-443277-7			●
Air, Kitty Benedict, 0-88682-547-4			●
Air Is All Around You, Franklyn M. Branley, 0-06-445048-1			●
Alice in Wonderland, Lewis Carroll, any version		●	
Animals That Glow, Judith Janda Presnall, 0-531-20071-X			●
Arrow to the Sun, Gerald McDermott, 0-670-13369-8		●	
Ashanti to Zulu: African Traditions, Margaret Musgrove, 0-8037-0308-2			●

B

Title	Featured Book	Fiction Book	Nonfiction Book
The Balancing Girl, Berniece Rabe, 0-440-84277-8		●	
The Banza, Diane Wolkstein, 0-14-054605-7	★	●	
The Black Snowman, Phil Mendez, 0-590-44873-0	★	●	
Bringing the Rain to Kapiti Plain, Verna Aardema, 0-14-054616-2	★	●	

C

Title	Featured Book	Fiction Book	Nonfiction Book
Carousel, Donald Crews, 0-688-00908-5	★	●	
Catch the Wind!: All About Kites, Gail Gibbons, 0-316-30955-9			●
Circus, Lois Ehlert, 0-06-020252-1		●	
The Cloud Book, Tomie dePaola, 0-8234-0531-1			●
Cooking the African Way, Constance Nabwire & Bertha Vining Montgomery, 0-8225-9564-8			●

D

Title	Featured Book	Fiction Book	Nonfiction Book
Drought, Christopher Lampton, 1-878841-91-2	★		●

E

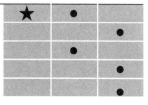

Title	Featured Book	Fiction Book	Nonfiction Book
The Emperor and the Kite, Jane Yolen, 0-399-21499-2	★	●	
Eskimo Boy, Russ Kendall, 0-590-43696-1	★		●

F

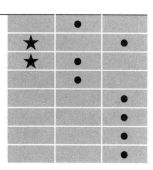

Title	Featured Book	Fiction Book	Nonfiction Book
50 Below Zero, Robert Munsch, 0-920236-91-X		●	
Fireflies, Caroline Arnold, 0-590-46944-4	★		●
Fireflies!, Julie Brinckloe, 0689-71055-0	★	●	
Flat Stanley, Jeff Brown, 0-06-440293-2		●	
Food, Terry Jennings, 0-516-48402-8			●
Food: Feasts, Cooks, & Kitchens, Richard Tames, 0-531-15711-3			●
Force and Motion, Peter Lafferty, 1-879431-85-8			●
Fun with Light, Maria Gordon, 1-56847-308-7			●

Title, Author, and ISBN

Title, Author, and ISBN	Featured Book	Fiction Book	Nonfiction Book
G			
George Shrinks, William Joyce, 0-06-443129-0	★	●	
Gilberto and the Wind, Marie Hall Ets, 0-14-050276-9		●	
Good Morning, Let's Eat!, Karin Luisa Badt, 0-516-48190-8	★		●
Gregory, the Terrible Eater, Mitchell Sharmat, 0-590-43350-4	★	●	
H			
Harry and the Terrible Whatzit, Dick Gackenbach, 0-89919-223-8		●	
I			
Iva Dunnit and the Big Wind, Carol Purcy, 0-14-054651-0		●	
J			
The Jacket I Wear in the Snow, Shirley Neitzel, 0-590-43945-6		●	
Jambo Means Hello: Swahili Alphabet Book, Muriel Feelings, 0-8037-4428-5			●
K			
Keeping Warm, Keeping Cool, Joan Elma Rahn, 0-689-30995-3			●
The Kite, Alma F. Ada, 1-56014-228-6		●	
Kite Flier, Dennis Haseley, 0-689-71668-0		●	
The Klutz Book of Magnetic Magic, Paul Doherty, 1-878257-86-2			●
L			
The Lazy Bear, Brian Wildsmith, 0-19-272158-5	★	●	
Light, David Burnie, 1-879431-79-3			●
M			
The Magic School Bus in the Haunted Museum, Linda Beech, 0-590-48412-5		●	
Mama, Do You Love Me?, Barbara Joosse, 0-87701-759-X	★	●	
Mike's Kite, Elizabeth MacDonald, 0153003200		●	
Mirandy and Brother Wind, Patricia McKissack, 0-394-88765-4	★	●	
Mirette on the High Wire, Emily Arnold McCully, 0-399-22130-1	★	●	
The Mitten, Jan Brett, 0-399-21920-X		●	
Moja Means One: Swahili Counting Book, Muriel Feelings, 0-14-055296-0			●
The Most Wonderful Egg in the World, Helme Heine, 0-689-50280-X		●	
Multicultural Cookbook for Students, Carole Albyn, 0-89774-735-6			●
N			
Nature's Living Lights: Fireflies and Other Bioluminescent Creatures, Pamela Carroll, 0-316-79119-9			●
O			
One-Hour Kites, Jim Rowlands, 0-312-03218-8			●

Title, Author, and ISBN	Featured Book	Fiction Book	Nonfiction Book

P

Title, Author, and ISBN	Featured Book	Fiction Book	Nonfiction Book
Planting a Rainbow, Lois Ehlert, 0-15-262610-7	★	●	

R

Title, Author, and ISBN	Featured Book	Fiction Book	Nonfiction Book
Rainbow Crow, Nancy VanLaan, 0-394-89577-0		●	
The Rainbow Fish, Marcus Pfister, 1-55858-009-3	★	●	
Rainbow Rider, Jane Yolen, 0-690-00301-3		●	
The Rains Are Coming, Sanna Stanley, 0-688-10948-9	★	●	
Rechenka's Eggs, Patricia Polacco, 0-399-21501-8	★	●	
The River that Gave Gifts, Margo Humphrey, 0-89239-027-1	★	●	

S

Title, Author, and ISBN	Featured Book	Fiction Book	Nonfiction Book
The Science Book of Air, Neil Ardley, 0-15-200578-1			●
The Science Book of Color, Neil Ardley, 0-15-200576-5			●
The Science Book of Light, Neil Ardley, 0-15-200577-3			●
The Science Book of Sound, Neil Ardley, 0-15-200579-X			●
The Science Book of Weather, Neil Ardley, 0-15-200624-9			●
Science Crafts for Kids, Gwen Diehn and Terry Krautwurst, 0-8069-0283-3			●
Science Magic (Series), Chris Oxlade			●
The Secret in the Matchbox, Val Willis, 0-374-46593-2		●	
Sound Experiments, Ray Broekel, 0-516-41686-3			●
A Story-A Story: An African Folk Tale, Gail Haley, 0-689-71201-4		●	

T

Title, Author, and ISBN	Featured Book	Fiction Book	Nonfiction Book
Transport on Land, Road, and Rail, Eryl Davies, 0-531-15741-5			●
The Twelve Circus Rings, Seymour Chwast, 0-15-200627-3		●	

U

Title, Author, and ISBN	Featured Book	Fiction Book	Nonfiction Book
Ukrainian Easter Egg Design Book, Luba Perchyshyn, 0-960-25024-7			●
The Ultimate Kite Book, Paul and Helene Morgan, 0-671-74443-7			●

W

Title, Author, and ISBN	Featured Book	Fiction Book	Nonfiction Book
The Wartville Wizard, Don Madden, 0-689-71667-2	★	●	
The Way Things Work, David Macaulay, 0-395-42857-2			●
Weather Forecasting, Gail Gibbons, 0-689-71683-4	★		●
Wheels, Byron Barton, 0-690-03951-4			●
When Blue Meant Yellow: How Colors Got Their Names, Jeanne Heifetz, 0-8050-3178-2			●
Wilbur's Space Machine, Lorna Balian, 0-8234-0836-1	★	●	

Z

Title, Author, and ISBN	Featured Book	Fiction Book	Nonfiction Book
Zack's Alligator, Shirley Mozelle, 0-06-444186-5	★	●	

● Shopping List

The activities in this book primarily use common materials available at most discount, grocery, or hardware stores. However, several lessons use materials (some of which are optional) that must be ordered from special suppliers. We provide ordering information in each lesson; the list below is for your convenience in preparing a "shopping list" of items you will probably need to order in advance. This is not an exhaustive list of all materials required; complete lists are provided in the activities.

Suppliers

Allen-Lewis Company	P.O. Box 16546, Denver, CO 80216	800/525-6658
Creative Educational Surplus	9801 James Circle, Suite C, Bloomington, MN 55431	800/886-6428
Delta Education	P.O. Box 3000, Nashua, NH 03061-9913	800/442-5444
Fisher Scientific	1600 W. Glenlake Ave., Itasca, IL 60143	800/766-7000
Flinn Scientific	P.O. Box 219, Batavia, IL 60510-0219	800/452-1261
Frey Scientific	905 Hickory Lane, P.O. Box 8101, Mansfield, OH 44901-8101	800/225-FREY
Hearthsong	6519 N. Galena Rd., Peoria, IL 61614	800/779-2211
K&B Innovations	141 Cottonwood Ave., Hartland, WI 53029-2014	414/367-8266
Metro Magic	1855 South University Dr., Davie, FL 33324	954/473-2385
Oliphant Research International	772 W. 1700 South, Salt Lake City, UT 84104	801/972-1448
Oriental Trading Company, Inc.	P.O. Box 3407, Omaha, NE 68103-0407	800/228-2269
Science Kit and Boreal Laboratories	777 E. Park Dr., Tonawanda, NY 14150-6782	800/828-7777
World of Science stores	For the nearest location, call	716/475-0100

Lessons Requiring Ordered Items

Are Mittens Warm?

*   dial thermometer (also called "pocket test thermometer"), #80-070-4923, **or**
    V-back metal thermometer, #80-200-1340; Delta Education

Babushka's Eggs'periment

*   wax crayon **or**
    egg dyeing kit containing beeswax, dyes, and tools; Hearthsong

Chemiluminescence

*   lightsticks; Oriental Trading Company
*   (optional) V-back metal thermometer, #80-200-1340; Delta Education

Chromatography Garden

*   9-cm diameter filter paper, #80-060-4009, **or**
    15-cm diameter filter paper, #80-060-4086; Delta Education
*   24-cm diameter filter paper, #09-795J; Fisher Scientific (for an extension)

Colors of the Rainbow

*   unbreakable acrylic prisms, #80-160-5130; Delta Education
*   (optional) giant prism, #80-160-7847; Delta Education
*   break-resistant 3-inch x 5-inch mirrors, #80-130-2113 (Other mirrors will work); Delta Education

Glitter Wands

- size 2, grade XX cork, #F02556; Frey Scientific
- (optional) clear plastic tube (about 4–4½ inches long) with screw-on cap, #808; Creative Educational Surplus

Growing Gators

- Magic Animal Alligators; World of Science stores, **or**
  Grow Dinosaurs; Allen-Lewis Company

Iron for Breakfast

- U-shaped ceramic magnet, #80-130-0463, **or**
  rumen magnet, #80-130-4632, **or**
  romax magnet, #80-130-7052; Delta Education
- iron filings, #80-060-0313; Delta Education
- 60-mm diameter petri dishes, #F07445; Frey Scientific

Is It Really Magic?

- simple magic tricks such as "magic nail box," "penny change to dime," "magic ball," and "magic coloring books";
  Metro Magic (also available from toy stores or magic stores)

Shrinky Plastic

- blank sheets of "frosted" shrinkable polystyrene; K&B Innovations

Weather Forecasters

- cobalt chloride hexahydrate crystals, #C0225; Flinn Scientific

Whirling Colors

- animation flip book (set of three), #80-060-0808; Delta Education
- (optional) white plastic top, #80-201-0128, and dry-erase markers, #80-130-8691; Delta Education
- (optional) Color Top; Oliphant Research International
- (optional) Toptical, #F17616; Frey Scientific
- Newton Color Disk, #65601; Science Kit and Boreal Laboratories, **or**
  Newton Color Disk, #F990868; Frey Scientific

Teaching Physical Science through Children's Literature

● Activities Indexed by Science Topics